Hideo Kojima

Influential Video Game Designers

Series editors:
Carly A. Kocurek
Jennifer deWinter

Previously published titles in this series:

Shigeru Miyamoto: Super Mario Bros., Donkey Kong, The Legend of Zelda
Jennifer deWinter

Brenda Laurel: Pioneering Games for Girls
Carly A. Kocurek

Jane Jensen: Gabriel Knight, Adventure Games, Hidden Objects
Anastasia Salter

Todd Howard: Worldbuilding in Tamriel and Beyond
Wendi Sierra

HIDEO KOJIMA

Progressive Game Design from
Metal Gear to *Death Stranding*

Bryan Hikari Hartzheim

BLOOMSBURY ACADEMIC
NEW YORK • LONDON • OXFORD • NEW DELHI • SYDNEY

BLOOMSBURY ACADEMIC
Bloomsbury Publishing Inc
1385 Broadway, New York, NY 10018, USA
50 Bedford Square, London, WC1B 3DP, UK
29 Earlsfort Terrace, Dublin 2, Ireland

BLOOMSBURY, BLOOMSBURY ACADEMIC and the Diana logo are
trademarks of Bloomsbury Publishing Plc

First published in the United States of America 2023

Cover design by Alice Marwick
Chinook military helicopter © Jozsef Soos / Getty Images

A catalog record for this book is available from the Library of Congress.

ISBN: HB: 979-8-7651-0168-1
PB: 979-8-76510-169-8
ePDF: 979-8-7651-0166-7
eBook: 979-8-7651-0165-0

Series: Influential Video Game Designers

Typeset by Deanta Global Publishing Services, Chennai, India
Printed and bound in Great Britain

To find out more about our authors and books visit www.bloomsbury.com and
sign up for our newsletters.

CONTENTS

FIGURES

PREFACE

In 2016, Guillermo del Toro and Hideo Kojima sat on a D.I.C.E. summit stage for a combined interview. Del Toro of cinematic fame (*Pan's Labyrinth* [2006], *The Shape of Water* [2017], *Pinocchio* [2022]) reflects on his friend Kojima, proclaiming him "a creative powerhouse." The trials and tribulations that Kojima faces, according to del Toro, will make him an even better artist.

Few video game designers have been as purposeful and as successful in curating an auteur persona as Kojima. In other books in this series, we talk about the importance of interrogating the role of game designers in game studies with the same care that we attend to film directors, authors, and visual artists. Doing so enables us to understand the labor of games as a created form and to develop complex languages and theories of design in this space as human activity. In this book, we are able to see a game designer who, from the beginning, was very aware of the importance of curating that identity. So while Bryan Hartzheim carefully includes Kojima's team as a creative and important part of a design process and vision, colloquially, the team disappears and Kojima is celebrated as a capital "A" Artist and a capital "D" Designer. An *auteur*, if you will.

What probably plays a part in this persona making is the close allegiance that Kojima has to cinema. Kojima always talks about the importance of film in his childhood and adult formation. He sees cinematic techniques as essential tools to be used in games. And to be frank, he dresses like a cinephile rather than a game designer. His clothes are sleek and artistic, his hair well-kept and stylish. We can imagine him conducting architecture desk crits or blending seamlessly into the milieu of prestige film festivals like Sundance. From how he dresses and presents himself visually to what he says and does in the media, Kojima's care and attention to his own brand as an artist and designer is evident.

Why harp on this affect so much in this forward? Because game designers are important actors in complex nodes of creation, yet many designers tend to align themselves to programmer/tech personas rather than artistic personas. The wardrobes of game developers are so often punchlines—a restrictive anti-fashion statement of free t-shirts and hoodies with carefully worn in jeans—and so radically separate the professional aesthetic of video gaming from that of other commercial arts. What emerges in this book is twofold: first, a careful consideration of design vision and philosophy and how the games instantiate those; and second, an analysis of a self-constructed Designer, a person with artistic vision, who is instantly recognizable and validated by artists in other media. Kojima's reputation and professional and creative trajectory show so clearly how games have moved from niche hobby to cultural and industrial powerhouse. Kojima's creative vision has steered multiple critically and commercially successful games, but it has also helped demonstrate how seriously games can and should be taken as a form of human expression alongside visual and media arts like photography and cinema. And when the games fail, that's fine. It's swallowed in the narrative of an artist taking risks.

This all sounds rather serious, and much of what Kojima does is quite serious—as Hartzheim so clearly highlights, Kojima often engages with current issues in a thoughtful and reflective way, raising key questions about technology, society, and the future. But that's not all. Kojima is also playful, sometimes even irreverent. Let's talk about cardboard boxes.

Cardboard boxes pop up as visual and as tool throughout the Metal Gear series, where player characters can use boxes in a variety of ways. Hiding in a box, of course, is obvious, but it's the less obvious uses that have made the humble cardboard box a true gaming icon: for example, in *Metal Gear Solid* (Konami 1998), a box that has been urinated on by a wolf can protect the player from wolf attack. The uses of the cardboard box range from practical to fantastical, from high stakes to absurd. In *Metal Gear Solid: Peace Walker* (Konami 2010), the player can take Kazuhira Miller to cuddle inside a cardboard box on the beach—a weird date, perhaps, but not the worst we've heard of. In real life, as in the games, the cardboard box is an artifact ripe with potential. It can be a tool, a building material, an art supply, or a toy. It can even help real-life US Marines fool a high-tech AI robot—giggling the whole time (Scharre 2023). In Kojima's hands, video games are a cardboard box, their possibilities bounded only by creativity and potential, sometimes serious, sometimes absurd, always compelling.

FOREWORD

Peter Tieryas

As long as I can remember, I've been playing the games of Hideo Kojima. From the original *Metal Gear* (Konami 1987) on the MSX and NES, to the recent *Death Stranding* (Kojima Productions 2019), he's always pushed the boundaries of what constitutes gaming with prescient stories that explore complex philosophical and social themes. His influence is vast in the gaming industry with the number of games inspired by his works being countless, but it reaches beyond that into the broader world of media and culture. Guillermo del Toro considers himself a fan. So does acclaimed director, George Miller, who praised *Death Stranding*, stating, "The skill that I see in great filmmakers, I now see in Kojima-san's work." J. J. Abrams called Kojima a "master of his form." The accolades throughout the years are too numerous to list.

Much like the films of Stanley Kubrick, Kojima uses genre as a tool and launching point to paint an entirely original canvas; the existential pigments he mixes together have a totally unique twist to them that push the very definition of gaming, whether it's using the second controller on the PlayStation to fool the mind-reading Psycho Mantis in *Metal Gear Solid* (Konami 1998), drawing on the actual sun to recharge the Gun del Sol in *Boktai* (Konami 2003), or the best mecha controls I've experienced in a game in *Zone of the Enders* (Konami 2001). Kojima guides players out of their comfort zone, both the philosophical kind and gaming one as well.

As both a novelist and narrative director in games, I know what he's doing is hard. Really, really hard. To pull it off as consistently and on as epic a scale as he's done is just unparalleled, something only a handful of people have done. Before every major project I undertake, I usually have several works I revisit for inspiration. The essentials include the *Metal Gear Solid* games, *Snatcher* (Konami 1988), and now *Death Stranding*. Every character, from the various specialists advising Snake via Codec to the menagerie of villains within, is incredibly memorable. The dialogue is riveting and even when I know the plot twists that are coming—as I've played them so many times—I'm still at the edge of my seat, unable to take my eyes off. Kojima's works incorporate the political, economic, scientific, and cultural zeitgeist to weave together a unique commentary that has more impact and immediacy for the characters since they live on the edge of mortality, skirting around death and pushing their ideological concerns to the extreme. Even if we disagree with the villains, we can't help but sympathize, even empathize with the worst of them. Kojima's attention to detail permeates every element of the world-building, from the menu descriptions to the technical information behind each piece of equipment like the voluminous data entries stored in the encyclopedic Jordan computer from *Snatcher*.

I still remember how I felt after each Kojima game. One of the most memorable for me was *Metal Gear Solid 2: Sons of Liberty* (Konami 2001). I was at LucasArts when the game came out. I asked my boss at the time if I could take a few days off to play it. I finished the game and was floored, so mesmerized by the themes that I had a hard time physically moving. There were issues *Metal Gear Solid 2* brought up that I still don't have answers to and that come back to me now with the arrival of ChatGPT, AI deep learning, and the implications for the future of social media and humanity.

For *Death Stranding*, I played it shortly after my daughter was born. I was deeply moved by Sam's experience wandering a postapocalyptic world with his baby. It was symbolic for me of how that first year had felt, trying to navigate the numerous intricacies of being a parent and keeping my baby healthy. The game took on even more significance with the pandemic as I'd often take her out for long walks in a baby carrier while navigating the empty streets of what had once been a teeming city. What did the future portend?

I've had the honor of meeting Hideo Kojima a few times throughout the years. What's struck me most is his generosity, creativity, and brilliance. I've asked him for advice a few times on works I've struggled with. The way his mind works is so ingenious, I was inspired just by the quick recommendations he made, unlocking the story puzzles in a way that made me wonder why I'd struggled with them in the first place. It was really special getting to see his "creative gene" in action.

I'm excited about this book because it'll give readers a chance to understand what makes Hideo Kojima's games so impactful and powerful. The level of research and insight is illuminating and, while I consider myself a huge fan, there was still so much I learned within its pages. There has never been a creator like Hideo Kojima. Let Bryan Hartzheim show you why.

ACKNOWLEDGMENTS

Much like Hideo Kojima's game design, this book is a synthesis of many influences. I'd first like to acknowledge the many brilliant colleagues and professors at UCLA who were instrumental in my education. I am particularly indebted to two role models: John Thornton Caldwell, for his wisdom, mentorship, and constant inspiration, and Steve Mamber, whose Video Game Theory seminar provided me the first glimpses of this world. Thank you, Steve, for not discouraging my feeble attempts at analyzing Shigeru Miyamoto's games. In many ways, this book started in your class.

Series editors Carly Kocurek and Jennifer deWinter tirelessly provided sharp feedback and a keen rhetorical eye over the years of this book's construction. It is wild to think that this idea originated while getting career advice from Jennifer in a Shibuya beer bar. The SWPACA Game Studies community warmly welcomed me, always provided kind and constructive feedback, and offered great game recommendations, particularly David O'Grady, Jim Fleury, Harrison Gish, Judd Ruggill, Ken McAlister, Steven Conway, and Matthew Thomas Payne. Two anonymous peer reviewers contributed detailed suggestions that significantly improved the book's structure. Katie Gallof and the entire team at Bloomsbury deserve credit for their editorial assistance. Trial demos of this book were presented at the friendly Mechademia and Replaying Japan conferences. Martin Roth, Rachael Hutchinson, Marc Steinberg, and Stevie Suan gave feedback or other vivid ideas that made their way into the golden master.

Waseda University provided institutional backing, research flexibility, and a generous grant in my first year that enabled me to acquire some expensive special editions of games. I thank the staff and faculty of the School of International Liberal Studies and the Graduate School of International Culture and Communication Studies, particularly Graham Law, Greg Dvorak, and Mitsuhiro Yoshimoto, for their support, guidance, and fellowship. Many of the ideas in this book were refined through discussions with such terrific undergraduate zemi and graduate students, particularly those in my Video Game Studies seminar. Special thanks to Victoria Duan, Kenta Kato, Jin Huizi, and, especially, Nave Barlev for being truly wonderful and talented TAs.

I am still in debt to Goh Wakabayashi, Reiko Sasaki, and Hiromi Seki for everything they did to help and educate a clueless graduate student about media production. Joseph Rodon and the first-rate Game Preservation Society in Setagaya fielded my requests for obscure copies of *MSX Magazine* and showed me original copies of *Metal Gear*. I am truly grateful for my amazing friends; thank you for your companionship and for playing and talking about games with me over the years. None of this book would have been possible without the support of big-hearted family. My aunt and uncle, Atsuko and Tokumasa, who housed an annoying fifth grader for a summer in Nagoya and taught him Japanese. My brother, Nick, for decades of gaming competition and camaraderie. My grandmother, Cathy, who bought my first NES when I was five. And most of all my parents, Joel and Yuriko, who were not happy about that NES purchase but always believed in me and supported my interests. Mom and Dad, this book is dedicated to you. Finally, to Rumiko: thank you for making me laugh, nursing my injuries, and sticking by my side through some rough times and many, many more great times. I couldn't have done any of this without you.

NOTE ON TRANSLATION AND NAMES

All translation of Japanese sources into English are by the author unless otherwise indicated. Japanese names appear in Western order, with given name followed by family name. This is due to the fact that figures such as Hideo Kojima and Yoji Shinkawa have been well-documented within English-language press and publications for over two decades. This name order is also adopted within the games themselves, which use Western order for English-language game credits (e.g., "A Hideo Kojima Game"). Considering the familiarity of these conventions to English-language readers, this book adopts Western order for all Japanese names to avoid confusion.

Chapter 1

INTRODUCTION

THE CULT OF KOJIMA

Hideo Kojima is a name even those only casually familiar with video games might recognize. For those unfamiliar, Kojima is the creator, designer, and frequent director of Konami's Metal Gear Solid franchise, a video game series that pioneered the "stealth game" genre and the cinematic action game in general. The Metal Gear franchise, including the first two titles for the MSX (Microsoft eXtended BASIC) home computer, spans over twenty-two games and game remakes. Of these, nine were designed, directed, produced, and cowritten by Kojima himself. These games have garnered positive critical reviews and game awards, with a select few included regularly in lists of the greatest video games ever created (EGM Staff 2003; Campbell 2006; Wilson 2012; IGN Staff 2022). Further, this is also one of the most commercially successful series in video game history, with nearly every Kojima-directed iteration selling in the millions. Including the various spin-offs, the Metal Gear franchise has moved over 50 million units globally.

When Kojima entered the games industry in the 1980s, contemporary combat games required players to proceed by killing enemies. *Metal Gear* (Konami 1987) introduced a new approach to the action game: of *avoiding*, rather than eradicating, enemy conflict in order to accomplish missions. Players were encouraged to scrutinize and chart paths through levels that would enable them to sidestep enemy combatants by hiding behind crates or ducking into doorways. With the Metal Gear series, Kojima introduced a style of gameplay in the action genre that rewarded patience, planning, and a sensitivity to the movements of avatars and layouts of environments. This type of gameplay ultimately became its own genre—the stealth game—comprising franchises such as the *Splinter Cell*, *Assassin's Creed*, and *Hitman* series. But stealth gameplay is now ubiquitous and can be observed in many franchises and games that aren't about spies or mercenaries, from sneaking segments in the action-adventure *The Legend of Zelda* games to quietly taking out enemy encampments in the open world *Red Dead Redemption* series to playing a goose who causes sneaky havoc in the 2019 indie hit *Untitled Goose Game*. While Kojima did not totally create this type of gameplay, the Metal Gear franchise unquestionably polished, popularized, and made it a type of play that is familiar in a variety of games today.

But Metal Gear was not just its gameplay systems. It was equally inventive for its particular approach to genre-bending storytelling, mixing plots of contemporary geopolitics and political intrigue with settings and characters inspired by espionage films and anime sci-fi. Moreover, the game was directed with a visual panache unique for its time, incorporating John Woo-like action sequences with archival footage of nuclear missile explosions. Here was a game that broke ground with its gameplay and style and also had something important to say. This influence, too, can be seen in the many games that have emerged from its wake that attempt to create a more cinematic presentation.

As the architect of the series, Kojima became the official spokesperson for the franchise as it grew larger and ever more widely recognized over three decades of sequels and spin-offs. This type of consistent association between a single creator and a commercial game series for such a long period is rare in the games industry, especially in Japan, where games function as brands that companies tightly control, and designers are often promoted to upper management or leave to start their own enterprises. The fact that Kojima was able to be consistently involved in these AAA titles for Konami helped endear him to players but also distinguished him and the series from other game franchises. While Metal Gear was and is a Konami brand, it became known as a Kojima *creation*, with a particular sense of design associated with him. It is this design sense and process which I map in this book, which looks at Kojima's design practices in *Metal Gear* and beyond. I argue that Hideo Kojima as a game designer helped to introduce complex themes and messages in commercial games while consistently innovating gameplay systems and modes of presentation to reinforce those messages. By doing so, his games ultimately encourage a type of play that goes beyond the confines of "video games" to engage with society as a whole.

Kojima has become a celebrated figure within gaming circles for these very reasons. Following the success of *Metal Gear Solid* (Konami 1998), each subsequent release in the franchise became an event, and Kojima himself became its most significant celebrity. Whenever Konami debuted a new Metal Gear title at various international game conventions and events, Kojima would be present, ensuring that his name and face were tied to the game in a way that is more typical for film directors or movie stars. Thousands of fans descended to chant Kojima's name and deify his presence, the "cult of Kojima" loyally spreading the director's words or dissecting his games on internet forums and social media platforms. This tradition has continued with Kojima's independent studio Kojima Productions and its debut title, *Death Stranding* (Kojima Productions 2019), as Kojima has led breathless presentations at game show conventions while audiences await his every word. And once the games are released, Kojima attempts to be transparent about the production process, publishing documentaries and bonus DVDs or providing interviews for countless books and guides that curate the behind-the-scenes details of the production process. These paratextual materials reflect Kojima's desire for audiences to take the medium of video games, as well as his status as a creator, seriously. Perhaps unsurprisingly for someone whose games are filled with cryptic messages and puzzles, he is the rare designer who makes games that fans are talking about well before and after the release. There are few designers who have more message boards, fan pages, and even books dedicated to them (see Golden Joystick 2015; Chami 2016; Wolfe 2018).

These are all examples of a secondary consequence of Kojima's association with Metal Gear: how he and Konami encouraged greater public recognition for the role of game designers. In contrast to early industry practice, where game companies refused to credit designers in order to control their intellectual property and reduce employee bargaining power, Kojima has been tied to Metal Gear in its promotion as well as its creative production. He has won a number of plaudits from the Japanese games industry, such as the PlayStation Awards and routine top scores in periodicals such as *Famitsu*, while also receiving recognition from the global games industry, with lifetime achievement awards from MTV, the Game Developers' Conference, and D.I.C.E. He was given a standing ovation at The Game Awards in Los Angeles upon being presented with its "Industry Icon Award," signaling the respect he has received from peers and fans around the world (see Figure 1.1). This recognition, moreover, transcends the gaming medium; in 2002, he was included in *Newsweek*'s annual "Who's Next" cover story of ten influential people (Itoi 2001). He has been compared to the games industry equivalent of James Cameron, Steven Spielberg, and Peter Jackson for his ability to blend art, entertainment, and financial success (Kohler 2016; Gates 2018). Unique among game developers, even creators outside the games industry—from feature filmmakers to musicians to graphic novelists—cite his influence.

Figure 1.1 A crowd applauds Hideo Kojima as he receives the Industry Icon Award at The Game Awards in 2016. Source: thegameawards on Youtube (2016).

Fans and critics delight in noting what makes a "Kojima Game," though no one definition exists, and seeming contradictions abound. The Metal Gear franchise encourages players to complete missions by sneaking around and avoiding armed conflict with enemies, building narratives around pacifist themes and the dangers of the war machine. Yet each of the games also indulges in sophisticated weapon physics and increasingly realistic depictions of violence and warfare. The franchise is famous for its integration of high-octane cinematic techniques inspired by Hollywood action cinema, often displayed in elaborate cut scenes to increase dramatic tension. But these cut scenes sometimes meet with critical derision, as they can come at the expense of the player's interaction. Every successive game in the franchise has responded to technological improvements via new platforms and engines, introducing increased levels of immersion via real-world weather and time effects, sophisticated enemy and support AI, and a bevy of customizable equipment. However, each game also seemingly breaks this immersion, reminding the player that they are playing a game and highlighting the artifice of the gaming medium. Depending on your preference, each of these attributes is a reminder of the human creator behind the system or a maddening inconsistency that gets in the way of the gameplay, but are all facets of what might be described as the experience of playing a "Kojima Game."

One unmistakable fact is that, as the director, Kojima is viewed by the public as the figure in charge. Central to Kojima's design is his direction, which early on meant taking on a wide variety of roles, from planner, to scenarist, to map designer, to cinematics editor, to even character designer and storyboard artist. Games are also not the limit of his creative activities. Outside of game design, Kojima has also penned essays and film criticism articles, hosted radio shows and podcasts, and helped run Konami as a producer and vice president. Like protean directors in the film industry such as Mamoru Oshii and "Beat" Takeshi Kitano, who traffic in animation, comedy, and writing in addition to directing celebrated films, Kojima is a man of many talents (Ruh 2013; Gerow 2007). These many roles illustrate what Kojima is not, namely, a programmer or illustrator, but they do highlight his skills in storytelling, ability to communicate his ideas effectively to others, and adaptability to multiple media formats, characteristic of many contracted multitalented performers in the Japanese entertainment industry. This desire to control and integrate various aspects of storytelling is a key element of Kojima's game design.

The Progressive Game

Kojima's embrace of game direction shortly after beginning his career at Konami was a way to grasp control from the programmers and engineers who held the digital tools to creative expression. This emphasis on control is one reason why some have likened Kojima to gaming's first "auteur" (Screenrobot 2019). The "auteur theory" developed in the 1960s to identify exceptional directors in films known for exerting their personality on the final product (see Hartzheim 2016). However, the theory has been criticized for placing too great an emphasis on the agency of the director and not enough on the specific contexts of production or on other individuals involved in the creative process. These criticisms can extend to game development as well. Commercial games, like films, are often collaboratively produced at large studios with diverse teams, meaning that a single person's precise role in game development is inherently limited and can be difficult to ascertain from an outside perspective. And while Kojima is a "director" who employs (and occasionally indulges in) the language of cinema for his games, games must account for player input, various interfaces and mechanics, or responsive AI algorithms and cannot rely solely on cinematic devices to relay their meaning or effect.

Nevertheless, focusing on the director of a film or game also has its merits. When the critics of the French film periodical *Cahiers du Cinema* in the 1950s and 1960s prioritized the director in their discussions of who was most responsible for idiosyncratic and subversive cinema within commercial structures, they were doing so in reaction to the Fordist production of the Hollywood studio system and its inherent anonymizing of its filmmakers (Hartzheim 2016). Video game studios also did not identify the creators of their products openly, leading to designers such as Warren Robinett hiding his name in an "easter egg" for players to find in a secret room of Atari's 1978 *Adventure*. Kojima's ability to forge a creative identity in the Konami bureaucracy strikes a similar note of the individual finding his voice within the corporate machine. Even if Kojima must sublimate that voice to the commercial imperative of making games that sell, it is useful to see how his games work against industry practices. Concentrating on Kojima the director also allows us to see how developers in a large studio can coalesce under a smaller department that channels their like-minded energies. Thus, a focus on the director allows us to understand the designs and contributions of Kojima, the individual game designer, but can also shed light on the contributions of his teams and what allowed them to create unconventional games while still drawing upon the sizable resources of commercial game development. Ultimately, working with Kojima under Konami allowed his teams to radically experiment with existing game genres, models, and programs. This enabled them to incorporate characteristics of multiple media forms to create interactive experiences that got players thinking about socially and politically meaningful ideas.

In this book, I argue Kojima's approach to game creation is that of a *progressive game design*, one that seeks to expand the boundaries of commercial video games by disrupting established game forms, narratives, or genres relative to the time in which they were produced. The term "progressive" is not to be confused with Jesper Juul's (2002) classification of games of "progression" and "emergence," used to distinguish between games that are linear and predetermined versus games that are nonlinear and unstructured (324). "Progressive" is employed here to define games that are interested in finding or making use of alternative ideas, opportunities, and modes of expression. This focus on a "progressive game" aligns with what the later editors of *Cahiers du Cinema* Jean Louis Comolli and Jean Narboni (1990) have called the creation of a "progressive" text in cinema. Comolli and Narboni argued that "all films are political" or, more specifically, that all films reproduce a society's dominant ideologies and systems of production, but certain films could work against these dominant ideologies by challenging established values and techniques (27–36). In response to the authors, Barbara Klinger (2003) has mapped the characteristics of the "progressive film genre," focusing attention on critics' affinity for films that depart from Hollywood conventions, such as pessimistic world views and themes that challenge existing social institutions; narratives that elide spectator identification, clear moral dichotomies, or formal closure; and visual styles that excessively call attention to themselves (81–4). Though critical of the goals of the authors, Klinger highlights how a "progressive film" became constituted through the discourse of liberally minded critics who sought out ruptures not only in ideology but also in contemporary film form and structure.

Within games studies, scholars have attempted to account for how radical games can potentially act as sites of social, cultural, and political resistance. Alexander Galloway's (2006) "countergaming" borrows from Peter Wollen's concept of "countercinema" to examine how an "avant-garde" comprising game mods "exists in opposition to and outside the gaming mainstream" (109). Building upon arguments formulated by Michael Hardt and Antonio Negri, Nick Dyer-Witheford and Greig de Peuter's (2009) "games of multitude" are games which "fight back against games of empire" and, in turn, propose new subjectivities, movements, and alternatives to games that depict and reinforce global capital (187). In their all-encompassing study of "metagames" or games of games, Stephanie Boluk and Patrick LeMieux (2017) attempt to "uncover alternate histories of play defined not by code, commerce, and computation" but through the relationship between human players and "nonhuman operations" (4). Most recently, Noah Wardruip-Fruin (2020) uses the concepts of "operational logics" and "playable models" to "show how game creators push boundaries to communicate new things, and create new opportunities for play, through video games" (xxv). These authors focus on "alternative" games that work against the established logics and practices of contemporary commercial game development to argue for transformative and meaningful play.

The closest approximation of a "progressive game" design might be found in Mary Flanagan's (2009) provocative idea of "critical play," where she argues that certain games exhibit subversive qualities that are designed to upset or undermine the status quo (10). Flanagan singles out the concept of "disruption" in particular as an action in-between total subversion, which seeks to overturn or overthrow existing laws, rules, or systems, and intervention, which involves direct action and engagement with political or social issues. Referring to "Disruption-Innovation" theory in the IT business arena, Flanagan argues that disruption "is a creative act that shifts the way a particular logic or paradigm is operating" (12). From Dell computers to Starbucks coffee, various innovators introduced disruptions to existing industries that created entirely new markets. Applying this idea to game design means having players "explore what is permissible and what pushes at that boundary between rules and expectations, and a player's own agency, within any given play environment—no matter how structured that play is" (13). Games that engage in creative disruption might emerge within existing game genres or forms of play, though the innovations and reorientations they introduce can lead to the creation of entirely new genres and styles of play.

Flanagan restricts her idea of critical play toward mostly activist and art games and their potential for critical reflection, hence their strongly oppositional and critical stances toward commercial games (a quality shared with other critical game scholars). But what happens when we apply this framework to games and game designers working within the commercial games industry? Is it possible to be both critical of commercial games while also working within their existing structures? Answering these questions is my goal in this book, and what I argue is ultimately the type of design Kojima has continually emphasized in his various games. Drawing inspiration from Klinger's categorization of progressive film and Flanagan's idea of critical "radical" play, I examine the disruptions that Kojima's games have introduced through their oppositions and challenges to dominant games and trends at the time. Unlike what is often thought of as "progressive cinema," Kojima's games do not simply challenge formal and sociopolitical conventions but also ludic and industrial ones. And unlike "critical play," Kojima's games are still commercial games that must also work from and within established commercial game genres and developmental structures.

Thus, in contrast to cinematic and ludic scholarship which emphasizes ideological modes and readings, I employ the term "progressive game design" to refer to how Kojima is both critical and constructive in his games. While this definition intentionally downplays the political connotation of the term "progressive," this does not mean that Kojima's games are apolitical or do not display consistent political arguments. The term "progressive" might also signal to readers stereotypes of evolutionary technological progress that the media industries have indulged in for decades, though such outcomes in any media are subject to critical debate. For the purposes of this book and its focus on game design, I limit the use of "progressive" here to specific intentional design categories. I argue that Kojima and his teams simultaneously employ and disrupt established game genres and representations in order to build alternative game models informed by other cultural media. In other words, in an attempt to advance the expressive potential of the medium of games, Kojima's "progressive game design" takes existing game genres and models to create new ones.

To explore this design approach, I map each Kojima-directed game through its progressive game design practices as documented by Kojima and his development teams. And to accomplish this, I employ several methods of analysis that incorporate distinct registers of information. The primary method is archival, using periodical and paratextual materials to map the games' basic design and development. Supplementing this archival material is discursive analysis of primary media sources to understand the games' contemporary production and reception contexts. Throughout, I incorporate relevant secondary sources in game studies and related media disciplines to provide critical context to this industrial discourse. Finally, I apply close ludic and textual analysis of the rules, mechanics, style, and narrative of several of Kojima's games in order to see how these design practices were implemented (or not) within the games themselves.

Through this mix of approaches, I engage with four aspects of Kojima's progressive design that consistently emerge to disrupt existing game conventions: socially relevant narratives, mixed-media aesthetics, thematically connected rule-based systems, and reflexive spaces. Though I analyze these design elements separately, they are not discrete or disconnected from one another in the design process. They inform and modify one another as part of an integrated whole and should be viewed as a complementary approach to game design (see Figure 1.2).

Together these elements create play experiences that evoke twin aspects of Kojima's progressive game design. On the one hand, his games emphasize the need for players to be aware of and interested in humankind's *social progress*. This commentary is reflected in narratives

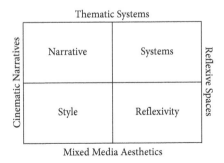

Figure 1.2 Progressive game design matrix.

that integrate contemporary conflicts, such as the widespread use of nuclear energy or the dissemination of fake news. Due to the games' commercial imperatives, these issues are allegorized via genre fiction such as mystery, sci-fi, and horror but are nonetheless critical of existing institutions, technologies, or political histories and alignments. This approach borrows not only from literature and cinema but also from popular fiction common to Japan's broader media landscape such as anime and manga. Using these popular forms, Kojima's games ask players to become conscious of these real-life issues and seek out ways to solve them.

On the other hand, his works embrace video games' ability to combine multiple media forms to create *industrial progress*. Hence, his games have been credited with redefining the boundaries of play, pioneering cinematic presentation, and creating new play systems/ mechanics such as the stealth genre. When paired with narratives of social progress, these systems also become challenges to conventions in existing popular industrial genres and structures, from mystery to action to horror, encouraging players to be critical of formulaic games (and ideas) such as the war game and its mechanics of violence to resolve conflicts. And even when these systems become absorbed and replicated by the larger commercial games industry, Kojima and his teams consistently attempt to innovate within these newly established structures. The resulting games occasionally invite criticism for their reliance on more linear media forms such as text, cinema, and animation but are also unique for their genre-bending, gameplay-innovating, and socially relevant experiences.

In a sense, Kojima's games are what he wanted to do with the many films and books he read as a youth all along: not to recreate them or even reenact them but to incorporate their conventions into digital game genres and interact with them. This means that Kojima's progressive design is highly tied to viewing video games as *multimedia*. That is, he freely draws from textual, audiovisual, and communicative conventions from existing media genres within the novel, radio, film, television, and social media mediums. These games often become simulated experiences of popular film or animation genres, reflecting Kojima's preference for genre entertainment. But they also have the power to stay with the player long after the completion of the game due to their ability to integrate real-world concerns. This inclusion of contemporary issues and problems disrupts the space and flow of play by ultimately bringing real-world issues into the diegetic or "in-game" reality of the game. The expanded game space conversely *increases* player immersion: as players realize that the fictional experience they believed they were playing is referencing their lived reality, the game and real-world converge, disrupting the limits of the ludic space. In other words, Kojima's game designs are constantly pushing at the boundaries of what industry, players, and larger society think commercial games can and should be. His games redefine the boundaries of what commercial games can talk about, how they can look, or what goals they can have, transforming our conceptions of them in the process. Where Comolli and Narboni asked, "What is a film?," Kojima asks, "What is a game?"

Structure of the Book

While Kojima's games are today most well known for appearing exclusively on Sony game platforms, his games have also appeared on a host of (mostly) Japanese home consoles and personal computers over the years such as Microsoft/ASCII's MSX standard, NEC's PC Engine, the 3DO, Sega's Saturn, Nintendo's Gameboy and GameCube, and the various Sony home and portable PlayStation systems. Though Kojima's games have become celebrated by the international gaming culture, understanding his games produced for Konami is to not only understand his particular approach to experiential game design but have a better understanding of a Japanese commercial studio approach to game development at the turn of the twenty-first century.

The second chapter of this book begins with how Kojima entered and made his first games in this incubated industry, examining Kojima's childhood influences from international cinema and genre fiction as a student, his early years at Konami in the planning department as a new university graduate, and his first game designs for the MSX home computer. The emphasis in this chapter is twofold. First, I establish how Kojima learned and grew from the late 1980s production context and development culture at Konami to design gameplay concepts around limited technological affordances. Second, I show how Kojima began to channel his literary and cinematic ambitions into what I argue is the essence of his progressive game design.

In Chapter 3, I examine the development and design of Kojima's adventure games, *Snatcher* (Konami 1988) and *Policenauts* (Konami 1994). Unlike the Metal Gear games and their influences from international action cinema and espionage fiction, these were games that developed from Kojima's lifelong love of detective mysteries and Japanese sci-fi television shows. Moreover, these were the first games where Kojima's design and direction merge as he was able to wrest a measure of control from programmers through scripting systems that enabled him to precisely direct the game's presentation and interactivity. The game's incorporation of animation production flows and, particularly with *Policenauts*, constant stylistic modification from version to version show how Kojima and his teams—first formed here as the "Kojima Clan"—viewed his games as forums for experimentation to present richer storytelling, worlds, and interactivity.

In Chapter 4, I look at the entirety of the Metal Gear Solid series developed for the Sony PlayStations 1, 2, and 3. Covering the entire series in a single chapter is an impossible task considering the complexity of their gameplay experiences and the richness of their themes. Moreover, the largeness of the games' AAA development meant that Kojima was increasingly less able to exert a martinet control over every aspect of production. Thus, the analysis is limited here to two interrelated areas. First, understanding how Kojima's progressive design carried over into the Metal Gear Solid series and how various developers assisted in and eventually took ownership over carrying out these designs. Second, showing how the franchise was able to resist an iterative approach to the trappings of formulaic video game franchise design by creating significantly different procedural experiences in each game. While this chapter argues that each PlayStation game carries the legacy of innovating story, style, systems, and reflexivity from the MSX Metal Gear games, Kojima's progressive design of the Metal Gear Solid games consistently alter *how* these four aspects are approached.

Following his fourth game in the Metal Gear Solid series, Kojima's game design takes a radical shift toward more open-world rule-based systems. In Chapter 5, I survey Kojima's games designed for portable game consoles such as the Game Boy Advance and PlayStation Portable to show how they would influence his design for *Metal Gear Solid V: The Phantom Pain* (Konami 2015) and, particularly, his first sole venture outside of Konami, *Death Stranding*. These games feature nonlinear systems of play that complement antiestablishment themes and narratives critical of American foreign policy. While the games are much more self-aware in their referencing other games and game genres, they simultaneously problematize the implicit rhetoric in these games as well.

The book concludes with an epilogue examining the legacy of Hideo Kojima's games and Kojima Productions, the designer-director's self-named studio that launched and shuttered while at Konami and was reestablished as its own independent game development studio in 2016. Kojima Productions carries on Kojima's design methods into new titles, particularly his concern for creating games that reflect real-world issues but also his desire to influence game developers through fostering a love for and fascination with other media, particularly cinema.

The following chapters in this book draw upon the words of Kojima and his "clan" of developers and designers, much of it derived from extensive paratextual materials produced for each of the games, including magazine features, interviews, strategy guide commentary, TV profiles, making-ofs, trailers, interactive documentaries, radio shows, and a wide array of social media activity, including Kojima's own very active Twitter feed. The bulk of this archival material has been obtained from Japanese and English-language game magazines and newspaper columns. Some of this material was difficult to acquire, and its availability was made through game history archives such as the web-based Internet Archive, the Setagaya-based Game Preservation Society, and, toward the end of the project, through the increasing amount of user-archived and translated materials by game historians and fans of Kojima's games.

Kojima is unique not only in the Japanese games industry but in video game development proper for his desire to constantly disclose the development process of his games to the public. These industrial disclosures function as part of a method of studio and self-promotion; Kojima has become an internationally recognized name in part due to his and Konami's diligence in promoting his work and status as a "game director" and a desire to claim authorship over collectively assembled game experiences. He and Konami have shaped his reputation as a designer who uses elements of multiple media, particularly cinema, for the direction of emotionally and thematically resonant games. One must be careful in attributing large amounts of collective work to a single author, no matter how influential. A potential harmful side effect of focusing exclusively on Kojima the designer/director is how the contributions of other developers can be sadly neglected or forgotten in the digital dustbin of history.

Kojima himself, thankfully, is aware of this problem. He credits his teams often in game credits, promotional material, and even his podcasts. As he is not a programmer or artist, it is also somewhat simpler to pinpoint what his specific influence is in the design of his games. A large part of this project is to demonstrate how one can conduct research on game designers that unravel the tangled threads of development to shine light on the particular contributions of individual staff members. This, of course, includes Kojima himself, whose outsized presence in the games industry is a welcome correction to the hundreds of talented designers who are still not acknowledged in the same way as their filmmaking peers. In an age of studio conglomeration where stars and talent have less control over their image or work and in a time where popular and casual mobile gaming has anonymized game designers and developers, Kojima's status of designer as superstar is a good reminder of how even the biggest AAA games can show the tastes, personalities, and design philosophies of their esoteric creators.

Chapter 2

ENTER KONAMI

DESIGNING EXPERIENCES FOR THE MSX

Hideo Kojima's reputation as a cinematic games creator is fed by both his fans and his own discourse. In his book, *The Gifted Gene and My Lovable Memes* (Kojima 2019), Kojima discusses the various books, music, and especially films that inspired him as a game designer and director, with asides in several chapters stating how a particular character or setting influenced a game design choice later in his career. While it is tempting to read Kojima's critical and promotional activities into his games, his designs are formed not just by Hollywood cinema influences but also by a number of domestic and international factors (Kojima 2008). In fact, the seeds of Kojima's progressive game design and his embrace of game direction emerged through a combination of three key aspects: one, his childhood background growing up in the Kansai region of Japan; two, his informal education through Japanese television, international cinema, and genre literature; and three and possibly most significantly, his early years working as a designer in small teams at Konami Entertainment in Kobe, Japan. These experiences led Kojima toward the people and conditions that would allow him to exert control over game creation in ways that few designers at large game studios ever have.

In this chapter, I examine Kojima's formative years in Kansai,[1] with an extensive analysis of the production context and game design of the two MSX games Kojima directed that would lead him to greater recognition many years later: *Metal Gear* and *Metal Gear 2: Solid Snake* (Konami 1990). This chapter is influenced by Nick Montfort and Ian Bogost's approach to "platform studies," charting how developers create game expressions by working through the specific affordances of computational systems (Montfort and Bogost 2009). Though Kojima initially wanted to make games for arcades or Nintendo's Famicom, he was instead tasked with making games for the MSX, an 8-bit standard computer that was jointly produced by Microsoft and ASCII Corporation. While the system today is hardly known outside of Japan, it had a loyal following of dedicated gamers who supported it for many years. The system was less prioritized within Konami compared to the Famicom, but it also afforded developers a degree of creative freedom that resulted in esoteric and experimental game concepts. This less regimented structure tasked planners for the MSX department with overseeing all aspects of game development. As Kojima described it: "We were in charge of everything from the game package to the ad copy to the design to the instruction manuals" (MSX Magazine 2003, 154). The ability to oversee the development pipeline was ideal for a novice like Kojima, who was able to quickly learn the different roles in game development, but also likely instilled in him the habit and desire to participate in many aspects of the development process.

"70% Made of Movies"

Hideo Kojima was born in 1963 in Setagaya-ku, Tokyo, the second of two boys to parents employed in the pharmaceutical industry. His life in the capital was short lived, as his father was transferred to Kawanishi City in Hyogo prefecture, and the family moved to the Kansai region when Hideo was three. Both of Kojima's parents were unusually employed full time, and he recalled coming home to an empty house every day after school as a latchkey child: "I still remember those feelings of solitude" (Edge 2004).

Kojima wasn't interested in school but soon found a wise and understanding friend: his television set. He began watching television voraciously: *tokusatsu*, or "special effects" superhero shows, animation serials, detective mysteries, and especially foreign movies. It was here that he began to develop the love of cinema that would influence the plots and settings of his games through watching dubbed versions of James Bond spy movies, Alfred Hitchcock thrillers, German war movies, and space adventures like Franklin Schaffner's 1968 *Planet of the Apes*. He loved stories about outer space in particular, having watched the Apollo moon landing on TV, but from early on had a strong interest in technology and its impact on social and cultural change. Upon experiencing the space-related pavilions and other exhibits related to state-of-the-art technology at the World Expo held in Osaka in 1970, he remarked, "One pavilion titled 'Humanity's Progress and Harmony' was really beautiful to me as a child" ("Kojima Hideo" 2000, 59).

Kojima's movie-viewing habits were encouraged by his parents, who began a ritual of watching a movie every night as a family after dinner. Once the movie was finished, his parents would ask him to critique what aspects of the film he thought were good or bad. "They wouldn't just show me kids' films," he said. "I'd even see the sex scenes" (Parkin 2012). The ritual continued when Kojima began attending movies in theaters like the Umeda Navio Hankyu and OS Gekijo in Osaka on his own. "The Asahi-za was the best," he said. "The owner would play *Cinema Paradiso* on the first floor screen, and Jean Claude Van Damme's *Cyborg* on the second floor screen" (Kojima 2008, 206). Kojima's parents gave him ticket money provided he give them a synopsis and critique when he got home. These critical faculties stayed with him his entire life, and he would eventually pen film criticism in his spare time. Even today, Kojima claims in his Twitter bio that "70% of my body is made of movies."

Studies have shown that practices such as "co-viewing" and "active mediation," or discussing media content after watching, help to encourage media literacy in children and assist in their ability to resist messages of violence and aggression (Mendoza 2009; Rasmussen 2014). Among their many talks, Kojima has remarked that his parents—a well-read couple who lived through the brutality of the Second World War—impressed upon him the horrors of war, a lesson that he would return to again and again when creating his own stories. His father, in particular, would tell him stories about the bombing of Tokyo. "He was running the streets searching for shelter from the bombs and fires. He told me he carried wounded children to safe places. His stories had a tremendous impact on me," Kojima said. His father was also a significant influence on his own fascination with Americana: "It was like walking a tightrope," Kojima explained. "He hated the Americans for the war, but when he got older he made contact with the United States and accepted, and finally fell in love with, American culture. I believe that I share this tightrope ambiguity with my father" (Edge 2004). In this way, Kojima's interest in cinema and cinema-viewing through television not only shaped the types of American-infused stories and settings of his future games but also his critical engagement with issues of American society through being prodded by his parents to reflect on the messages of media as a child.

Kojima's parents encouraged his artistic proclivities, and from an early age, he began experimenting with storytelling and writing. He naturally gravitated toward cinema and began writing scripts and shooting his own 8mm films with his junior high school friend, Tatsuro, for his boutique studio, HideTatsu Pro, which made a series of detective dramas and zombie horror films to show at school festivals and hawk to fellow classmates for pocket change (Konami 2005a, 144–5). But during this period, he also became a voracious reader—detective fiction, sci-fi, adventure, and fantasy—from a range of genre authors such as Agatha Christie, Isaac Asimov, Richard Matheson, Michael Crichton, and Kobo Abe (Onoue 2016), developing a strong affection for descriptive prose/dialogue and fantastical worlds/scenarios that would later inform the dense, sci-fi plots of his future games. He began to harbor ambitions of moving back to Tokyo and becoming a novelist, but he abandoned those plans when his father passed away when he was thirteen. When he was set to graduate high school, instead of heading to art or trade college and developing his storytelling urges in a more structured environment, Kojima stayed close to home, entering university to study economics. But this formative "research" period of creative reading and writing continues to inform Kojima's affinity for narrative complexity, social engagement, and specific genres—mystery, sci-fi, and political fiction most prominently.

Like much of his childhood, Kojima grew frustrated being surrounded by a student body that lacked interest in his own passions. "During this time, you could find me sleeping in a game center, porn theater, or a friend's house," said Kojima ("Kojima Hideo" 2000, 62). While Kojima had slowly abandoned his dreams of becoming a novelist or film director, he purchased a Nintendo Family Computer (Famicom, for short) and grew increasingly fascinated with the medium of video games and their nascent ability to express stories and worlds. In one interview, he cites several games that had the greatest influence on him as a young designer, including Nintendo's *Super Mario Bros* (1985), Namco's *Xevious* (1982), and Enix's *Portopia Serial Murder Case* (1983). One common thread in his explanations of why he found these games attractive is their purported ability to express hidden depths beneath the surface of the gameplay. In describing *Xevious*, for example, he says, "From the backgrounds and enemies to the mecha designs and even sense of naming, it showed me that games could have strong worlds" (Takei 2008).[2] In short, where the path to novel writing was cut off and the path to filmmaking was unclear, the path to games showed Kojima a burgeoning medium where he could still express his own personality via his storytelling and world-building urges.

Learning the Ropes

Nearing graduation from university, Kojima began applying to various toy and game companies, though he was particularly drawn to Konami for a few reasons. The first was logistical, in that the company was based near home and his mother in Kobe, and he was attracted to the headquarters located in the hi-tech Port Island. The second was practical: one of his economics professors recommended the company to him because it was listed on the Tokyo Stock Exchange and would therefore provide a semblance of security and social respect compared to newer and less reputable game companies. The third was an affinity for the company itself: he had played early 1980s Konami games like *Frogger*, *Pooyan*, and *Yie Ar Kung-Fu* in arcades and was drawn to their comical spirit.

Konami hired Kojima as an MSX planner (the rough equivalent in Japan of a game designer) in Development Division 3 (*kaihatsu sanbu*), a first for the company that had theretofore hired new employees only as programmers and artists (Konami 2005a, 177). The first game that Kojima provided planning support for was *Penguin Adventure* (Konami 1986), the sequel to the 1983 *Antarctic Adventure*, an endless runner type of scrolling platformer where the player controls a penguin who must race to various international research stations in a limited time while dodging obstacles like seals and crevasses. Though it was, in Kojima's words, a *kusogé*, or "shit game" ("Kojima Hideo" 2000, 64), he was evaluated favorably enough for his work on it to be assigned to the concept and design of another MSX title called *Lost Warld*, a project assembled from the scrapped remains of an action game called *Masked Fighter*. "The title was world but with war like a cross between war and world," he explained. "It was a Mario-esque action game with a story" (Kent 2005). Kojima was in charge of taking the game from concept— the "masked fighter" was replaced with a Lara Croft-like female explorer—to completion, and his team of newbie developers packed the game with various objectives, bonuses, and mini-games. But the team was inexperienced, found little in the way of support from the veteran staff, and was scolded by management for running behind schedule. Eventually, *Lost Warld*, too, was scrapped, culminating in six months of wasted work in what Kojima has called the "biggest disappointment of my life" ("Kojima Hideo" 2000, 65).

Kojima would move around to other projects such as the 1986 shoot 'em up *Knightmare*, providing planning assistance but without being given lead design duties. While learning on the job, two designers became mentor-like figures for Kojima during this time: Ryohei Shogaki, the director of *Penguin Adventure* and a planner on *Yie Ar Kung-Fu*, and Naoki Matsui, the designer for Konami's 1987 *Nemesis 2*, an MSX sequel to its port of the arcade shooter *Gradius*. The three would write design proposals all day, trying to one-up each other's ideas in a "jet stream attack." When Matsui and Shogaki went home, Kojima would continue late into the night, bouncing ideas off of other developers: "I would ask everyone (laughs). By doing that, I could see their reactions, and I could rethink ideas if needed. It's important to discuss new ideas with others, and it's something I still do to this day" (Konami 2005a, 177–8). Shogaki and Matsui had opposing leadership sensibilities. Shogaki was more of a motivator, pushing his team forward with insistent encouragement even when they came up against difficult situations. Matsui was more practical; if there was a problem, he would round up all of the programmers and go through each issue one by one using logical directions. As game designers, and not just project managers, they had a lot of influence within Konami, and Kojima credited them for his own approach to game design: "My style is if you combined them and then divided them by two" (Konami 2005a, 178).

One small consolation during this challenging period for Kojima was in realizing the joy of working on a project with a team; Konami provided the kindred spirits he longed for as a lonely student working on stories by himself. "They were failed manga artists, failed band musicians, failed writers and designers, and programmers who just lived to program," Kojima said ("Kojima Hideo" 2000, 66). It was an environment where the staff was itching to create to prove themselves. "The industry was full of dropouts, people who felt like games offered them another chance," he said. "I met many people in that same situation; we bonded together through that in some sense" (Parkin 2012). Konami—lush with bubble-era cash, a string of arcade hits, and the audacity to give out motorcycles to winners of anniversary party raffles—was willing to indulge their ambitions if it would bring about good business. But Kojima would have to win over his superiors with *solid* game concepts first.

The Birth of the Stealth Game?

One game had been giving developers at Konami trouble for months. It was a combat game codenamed project N312, designed in the vein of scrolling "combat" platformers at the time such as Capcom's *Commando* and SNK's *Ikari Warriors* that were heavily inspired by the popular *Rambo* films. Players controlled mercenary avatars, shooting and killing hordes of enemy soldiers over a scrolling jungle background. Konami's project for the new MSX2 standard—a slightly more powerful successor to the MSX—was designed to capitalize on this trend. The problem, however, was that the system's limitations made such combat difficult to achieve. It was from such limitations, however, that the idea for *Metal Gear* was created.

Limited affordances have birthed many significant innovations in game design, with the works of Nintendo's Game Boy designer Gumpei Yokoi ("lateral thinking with withered technology") being one of the most prominent examples (Yokoi 1997). The MSX2 was not technically inferior to more popular game consoles like Nintendo's Famicom; as a newer computational standard, it boasted a significantly more powerful Zilog Z80A CPU (with a clock speed of 3.58 MHz vs. the Famicom's 1.8 MHz), much more memory and video RAM (64 KB vs. the Famicom's 2 KB), and a much larger screen resolution and color palette (512 vs. 25 displayable colors). Games released for both the Famicom and MSX2 tended to look sharper and display a deeper range of colors on the MSX2. The problems, however, were in two processing areas that were debilitating for a scrolling combat game. First, while the MSX2 had a vertical scrolling register, it lacked a horizontal scrolling one to smoothly process horizontal scrolling per pixel. To work around the lack of a specific horizontal scrolling register, programmers for any game could manually adjust the screen location—dropping off and adding background tile graphics each time the player moves horizontally across the screen—though this would still result in the persistent appearance of choppy frames at the edges of the screen. A second, larger issue was the system's limited capacity to display simultaneous sprites on a screen. The MSX2 could display up to thirty-two color sprites at a time, though only eight sprites could be displayed on a horizontal line. Once this sprite limit was exceeded, the video display processor (VDP) prioritized certain sprites and dropped others. Simply put, if too many sprites in a game were lined up on screen, some of them would flicker since they had exceeded the system's single-screen sprite capacity. For a combat action game, this limitation meant that the action could be incomprehensible if multiple avatars entered the screen and both sides began firing bullets. Programmers would have to significantly scale back the details of avatars, restrict player or avatar movement to avoid lining up avatars horizontally, or reduce the total number of sprites that could appear on the screen. This last idea is seemingly the worst option, as a reduced number of enemy combatants in a shoot 'em up drastically makes the gameplay less challenging. But it was this option that Kojima innovated with project N312.

Fresh off the failure of his recently canceled game, Kojima was assigned to try and make a combat game from the limited affordances of the MSX2. He initially felt uneasy about making a war game considering the anti-war teachings of his parents, but he used this stance to his advantage by coming up with a solution to the hardware's limitations. "Rather than put out a bunch of enemies," he said, "I thought we could make a game full of thrills by having the player avoid a small number of enemies" (MSX Fan 1995, 5). Citing the influence of the Second World War adventure epics *The Great Escape* (Sturges 1963) and *The Guns of Navarone* (Thompson 1961), Kojima conceived of a war game where the player would not engage with enemies directly but would try to sneak *around* them in order to execute an infiltration and rescue mission (Kojima 2008, 134–40). The player would need to proceed through an enemy base without being spotted. In short, the creation of the "stealth game" was due to Kojima's acknowledgment of the limited affordances of the MSX2 hardware and a design of a concept that not only worked around those limitations but also around his discomfort with the goals of the war game genre.

While Kojima in interviews has often mentioned his inspiration for the original *Metal Gear*, which was initially titled *Intruder*, what is somewhat less discussed is how much resistance he faced from Konami staff upon his proposal. The stink of the failed *Lost Warld* meant developers were unwilling to see the potential in Kojima's proposed system, so he created detailed maps of the different base areas in order to convince them. This would set an early precedence for Kojima and his teams to visualize game concepts through maps, image boards, and other material designs that could be revised and iterated upon. Through these early rejected concepts, one can see how Kojima laid out the basic system of *Metal Gear* that would overcome both the sprite limitations and the lack of a scrolling function for the MSX2 (Kojima 1987). Early plans of the game's maps, for example, made possible the sort of continuous yet varied action that the game would require, but from a game design perspective, it also emphasized guiding the player through detailed, discrete environments that would become a recurring structural component of all of his adventure games. The game map was laid out in a flip screen overhead perspective, where the player would proceed from screen to screen with some amount of multidirectionality (see Figure 2.1). Each screen featured a different layout and one or two enemy soldier nonplayable characters (NPCs) or stationary cameras, whose path of movement or field of vision is indicated by arrows. The player would need to figure out how to proceed from one end of the screen to the other without moving into the enemy NPC line of sight by quickly grasping the enemy NPC movement loop. To give a sense

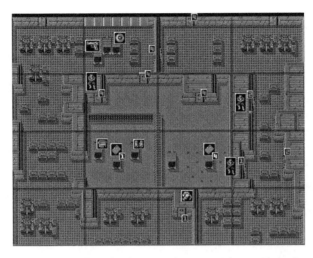

Figure 2.1 Map of a floor level in *Metal Gear* similar to Kojima's rejected proposal. Source: "Metal Gear MSX Floor Map" by Procyon, used under CC BY 3.0/ from StrategyWiki.

of progress, some screens also contained numbered items hidden in trucks or rooms that unlocked new abilities or accessible areas, while other screens contained characters who reveal important narrative information. In this way, the initial concept maps illustrate player progression at the microlevel (what to do in each screen) and macrolevel (the order of larger structural goals).

Eventually, Kojima gained the sympathetic ear of Naoki Matsui, who said he would push Kojima's proposal to his bosses if he could get it ready within a week. To his game design, Kojima added a fictional setting that drew upon his years reading war, spy, and adventure fiction as a youth. The game was set in the year 199X, where a legendary mercenary has established a rogue military nation 200 kilometers north of South Africa called Outer Heaven, which is rumored to be developing a weapon of mass destruction. Big Boss, the commander of the elite special forces unit FOXHOUND, sends operative Gray Fox to investigate. However, Gray Fox is captured days later; the only communication he sends back is the cryptic phrase "Metal Gear." Suspecting Metal Gear to be the feared weapon, Big Boss sends out another operative, the novice Solid Snake, to infiltrate Outer Heaven, retrieve Gray Fox, and find and destroy Metal Gear.

The game's basic system was completed in a month, and the entire game was released in July of 1987 after a development period of about four months, a timeframe not at all unusual for Konami or other studios

Figure 2.2 Side-by-side comparison of a promotional still from *The Terminator* (Orion Pictures 1984) and box cover art for *Metal Gear* (Konami 1987).

developing for the MSX2, which was used to releasing a game every three months. Kojima expressed difficulties with the production beyond the initial planning stages, as most of the team was more experienced than him. He didn't know many of the staff and had little say in aspects of the game's peripheral materials, such as its instruction manual art, which looks to have been designed by the same artist who did the instruction manuals for *Nemesis 2*, or its packaging, which modeled Solid Snake after the character Kyle Reese in James Cameron's (1984) action film, *The Terminator* (see Figure 2.2). According to his design docs, Kojima even intended for a more dramatic entrance of the opening credits and game title with fade-ins, but this, too, was replaced in the final version with the title flying in from the bottom of the screen. The game was able to at least realize his instructions for the intro logo's sharp sound effects.

The biggest innovation in *Metal Gear*'s design was in its redirection of player motivation in combat games from confrontation to escape via basic graphic and aural cues. Most combat action games at the time provided players with a cathartic feeling upon vanquishing a fleet of enemies, collecting power-ups, and becoming ever more powerful. The action itself varied little from stage to stage, and challenge came in the form of defeating more powerful enemies in greater numbers.

Metal Gear makes this catharsis very difficult to achieve by emphasizing mechanics of suspense. The game pressures players to avoid enemies and makes confrontation extremely unpleasant. If the player moves into the line of sight of the enemy NPC, a single exclamation mark appears above their head and their algorithm changes from a passive movement loop to actively follow Snake (see Figure 2.3). Once this algorithm is triggered, they will chase Snake down while shooting projectiles at him until one or the other is defeated. In some areas, two exclamation marks above the head of the enemy would indicate that enemy soldiers would continue to pursue Snake from screen to screen unless the player exits the area entirely; some areas even have enemies such as dogs that will constantly chase Snake from screen to screen. This stress, moreover, is augmented through the sudden change of the sparse score into frantic background music, enhancing the feelings of danger and panicking the player into frustration. Players would thus derive more satisfaction in proceeding through areas undetected and without killing enemies than if they were to directly engage them.

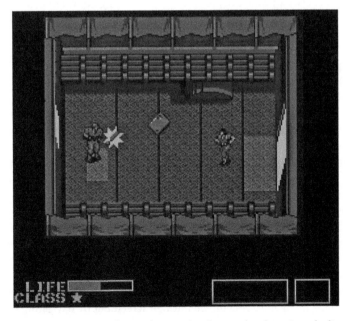

Figure 2.3 Walking into this truck immediately puts the player into the line of a soldier's sight. Smart players will wait until the soldier leaves the truck so as not to trigger his "alert" algorithm (*Metal Gear*, Konami 1987).

It would be incorrect to say that no other games had previously emphasized mechanics of enemy avoidance via stressful audiovisual cues. While recognized as the first "stealth game," *Metal Gear* was more of a puzzle-action game, one that actually had a lineage of early 1980s predecessors such as Taito's *Manbiki Shonen* and *Lupin III*, id Software's *Castle Wolfenstein*, and Sega's *005*, where gameplay involved collecting rewards while quickly avoiding the line of sight of enemies in top-down grid layouts. In these games, the core mechanic, or "essential play activity players perform again and again in a game," is *reacting* (Salen and Zimmerman 2004, 316). Specifically, players must react to the movements of the enemy AI and quickly move their avatar out of its line of sight, as the avatar is often ill-equipped with any other weapons or abilities than the input of movement.

Metal Gear, however, gave players a freedom of choice: fight or flight, even if one was encouraged more than the other. Players do not immediately encounter enemies upon entering a new screen, as the designers intelligently place them away from the screen where the player enters. Thus, players are given ample time to study each on-screen space before charting a course of progress. Players during this waiting time are not simply appreciating the scenery but are importantly memorizing the movement of the enemy AI in order to find the optimal path in which to proceed. Players must move through this maze of obstacles without triggering the enemy AI alarms, but if they are not able to "solve" each puzzle (i.e., they accidentally move into the line of sight of the enemy AI), they can also proceed by defeating the area's enemies through quick reflex shooting and dodging of enemy projectiles. Fighting is a last resort for frustrated players unable to chart a sequence of nonconfrontational progression, as progression in the game becomes considerably more challenging if players are not considerate of the details of the environment and the movement of the enemy AI. Thus, even in its early, puzzle-like stages, *Metal Gear* distinguishes itself from its quick-trigger stealth predecessors with what would become the core mechanic of the Metal Gear franchise: *waiting*. Or specifically, waiting to memorize the movements of enemy AI and proceed through levels undetected with a minimum number of stressful encounters. Kojima and the developers for *Metal Gear* thus created an alternative type of gameplay that provided tension and emotional release to players not by facing off against difficult enemies on screen but by navigating past them undetected.

Metal Gear is intricately structured, conveying a roguelike martinet direction over how players can proceed through the game. Most areas of the game are initially locked from player access via security doors that require progressively more powerful key cards, which the player acquires during the course of the game. The game guides the player to different rooms in the compound, and once those rooms have been exhausted for items, then other areas can be explored. While subsequent titles in the franchise open to allow for more flexible player exploration, *Metal Gear* is comparatively linear in the limited ways in which players can work through the environments. Most screens involve memorizing the loop of the NPC soldiers or surveillance cameras and then moving Snake quickly past them without getting into their line of vision. And few screens contain more than two enemies at any time, thus eliminating the MSX2 hardware's flickering sprite problem.

This linear progression also allows the game to place "bosses" at key junctions as obstacles for players to overcome, with their inspirations reflecting the protean influences from Kojima's childhood. The bosses are mercenaries who guard Outer Heaven, but despite the realistic trappings of the combat genre, they are drawn from the Japanese television shows that Kojima consumed as a child, particularly the *tokusatsu* Ultraman and Kamen Rider franchises, with their formula of having the titular heroes fighting a different, themed "enemy of the week." So while some enemies wield realistic weapons like machine or riot guns, others are made of cybernetic parts or hurl boomerangs from behind a wall of hostages. The enemies themselves are somewhat comical, with names like "Fire Trooper" or "Coward Duck," and also have backgrounds of their own, the information of which is included in the instructional manual. And of course, the eponymous Metal Gear mech itself would be out of place in a realistic war setting but is completely at home in Japanese mecha anime. Kojima was a fan of anime such as *Mazinger Z* (Katsumata 1972) and *Mobile Suit Gundam* (Tomino 1979) and included detailed diagrams of the Metal Gear mech for hobbyists in the game's instruction manner in a nod to *Gundam's gunpla* plastic model blueprints.

Paratexts like instruction manuals can flesh out narrative details difficult to convey within the game, but Kojima added an important and innovative function to the game itself that would convey both story and information: a transceiver device. Kojima did not realize the storage limitations of the MSX2 ROM at the time, packing the game with cut scenes that had to be removed for going over the ROM capacity; one of the few that were left was the opening scene in which Solid Snake swims up to the Outer Heaven compound, establishing that Snake must proceed from the bulwark without any equipment. The transceiver device was a separate interface that conveyed dialogue between Snake and another character. Players could also bring up the transceiver on their own by pressing a keyboard button and rotating a dial to the frequency of the character. Contacting and being contacted by different support characters throughout the game allowed the game to convey both the story and information that was lost by the removed cut scenes.

Most of the information relayed via the transceiver is in the form of mission objectives or hints in overcoming certain areas or boss fights, such as map tips from resistance leader Schneider. Depending on when players call during the game, however, allows them to access more humorous conversations. Placing a call to weapons expert Diane at the wrong time might connect you to her jealous partner Steve, who will quickly tell you she's "out shopping" or "in the shower." The big plot twist also comes via the transceiver calls, as Schneider tries to warn you that Big Boss himself is the legendary mercenary, only to be killed mid-sentence before he can drop the bombshell. Even Big Boss gets in on the action, telling you to give up and "turn off your MSX" when your pursuit of the mercenary gets you too close to the Boss himself, a humorous breaking of the "fourth wall" that would foreshadow many such moments in later Kojima-directed games (and which will be elaborated upon later in the chapter).

Despite the compressed timeframe and the lack of support Kojima received, as well as very little marketing or promotion of the game itself, *Metal Gear* was a mild commercial success, with the NES version of the game selling over one million copies (Kojima 1993a), even if Kojima himself had little do with a port he believed had "no sliver of appreciation for the players" (Hawkins 2011). Reviewers from both Japan and Europe viewed the game in a mostly favorable light. One critic from UK publication *The Games Machine* praised the "enormous area of play," the pacing of "action" and "suspense," the details in the world imparting a "sense of being there," and the game's addictive quality in how "the urge to get further in the game is quite strong" (The Games Machine 1987, 61). MSX fans in Japan were strident in their support, with the game quickly placing in the "Top 5" in *MSX Magazine*'s monthly polls and remaining there for months. One critic for the magazine even picked up on Kojima's brand of slapstick humor, singling out what would become a recurring humorous trope in future *Metal Gear* games of Solid Snake sneaking around using less-sophisticated equipment: "You can't help but laugh when you equip the cardboard box" (MSX Magazine 1987, 83). More importantly for Kojima, the game's release and recognition afforded him the respect of his peers and bosses, and a willingness from other developers at Konami to see his ideas through. Though the game was his "first child" (Kent 2005), there were seeds for the type of progressive games he would make in the future, with attention paid to the investigation of complex environments, multigenre story elements, humorous characterizations, and a desire to impart a message to the player, however obliquely.

The Making of Metal Gear 2: Solid Snake

The development team was given a week off following the release of *Metal Gear*, but for designers like Kojima, this simply meant time to come up with a new game concept. The idea that Kojima conceived, and would focus on for the next year alongside its role-playing adaptation, was the graphical adventure game *Snatcher*, which I examine in length in the next chapter. Kojima would not return to *Metal Gear* immediately, though Konami had responded to the game's success in the North American market with a sequel made by other Konami developers. Titled *Snake's Revenge* (Konami 1990), the game was only released outside Japan and had little to do, story or gameplay-wise, with Kojima's *Metal Gear*. Kojima, in fact, claimed he had not even heard of the project until a young developer who was working on the game approached him on a train ride home and begged him to make a true Snake sequel. Kojima got home and immediately penned a concept for what would be *Metal Gear 2: Solid Snake*.

Kojima's concept proposal was considerably more ambitious than his first child, with a noted emphasis on creating a deeper game experience on a sensory level. Instead of localizing the action to single screens, à la *Metal Gear*, Kojima envisioned a simulated real-time game environment. "The player must plan out a strategy not just for each screen, but for the entire map," he said. "The player's every action will affect the entire game world" (Kojima 1990). Enemies in the game would have their own loops, but the patrol area would expand to the entire map as enemies continued to "live" even if they weren't visible on the game screen (see Figure 2.4). Players would have to consider the entire movement of the area in a way similar to a simulation game. Another change that attempted to de-emphasize physical reflexes and draw on the player's "senses (sight and sound)" was in the form of more auditory cues: the sequel would emphasize sound effects (and de-emphasize background music) to add another layer for players to consider when moving around the environment. These sound effects

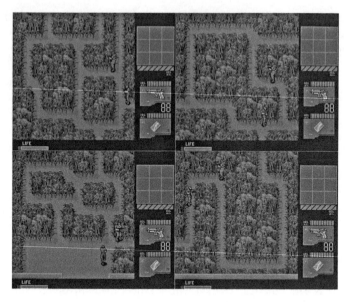

Figure 2.4 Tracking an enemy sentry in *Metal Gear 2: Solid Snake* (Konami 1990) demonstrates how enemies display "memory" from screen to screen for a more continuous experience.

made their way into the final game via the squeaking sound of Snake's footsteps on steel floors or the sound of a pulsating heartbeat when Snake sneaks through vent shafts (the team's idea of trailing a whistling soldier to the layout of a rescue target was left on the cutting room floor). Finally, the addition of a "crawling mechanic" was proposed to add a "sense of depth and three dimensionality" to the sneaking aspects of the game (Kojima 1990).

Konami's sales department needed convincing since the Famicom version of *Metal Gear* sold poorly in Japan. However, Kojima did not need to go to great lengths to persuade Konami's developers to create a sequel to his first game. He had gained their respect not only through *Metal Gear's* successes but also through the critical acclaim for the recently completed *Snatcher* and its detailed world and story. The development team even held a company-wide contest for designing the new Metal Gear D mech, with the winning designer, Tomohiro Nishio, going on to become the mecha designer for the game (Kojima 1993a). The game's development was not without its hiccups. Though development took six months, production was temporarily halted and the staff were moved to different teams due to complications with another game. The team also kept going over the ROM capacity, leading to changes in the game's specifications and a reduction in the originally planned character count (Konami 1991).

The much-anticipated release for *Metal Gear 2: Solid Snake* in July 1990 was almost exactly three years from the debut of *Metal Gear*. The game was only released in Japan, with sales figures difficult to determine, though, according to Kojima who went to a store on release day, "There was a long line of developers who had the faces of shrewd players" (Konami 1991, 6). The game met with strong critical acclaim from MSX publications. One review said that *Solid Snake*'s appeal lay in its "sense of suspense that you can't experience in other games (like an RPG or AVG)." The anticipation of the next set piece combined with the thrill of hiding from enemies "reveals a cathartic feeling that is a true pleasure." All of this gameplay, moreover, was buttressed by a "story that overflows with humanity" (MSX Fan 1990, 19).

The positive reception was notable, considering the title was Konami's last original game for the MSX2, a system beloved by its players for its eccentric games, and one in which Kojima developed a respect for despite an initial development reluctance. Working on the MSX also revealed Kojima's special ability to connect with game audiences and his desire for recognition from them. Kojima incorporated the MSX into several moments in the game—including an epilogue that follows the credit sequence—an homage to the system that comprised the first five years of his games career. The MSX was a "coming of age" for Kojima, who said that he was "learning and living together" with the system's players. Many gave him words of encouragement, which supported him during the early portion of his career. "I think we developed a kind of codependent relationship that went beyond the roles of simple senders and receivers," he explained (MSX Fan 1995, 9). Beyond Kojima's early recognition of and appeals toward his fan base, his relationship with players anticipates some of the effects of developers' higher visibility within the industry, as well as the rise of official and unofficial fan forums that invite players to comment on games in detail.

Directing an Experience: Progressive Game Design

While Kojima is recognized for innovations in Metal Gear Solid, his core design principles were developed by *Metal Gear 2: Solid Snake*. These principles revolve around what the designer-director and others have called the creation of *taiken* (MSX Magazine 1990, 45). Formed from the kanji characters of "body" (tai) and "to trial or attempt" (ken), *taiken* translates in Japanese as both "to experience" and the "experiences" themselves. The word suggests a practical, physical approach to trying out something to which one is unaccustomed. This was a key word used to explain the concept of *Solid Snake*. The instruction manual, for example, said the game's concept was developed from "both the feelings that you can only get from novels or films, but also the *experience [taiken]* of simulation that you cannot taste from novels or films." From this "simulated experience," the creators sought to make a "new convergent entertainment" that would move games from the "era of play" to the "era of experience."

The design of experiences in games is not exclusive to Kojima, and other designers such as his *sempai* Shigeru Miyamoto have also described their games as the play of everyday-inspired experiences. Jennifer deWinter has argued all game designers, in fact, are "experience designers." Therefore, "an auteur approach to game designers needs to attend to how game designers are trained to think about game experiences, how their cultural context shapes their worldview, and how their working conditions allow them to realize their visions" (deWinter 2019, 178). Understanding a specific designer's approach to game design thus means understanding multiple contexts—national, local, professional, industrial, and temporal—to decipher the *type* of experience the designer is aiming to create.

In an interview with the Smithsonian American Art Museum in 2012, Kojima stated the importance of considering the overall experience in his game design: "What would it be like if you were actually there? What if I could simulate this somehow in a game and have it be interactive? That's where I start my game designs from, looking at an experience and trying to re-create that experience." Kojima's early writing on game experiences also articulates the type of experience he intended to create via games. The language in the ad for *Metal Gear 2*, in fact, reflected what Kojima wrote in an internal memo to Konami employees in 1989: games were moving away from "play" and toward the "reading" of a "single created image (world)." Within that world, the images and settings are established, and the game elements are there merely to progress the world. Kojima identified that people were playing games not just to kill time but for the stories, visuals, settings, and a "source of cultural absorption" that was similar to what his generation experienced watching movies and reading genre fiction. For this new generation of players, games were a virtual reality device capable of simulating alternate ways of seeing and being:

I think that the "play" of games, first of all, has strong elements of "make believe," where we place ourselves in an imaginary world, decide on the rules and roles, and engage in a simulation of that fictional world. The games at the turn of the century will be able to reproduce these make-believe elements more realistically and make possible a make-believe play that is exceedingly close to the real thing. That will be less a game than a way to *taste the world* (emphasis in original), and will simulate culture, ideas, and many kinds of life necessities. These perfected games will take the reading elements of novels and movies and combine them with educational elements to create an "experience" game. (Kojima 2004)

From an early point, Kojima's approach toward game design was to contribute to the larger cultural discourse by simulating experiences derived from the films and genre fiction of his youth. His game designs after *Metal Gear* reflect not only this desire for cultural engagement but a larger impulse for games to simulate multilayered experiences as a greater range of affordances become available from more advanced computational systems.

Kojima and his team do this not by any one method but through embracing games as a conduit for synthesizing multiple kinds of media, combining "rule-based systems, non-linear elements and elements adapted from linear narrative media" (Stemmler 2019). By drawing upon the strengths of different media forms, Kojima directs experiences that not only simulate linear narrative media but also are capable of evoking deeper emotional responses and more varied intellectual output from players than games that emphasize mechanics or competition. These game experiences utilize contemporary discourses or technologies to "update" existing game genres and structures primarily through four means:

1. Blending fictional and real-world elements in novel-like linear narratives.
2. Remediating the aesthetics of more audiovisual-oriented media such as live-action cinema, animation, and motion graphic novels.
3. Reinventing rule-based systems around the emergent play of detailed environments.
4. Inserting or incorporating spaces for reflexive purposes.

I will examine these four aspects—narrative, style, systems, and reflexivity—in the following chapters presenting Kojima's games in greater detail, but each is already evident even in the 8-bit technology of the MSX2 with *Metal Gear 2: Solid Snake.*

Thematic Narratives

Unlike for the first *Metal Gear*, Kojima had a strong hand in shaping the scenario for *Solid Snake.* While Kojima's games feature narratives that are based in sci-fi and fantasy tropes, they are filled with events that reference real-world contemporary geopolitics and technological developments. Such references are not necessarily unique to Kojima's games and are quite common in games that exhibit "social realism," what Alexander Galloway has called "games that reflect critically on the minutia of everyday life, replete as it is with struggle, personal drama, and injustices" (2004). As Kojima's games are organized around spectacular situations, they don't necessarily exhibit social realism, but they are socially conscious, offering "direct criticism of current social policy" (Galloway 2004) in increasingly complex narratives that do not simply refer to contemporary social issues for the sake of topicality. Their progressivism stems from the fact that they provide critical commentary and even prescriptions to issues through the plots, characters, and gameplay.

Solid Snake's world is set in an alternate denuclearized 1999 (a plot point that would be retconned in future versions of *Metal Gear Solid*) that is also facing an energy crisis due to the rapid exhaustion of fossil fuels. A Czech scientist named Kio Marv invents a synthetic fuel called OILIX that could potentially solve the world's energy problems, but he is kidnapped en route to an academic conference by soldiers from Zanzibar Land, a rogue nation established by mercenaries in Central Asia after separating from the former Soviet Union. NATO discovers that Zanzibar Land's leaders intend to hold Dr. Marv hostage and take control of the world's petroleum supply; mercenaries there have collected nuclear warheads salvaged from old stockpiles marked for dismantling and are possibly creating a new nuclear weapon in the vein of Metal Gear. Roy Campbell, the new leader of FOXHOUND, calls in Solid Snake to rescue Dr. Marv on Christmas Eve and protect the world from a new nuclear threat. This brief description of the plot provided in the game's introduction evokes Cold War politics, projects Soviet Union developments, references the oil crises of the 1970s, anticipates the 1990 oil shocks that follow Iraq's invasion of Kuwait, and directly places the player in the role and perspective of America's human intelligence and security.

We can also see in *Solid Snake* an explicit antinuclear theme, as opposed to the implicit messaging of nonviolence in *Metal Gear*, along with exhortations to avoid the fear and tension of arms races. This is another example of how the media Kojima grew up with exerted an influence on the thematics of his games, as Japanese media has an extensive history of portraying or dealing with the aftereffects of nuclear weapons and energy and the fallout of the Hiroshima and Nagasaki atomic bombings, from the Godzilla film franchise to various manga and anime such as Keiji Nakazawa's *Barefoot Gen* and Sunao Katabuchi's *In This Corner of the World*. It should come as no surprise that Japanese video games also exhibit this nuclear discourse, with franchises such as the *Final Fantasy* series allegorically communicating antinuclear ideology. As Rachael Hutchinson (2019) has noted, such games can be even more effective in communicating their ideology than other forms of media, as "games demand action and decisions from players. This can create a more self-reflective environment, conducive to the reception of ideas" (130). *Solid Snake* does not allegorically deal with nuclear weaponry but instead directly represents and critiques nuclear arms proliferation through a narrative of mercenaries threatening the world with nuclear war. Indeed, the depressing endlessness of war is reiterated in the game as well, most shockingly in the form of war orphans who the player encounters living in Zanzibar Land; late in the game, it is even suggested that they will be trained as child soldiers and sent off as mercenaries into an unnamed battlefield.

These themes are part of a larger world, a narrative built across multiple eras, geographies, and games that evokes the serial manga and anime narratives Kojima consumed in magazines and on television as a child. *Solid Snake*'s history is a deep, alternate chronology of political events that Kojima had to revise several times due to changing global developments. "The Tianenmen protests, the Romanian Revolution, the German reunification," he said. "I wrote that the Berlin Wall would fall in the middle of the 1990s, so I was shocked when it actually fell [during the course of production]" (Konami 1991, 5–6). *Solid Snake* also references newly introduced characters who openly discuss Solid Snake's exploits from *Metal Gear* (now set four years earlier) regarding his defeat of Big Boss and take down of Outer Heaven. Characters from *Metal Gear*, moreover, appear in *Solid Snake* and directly reference their actions several years prior as if the time that has passed between games has passed for the characters in this world as well. This is most clearly seen in the evolution of Grey Fox, a victim in *Metal Gear* turned tragic villain in *Solid Snake*. This direct and repeated referencing of *Metal*

Gear's story provides the game with rare and sophisticated instances of intragame seriality, asking players to connect the references within *Solid Snake* not only to contemporary world politics but also to various narrative details between games made three years apart. Here, the benefit of having a single designer pen scenarios for both games is evident; while Kojima has often muddled details between games, the attempt to create an interconnected history via repeating narratives, characters, and world details from previous games, also even including allusions to *Snatcher*, makes the world of *Solid Snake* historically and thematically richer.

Mixed Media Aesthetics

Kojima's games stylistically evince many types of media modes, a concept referred to as "multimodality" (Kress 2010; Bateman and Schmidt 2012). *Solid Snake*, like many of Kojima's games, draws particularly from the aural, visual, and even textual elements of linear narrative cinema. This is by design, as the structure of the game was assembled like a screenplay to bring out the game's detailed thematic story in a playable experience. In the rough scenario for the game, one can observe how the game is organized not by levels or stages but via scenes titled by the action in the game. One scene called "Follow the whistling man," for example, is accompanied by a "hint" that indicates a clue presented to players, an "event," which states the sequence's objective and how it will resolve, and "story" that reveals the concealed mysteries of the plot. While *Solid Snake* presents large fortresses, jungles, and desert areas, each of these areas are actually composed of these scenes of smaller missions where players must complete specific objectives related to the narrative. Thus, Kojima's scenario design is not simply that of background history or character but of presenting players with specific scenes to experience. Each scene is designed for the player to interactively unveil the concealed narrative: tailing a soldier into the women's restroom or sneaking through sleeping quarters without being spotted results in the revelation of story details that incrementally reveal the stakes of the plot.

This is where Kojima's infamous lengthy cut scenes begin, with one magazine at the time stating that these were "the finest cut scenes ever seen in a Konami game" (MSX Magazine 1990, 45). Learning from their mistakes with *Metal Gear*, Kojima and his team quadrupled the ROM capacity from 1 Mbit to 4 Mbit to include the cut scenes from the planning stages (Kato 2014a). This is immediately evident

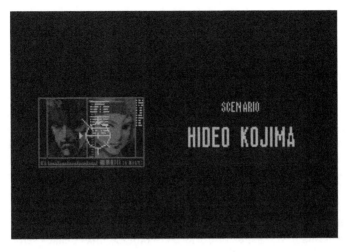

Figure 2.5 Opening cut scene for *Metal Gear 2: Solid Snake* (Konami 1990).

in the two opening cut scenes for the game—one that features the game's credits displayed alongside the construction of the Metal Gear D and another that narrates the backstory—that together are over six minutes long (see Figure 2.5). Accompanied by a dynamic score, they evoke the opening credits of a sci-fi action film directed by James Cameron or Mamoru Oshii (two directors for whom Kojima has openly expressed his admiration) despite the limited technology at the developers' disposal.

Cut scenes are not unique to *Solid Snake*, and games from *Tetris* to Namco's *Ms. Pac-Man* (1981) have included them as rewards from the stress of the gameplay, such as the cinematic featuring the moment when Mr. and Ms. Pac-Man first meet following the completion of the second stage. They also can introduce basic narratives, such as the opening cut scene to Nintendo's *Donkey Kong* (1981) that shows Kong kidnapping the princess, climbing the construction scaffolding, and challenging Jumpman (the player) to come rescue her (Kohler 2005; deWinter 2015). But *Solid Snake*'s cut scenes were more elaborate, often several minutes long when combined with radio conversations and created with the express purpose of allowing players to connect to characters on a deeper level than the typical avatar. Two of the most memorable cut scenes involve Natasha Marcova (later changed to Gustava Heffner), the former Olympic figure skater turned Czech state security operative, sent to rescue Dr. Marv from Zanzibar Land. When she comes across Snake, the two engage in some flirtatious back and forth, while also going into Natasha's sad childhood fleeing the Nazis and failed relationship with Frank Hunter, aka Gray Fox ("Our Berlin Wall was too high for either of us to climb"). Soon after reaching Dr. Marv, Natasha is attacked by a missile while crossing a bridge, destroying the bridge and leaving her for dead. The previous cut scene between Snake and Natasha sets up an emotional payout, where Natasha's death becomes a meaningful and tragic one, and one that will reveal itself once again in the game's final moments. The destroyed bridge, moreover, becomes a constant symbol of Snake's impotence; it stands in his and the player's way and takes over another hour of gameplay before it can be crossed in a cathartic cut scene when Snake sails over it on a hang glider. Finally, the cut scene introduces Gray Fox, who has survived the destruction of Outer Heaven and is now commanding troops in Zanzibar Land. The death of Natasha at the hands of his former comrade links Snake's sense of loss and anger to the player, creating an even stronger motivation to complete the game and exact revenge.

While Kojima's subsequent games would utilize 2D animation and 3D graphics for their cut scenes, his games are ultimately cinematic not because of lengthy cut scenes but because they were among the first to utilize the tools of cinema to present the story and gameplay, as well as reference existing films and actors, in a practice called "stylistic remediation." "Remediation" is the representation of one medium in and by another and is often used to describe how new media takes the form and iconography of older media (Bolter and Grusin 1999). "Stylistic remediation," on the other hand, is what Drew Morton (2016) calls "the remediation of formal and stylistic attributes that are specific to one medium or the other" (6). Kojima's own words explain this process quite well: "When I talk about games that are like movies, I don't mean just using FMVs. What I mean is a game that draws on the various elements and techniques of film such as its direction, script, or lighting" (Game Hihyô 1996, 56).

In the case of Solid Snake, the stylistic tools of cinema were used to enhance the audiovisual drama of the game. One can view the game, in fact, as a complex silent film, a comparison Kojima has made on his early career on multiple occasions: "Games were composed of simple actions like those seen in old Chaplin or Keaton movies: running, jumping, digging, throwing" (Parkin 2015). In a review of Charlie Chaplin's *Modern Times* (1936), Kojima wrote, "I am a creator from gaming's 'silent era.' Games were games; they aren't movies. Games had no sound or color originally. But they were still games" (Kojima 2008, 40). This combination of cinematic technique with interactive gameplay can be seen in the design of the spaces where the player controls Snake. The MSX's affordances were not ideal for a scrolling camera and shooting gameplay, so Kojima compensated for this limitation by emphasizing a wide shot lens that allows the player to view all of the action within the diegesis or on-screen action.[3] The game compensates for the lack of spoken dialogue, moreover, through remediating multiple cinematic aural and textual elements—sound and graphic effects to signal different alerts, a strong musical score that indicates tension in different environments, and a variation of intertitles in the various radio communications to convey plot, character, and even humor.

For all the comparisons to popular entertainment luminaries like Cameron or Spielberg, Kojima actually more closely resembles another, more eclectic auteur in Quentin Tarantino, whose encyclopedic and idiosyncratic knowledge of genre films inflects all of his films and the mythos surrounding his auteur personality (Semenenko 2004). This intertextual knowledge is reflected in Solid Snake in the many references to popular Hollywood films at the time, from its titular hero's name being a nod to Kurt Russell's Snake Plissken in Escape from New York (Carpenter 1981) to the Die Hard (McTiernan 1988) homage in setting Snake's rescue operation on Christmas Eve. But it is Solid Snake's original art design that most clearly signals the ambitions of its creator to stylistically remediate a cinematic experience with "talent" from films that Kojima personally enjoys. In both the instruction manual and radio communications, each of the characters' portraits is based on a real-life likeness: Snake (Mel Gibson), Big Boss (Sean Connery), Roy Campbell (Richard Crenna), Holly White (Brenda Bakke), Frank Hunter/Jaeger (Tom Berenger), and George Kesler (Dolph Lungren) all are imbued with a celebrity flavor despite the game's simple sprites. And unlike the largely uncontrolled experience Kojima had with regard to the art for Metal Gear, he had a much stronger say in the package design of Solid Snake, getting Yoshiyuki Takani—a famous illustrator of resin kits and promotional posters for early 1980s sci-fi anime titles such as Super Dimension Fortress Macross and Nausicaa of the Valley of the Wind—to design the dynamic package art for Solid Snake evocative of these other works.

Emergent Systems and Complex Environments

On the face of it, Solid Snake and the various games in the Metal Gear franchise are what Matthew Weise (2009) has called "procedural adaptation, or the taking of a text from another medium and modeling it as a simulation" (238). As mentioned earlier in the chapter, this means that *Solid Snake* simulates not only war espionage films like *The Great Escape* and *The Guns of Navarone* but also spy films and TV series such as the James Bond or *Mission: Impossible* franchises that focus on using sophisticated tools to sneak around heavily manned enemy compounds. These rule-based simulation systems are typically redesigned at the point of new console platform technology, where Kojima and his team create engines that account for the console's larger range of affordances. This was not the case with *Solid Snake*, as the game was made for the same MSX2 standard as *Metal Gear*. But considering *Metal Gear* was Kojima's first complete game, he was not a part of its initial planning, and he did not have much experience with or understanding of the MSX hardware at the time, *Solid Snake* could be considered the first *Metal Gear* title where Kojima was familiar with the processes of game development and the goals of game design. Where *Metal Gear* was primarily a puzzle game, *Solid Snake* is truly a stealth game, adding new movements for players and enemies that broaden the possibilities for more realistic sneaking mechanics similar to its cinematic inspirations.

Part of this realism was obtained by Kojima and his team doing extensive research, gathering books, films, toys, and anything military related they could get their hands on. At one point, there was a mountain of model guns on their desks, and some developers started showing up to work in full battle fatigues. They met and interviewed an author who was a former Green Beret member. They even practiced survival games in the mountains with laser guns, with some staff becoming the models for Snake's new crawling mechanic. Many of the photos of detailed weapons in the instruction manual and packaging were also apparently taken of the staff's own toy gun collections. According to Kojima, the process became all-consuming, like method-acting as design: "Our work became our hobby, we became otaku, and our everyday life became a game simulation" (Kojima 1993b).

The attention to realism shows up in a more immersive environment, most apparent in the newly intelligent enemy AI. Enemy soldier algorithms for routes are less predictable, with improved cones of vision that extend across the entire field and not just in direct lines. Further, enemies themselves can now move from screen to screen, with multiple enemies now able to appear on screen at once (even if they are not all firing bullets). This added enemy complexity would be impossible to navigate without a scrolling screen if not for the addition of a radar map in the top-right corner of the screen that shows the layout of the floor

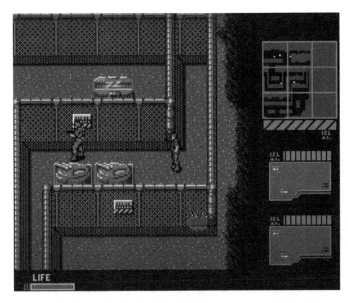

Figure 2.6 The radar screen in the top right shows both the map layout and the location of enemies. While helpful, it also has the unfortunate effect of drawing the player's attention away from the game field in *Metal Gear 2: Solid Snake* (Konami 1990).

and where enemies are located within it (see Figure 2.6). When spotted by enemies, the map is no longer visible due to an "alert mode" that does not disappear until Snake has hidden from his enemies for a set period of time. These various interfaces, modulated by the radar map, raise the stakes for players to proceed carefully by punishing them with more prolonged sequences of suspense if caught. The radar greatly increases the depth of stealth gameplay, as players now need to be cognizant of enemies both on- and off-screen, of diegetic *and* nondiegetic action, and its removal is highly punitive as it essentially casts players into the darkness.

The addition of details into environmental conditions and textures also adds to the stress of sneaking in a populated environment. Certain floors now make sounds when Snake walks on them, alerting guards to the player's presence. While elevators acted as a sort of magic safe zone in *Metal Gear*, they operate more realistically in *Solid Snake* as players must press a button to call them up and wait for them to arrive. This small act adds to the tension of specific areas, where players must order an elevator and slip into it quickly enough before being spotted by an approaching guard. And the environments themselves have a greater sense of interactivity due to the fact that Snake can crawl. Stationary tables, air vents, holes in fences, and even cardboard boxes that were once part of the background can be moved through, into, and hidden under. Despite the top-down 2D perspective, Kojima and his team were already thinking that deeper levels of interactivity—and true stealth mechanics—required a 3D depth of field that could balance the more intelligent enemy AI by giving players greater flexibility in how to proceed through environments. No longer single-answer puzzles, environments became emergent systems with multiple possible routes and options for player navigation.

Solid Snake, though, is not only a game that procedurally adapts the spy or espionage war film. It actively makes arguments about contemporary war, both directly through its narrative and more obliquely through the game's play mechanics. Presenting arguments through the game's mechanics is what Ian Bogost (2007) calls "procedural rhetoric" or the "process of persuading through processes in general and computational processes in particular" (3). As Nintendo's *Smash Bros.* and *Kirby* designer Masahiro Sakurai (2004) puts it, the Metal Gear series "pushed the anti-war philosophical message that the more you can avoid confrontation with the enemy, the better it was" (106). Players thus were encouraged not to sate frustration via aggression but by avoiding conflict. In a gaming culture that celebrated accumulating high scores via kills and victories, a system that rewarded players for considering nonviolent options was an especially novel innovation. But it also functioned as a moral commentary by questioning the logic of war games, its inherent trivialization of human life, and its positing of armed conflict as the solution to difficult objectives. Like the real world, diplomacy and nonviolent means of determent can also be much more difficult to accomplish, but the rewards to human (and player) life and social order can potentially be far greater.

Moreover, while each game in the Metal Gear franchise deals with similar topics such as the impact of war and technology on modern society, these topics are investigated in myriad ways depending on the social and temporal context in which the game takes place. This creates distinctive themes for each game, which are then in turn complemented by a system of play that corresponds to those themes and creates a slightly different procedural rhetoric from the preceding game. For example, where *Metal Gear Solid* deals with a general anti-war message and a stealth system that corresponds to avoiding enemy detection, in *Metal Gear Solid 4*, the war machine has created a world where heroes and villains are less distinct. As such, Kojima and his team constructed a system of play where the player can switch between sides of battle with a more flexible stealth mechanic. I will investigate these systems in more detail in Chapter 4, but while each Metal Gear game can be described generically as a "stealth" game, each also has its own rule-based system that distinctly communicates a unique procedural argument. This stands in stark contrast to most game franchises that typically iterate on existing systems for audiovisual or narrative details yet offer scant criticism or commentary on the various mediums they procedurally adapt.

Reflexive Spaces

The "fourth wall" is a term that originated in theater to describe an invisible wall that separates the fictional world on stage from the world of the audience (Bell 2008, 203). While the audience is aware of this separation between their reality and the fictional setting that is before them, the actors on stage are typically not. This illusion can be broken, however, if the actors address the audience directly, an action commonly known as "breaking the fourth wall." Some performances will intentionally break the fourth wall with actors addressing the audience for comic effect, while others, such as the works of playwright Bertolt Brecht, break the fourth wall for a "distancing effect" where the actor "appears strange and even surprising to the audience" (Willett 1964, 91). Applied to screen media such as film, TV, and video games, the fourth wall would refer to the barrier between the fictional world on screen and the physical space of the spectator or player. Fourth wall breaks are employed considerably less in games than in film/TV, though they do exist. Carter, Gibbs, and Harrop (2012), for example, refer to fourth wall breaks in games as an "action made by a player's character which makes use of knowledge that the character is not meant to be aware of" (13). This concept also has parallels with the idea of "the magic circle," a phrase popularized by Johan Huizinga's theories of play used to describe the separation between a game's fictional world, bound by agreed-upon rules, and the world of the player (1949, 10). A breach of the fourth wall or magic circle in games can mean that the fictional reality of the character in some way acknowledges the lived reality of the player.

Kojima's games have become famous for just such fourth wall breaks and magic circle violations. There are several examples of this in *Solid Snake* when characters will directly reference the world outside the game, particularly in the transceiver radio communications. For example, Roy Campbell tells you to "think like a game designer" when trying to overcome obstacles, and Dr. Kio Marv hides his formula for OILIX "inside an MSX cartridge." Another character named Master Miller is very concerned for your personal well-being, instructing you at various points to "wait 30 minutes after eating before playing games," not to "drink too much soda while playing," and to not "picture the GAME OVER screen, even when you make a mistake." These examples directly reference video games within the game itself, reminding the player that they are participating in a fictional experience and interjecting the fictional diegesis with game practices, technologies, and conventions of the player's world.

Indeed, there is an entire Wiki dedicated to instances of the fourth wall being broken in Metal Gear Solid. However, the practice is so common in Kojima's games that it is rendered practically meaningless to think of them in terms of violating a magic circle that is separate from the real world. Instead of thinking of Kojima's games as breaking or obeying the concept of a fourth wall, it is instead more instructive to see how he and his team open up the game diegesis beyond the boundaries of the screened world to consider other material aspects of the game and its environment. In recent years, scholars have challenged the concept of the magic circle, arguing that a separation of the real and fictional world of play is, in practice, an impossibility due to various factors such as the player's background and environment (Duncan 1988; Liebe 2008; Consalvo 2009). Steven Conway (2010) argues that, instead of thinking of such boundary-crossing games in terms of breaking imaginary walls, we think of them as "expanding" or "contracting" the circle as the fictional world of the digital game moves beyond its previous boundaries to incorporate other software and hardware. This "circular wall" conversely *increases* immersion since the screen's game world is now blurring with physical reality (147).

One common way in which Kojima creates this circular wall in his games is through the integration of its paratexts into the play experience. The literary theorist Gerard Genette (1997) defined paratexts as a "threshold" between the text and what frames it (2). This includes both formal framings, such as covers, titles, and notes, but also discursive framings, such as newspaper reviews and magazine interviews. Jonathan Gray (2010), applying this to media such as film and television, argues that some paratexts like toys, games, and spin-off novels and websites can "inflect or redirect the text following initial interaction" (35). Such a practice is ubiquitous in Japanese media, where the package design of analog media is as much a selling point as the media itself. Liner notes accompanying CDs, collector's boxsets for DVD films, and elaborate extras such as figures and fashion packaged with anime Blu-rays function as promotional devices and playful accompaniments to the featured media. Beyond the shopping incentive for fans and collectors, such packaging facilitates its own kind of ludic mastery in its encouragement of audiences to intensely search out exclusive information unavailable in the media itself (see Daliot-Bul 2014, 86–91). Kojima's games involve not just the design of the play experience but its paratexts and their incorporation as well: instruction manuals, box art, console interfaces, trailers, and even the physical discs themselves become possible means for extending the spaces of play.

With *Solid Snake*, the game's physical packaging is involved in the play of the game in several ways. Much of the game's story is fleshed out to an extreme degree in the instruction manual, authored by Kojima himself. Over half of the manual provides detailed information regarding the game's fictional world, including the background and formation of FOXHOUND; detailed backstories for the main characters such as Solid Snake and Big Boss[4]; the history, economy, and demographics of Zanzibar Land as well as reports of its top mercenaries; a copy of Operation Intrude F104, Snake's mission instructions; a scientific explanation of OILIX's chemical properties; and various explanations of Zanzibar Land's military vehicles, including five pages of blueprints and specifications for the Metal Gear D (see Figure 2.7). The manual is also referred to within the diegesis of the game. In one instance, Roy Campbell directs players to decipher a secret tap code using a grid provided in the game's instruction manual. The game's MSX box is even incorporated into some of the game's puzzles and challenges, such as when Roy Campbell instructs players to change radio frequencies but tells them that the new frequency is "found on the back of the game's software package."

Such details could easily be provided to players within the game, and the idea of moving players away from the screen would seem to break the spell of the "magic circle." However, it is more instructive to view such actions as not moving players out of the game world but expanding its parameters to that of the player's environment. By directing players to outside of the game space, *Solid Snake* delimits the boundaries of the magic circle and extends the possibilities of immersive entertainment. This multidirectional play extends the experience of being a spy to outside of the screened reality, with players now resorting to unconventional means to overcome obstacles and solve problems. Such

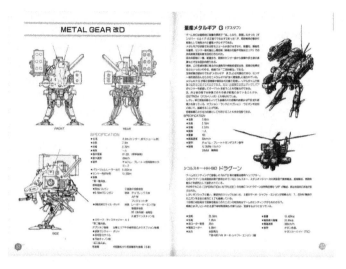

Figure 2.7 Mechanical and narrative details in the 55-page instruction manual for *Metal Gear 2: Solid Snake* (Konami 1990).

resourceful actions also indirectly reinforce the game's themes; as players become conditioned to connecting with the game even when they step away from the screen and controller, these boundless play spaces get players to continue thinking about the experience of the game long after finishing it. "I want to express something to players, leave them with something," reflects Kojima. "Something that doesn't just finish with the end of the game, but a first step that sparks interest in the real world" (Konami 1991, 7). Such an extended experience becomes the final step in Kojima's progressive design: narrative themes, aesthetics, and systems which draw from real life are incorporated with a larger goal of creating greater public awareness and, hopefully, social change.

The Best Is Yet to Come

Hideo Kojima's *Metal Gear* games for the MSX were well regarded among MSX owners, but without an international release for *Solid Snake*, his reputation outside of critical circles in Japan was nonexistent. The two games, however, would lay the seeds for the Metal Gear Solid franchise that would make him a household name. Importantly, they would allow Kojima to develop an approach to game design that he would employ in his career even through industrial and technological changes.

Like many designers during this period, Kojima was inspired by the genre fiction and cinema of his youth and surroundings. That he sought to incorporate the influences from the cinema, television, literature, and manga that he and his generation were interested in should come as no surprise. That fact that he was able to take these fictions into interactive experiences, however, was due in large part to the particular environment he found himself in during his first years at Konami. As a new designer, Kojima was tasked with essentially fixing a broken concept. Having to think through the limitations of the platform and create a mechanic that was still fun despite these restrictions forced Kojima to reckon with the fundamentals of commercial game development. Unburdened from the oversight and pressures of developing for more popular systems, he was then able to create and further refine the game experience through the relatively free and niche development culture of the MSX planning team and, by extension, the detail-oriented nature of its players. Such an environment asked planners to work with programmers and oversee multiple aspects of development, allowing Kojima to innovate not just a new type of gameplay but also embellish its drama by writing complex plots and scenes for the game and its paratexts.

Developing for the less popular MSX, then, was ironically a blessing for Kojima. It allowed him to work with and learn from more experienced developers, who he then had to convince of his own game concepts with detailed plans, diagrams, and explanations. Working through the limits of the platform's technical affordances eventually allowed him to indulge in the bounds of his inspiration and work ethic, a habit that would continue with other game genres and platforms with a greater range of affordances.

Chapter 3

SMALL TEAMS, BIG WORLDS

PLAYING DETECTIVE IN *SNATCHER* AND *POLICENAUTS*

Following the mild success of his first completed project in *Metal Gear*, Hideo Kojima was told to immediately think of his next game proposal. In a week, he came up with what would be his second cinematic game at Konami, a title approved for development on the NEC PC-8801 with the condition that it be simultaneously developed for the MSX2. This proposal would become *Snatcher*, a graphical adventure game released in 1988 that put players into a very different *taiken* than the puzzle and action infiltration of *Metal Gear*. Once again, Kojima found inspiration from Hollywood cinema, though in this case, a more contemporary and timely influence: *Blade Runner* (1982), Ridley Scott's film adaptation of Philip Dick's 1986 novel *Do Androids Dream of Electric Sheep*. The cyberpunk film is set in a futuristic Los Angeles and stars Harrison Ford as Rick Deckard, a plainclothes police officer tasked with tracking down and terminating rogue androids called "replicants." As Kojima explains it, "Sid Mead, Ridley Scott, Vangelis, Douglas Trumbull—all of these figures who I'd been attracted to were linked together here. Saying I simply like the film doesn't do justice to the deep feelings I have towards it" (quoted in Mashita 1992, 104). *Snatcher* is similarly set in a neon-soaked melting pot called Neo Kobe (a reference to both Konami and Kojima's origins) in the year 2042 (2047 for the Sega CD version), when half the world's population has been wiped out by a biological weapon. The player's perspective is from a similar detective-like character named Gillian Seed, a "junker" tasked with tracking down and terminating androids called "snatchers," who kill humans and take over their lives. Gillian suffers from amnesia and becomes a junker in order to discover his past with the help of his trusty sidekick robot, Metal Gear mk-II.

Six years later, Kojima would complete a second graphical adventure game, *Policenauts*, inspired by 1980s Hollywood action cinema, particularly the buddy action flick *Lethal Weapon* (Donner 1987). The film's pairing of loose cannon Martin Riggs (Mel Gibson) and straight-arrow Roger Murtaugh (Danny Glover) as they team up to stop a gang of drug smugglers created comedy out of the standard detective cop formula, relying instead on a buddy dynamic that Kojima found appealing: "I made *Snatcher* and *Policenauts* from my love of buddy movies, and I want my buddies to always be on the side of justice" (Kojima 2008, 82). *Policenauts* begins in a future dystopia called Old Los Angeles in the cluttered office of private detective Jonathan Ingram, a former cop-turned-astronaut recently woken from cryosleep after an accident on a space colony sent him adrift. Jonathan heads back to the colony, now a thriving advanced civilization called Beyond Coast, to investigate the death of his ex-wife and the disappearance of her husband. He contacts his former "Policenaut" buddy, Ed Brown, and as the two begin their investigation, they uncover a drug- and organ-trafficking operation that might be run by their old Policenaut comrades.

Other aspects link these two games beyond their cinematic inspirations and themes of justice and urban corruption. Specifically, both games were pivotal turning points for Kojima in his role as director. While critics point to the Metal Gear Solid series as when Kojima incorporated cinematic influences into modern games, *Snatcher* and *Policenauts* laid the seeds for his more well-known efforts. Both games were successful experiments with crafting a different type of experience centered around playing detectives inspired not only from the 1980s films popular with Kojima and his peers at the time but also by police procedurals that Kojima grew up watching as a child, like Richard Levinson and William Link's *Columbo* TV series and adaptations of Seicho Matsumoto's 1974 novel *Castle of Sand*. In both games, Kojima was able to exhibit a level of command over the development process that began with his commandeering of *Snatcher*'s game engine and culminated with the advertising of Kojima's direction of *Policenauts* as "A Hideo Kojima Game."

In this chapter, I examine the design processes of Kojima's two graphical adventure games from 1988 to 1996. Specifically, I look at how Kojima's progressive design was applied to the adventure genre of *Snatcher* and *Policenauts*, creating detective stories that pushed the boundaries of the genre and the video game medium through narratives, aesthetics, and systems that drew upon other forms of media. This focus on innovation is displayed through Kojima's incorporation of many of his childhood influences such as detective novels/TV serials, radio dramas, and sci-fi animation into the adventure game genre. But this experimentation was importantly borne out of the control afforded to

Kojima and his team at Konami's Kobe studio. They created extremely detailed world settings and scenarios, utilized sophisticated animation production processes and pipelines, and methodically iterated as new formats and processing capabilities allowed for the increased storage of information and more interactive affordances. This stable development environment allowed Kojima and his team to experiment with ideas, systems, and stories that emotionally draw players into the game's action and blur the boundaries of the real and game world. Such playfulness is mirrored by a real-world concern that players continue to think about the games they play and how they reflect social issues and dramas even after they finish playing them. This desire for games to inspire ongoing reflection by meaningfully disrupting game "flow" is a key design practice for Kojima and his teams.

World-Building Neo Kobe

When Kojima proposed what would become Konami's first adventure game in *Snatcher*, the genre was growing rapidly in Japan and around the world. Emphasizing environmental exploration and deep character interaction, graphical adventure games demanded longer play sessions and attention from players than coin-ops. Anastasia Salter (2014) defines the adventure game as involving "a player seeing a story through from beginning to end, following the experience of a viewpoint character—the player's avatar—on a quest shaped by the world and story crafted by the designer" (4). While the adventure game began as a series of text-based commands and responses on personal computers in the 1970s with titles such as *Colossal Cave Adventure* and *Zork*, the genre grew significantly in the 1980s through graphical bitmap illustrations, such as Sierra Entertainment and co-founder Roberta Williams' landmark *King's Quest* series (1984–), which cast players as a knight in a fantasy realm who must venture on an epic quest to protect his kingdom.[1] The development of point-and-click interfaces, such as those pioneered by *Maniac Mansion* (Lucasfilm Games 1987), combined complex narratives with mechanics that asked players to solve puzzles via exploring a colorful game space through a set of predetermined verbs such as "look," "talk to," and "pick up" (Fernandez-Vara 2008, 221).

In Japan, graphical adventure games proceeded along a different path owing to the country's deeply embedded comics and animation industries. One of the most influential, at least to Kojima himself, was Chunsoft and Enix's *The Portopia Serial Murder Case*, a mystery adventure scripted by *Dragon Quest* maestro Yuji Horii that Kojima claimed was "the rare game where the personality of the creator was evident in the world, design, story, and puzzles" (Takei 2008). Players assume the role of a detective ("Boss") who must investigate the murder of a bank president in Kobe. The perspective and narrative are entirely presented in the first person, and players must either type in or select from a menu of commands in order to proceed with the investigation. Despite technological limitations, the game effectively conveys an eerie atmosphere, complex characterization, and a killer plot twist, showing a young Kojima that "even games can depict human drama" (Takei 2008).

Horii's game was released for both the PC and Famicom, selling 700,000 copies (Iwamoto 2006, 201) and leading to subsequent investigative adventure games in the mid- to late 1980s such as Riverhillsoft's *J.B. Harold Murder Club* on the PC Engine and Nintendo's *Famicom Detective Club*. During this time, as personal computers from NEC became increasingly graphically sophisticated, adventure games that doubled as digital comics also emerged. Contemporary magazines reveal dozens of advertisements for adventure games based on animation properties such as Micro Cabin's game adaptations of Rumiko Takahashi's *Maison Ikkoku* and *Urusei Yatsura*, or Toho's game based on Hideaki Anno's *Nadia the Secret of Blue Water*. These games used similar interfaces to *Portopia*, though more for the purpose of advancing stories based on the animated properties rather than solving mysteries. Thus, while reviewers and even Kojima himself state that *Snatcher* is most influenced by Hollywood cyberpunk works such as *Blade Runner* or *The Terminator*, the game is equally a child of the Japanese games industry's trend toward mystery and anime-inspired adventure games in the 1980s.

While Kojima owed a debt stylistically to these films, what distinguishes *Snatcher* from them—and from other adventure games in Japan and even the United States at the time—was its dedication to creating a deep world or *sekaikan*. In Japanese, *sekaikan* translates directly to "world settings" or "worldview" but often is used to convey the atmosphere or lived-in quality of the fictional world that has been created. It can also refer to the particular feel of the world as created by its author. In his study of anime production, Ian Condry (2009) defines *sekaikan* as "the properties that define the world in which the characters interact" (141). As a concept in the English language, it is perhaps most similar to J. R. R. Tolkien's process of "subcreation," what Mark

Wolf (2012) has described as a system of "secondary world" creation that relies on not only geography or history of the created world but also its characters' experience of it. Manga creator and theorist Eiji Otsuka (2010) has written persuasively on the importance of *sekaikan* to consumption in Japan. As an editor for Kadokawa Entertainment, Otsuka was responsible for publishing works that could spawn a wide world of ancillary media and products. As Marc Steinberg (2015) argues, "world" in this instance refers to a "cosmology, the rules of the world, the chronology of events that take place in the world—and that give a sense of reality or verisimilitude to this fictional universe" (51). Such fictional rules, chronologies, histories, and geographies were in demand particularly in the 1980s due to the growth of passionate fans, or otaku, of anime, manga, and games. Deeply engaging and learning about the worlds of their favorite works became a key selling point to fans who wanted to better understand how every detail of a fictional world connects to and shapes the whole.

Kojima was aware of this fan-driven push for deep *sekaikan* and viewed *Snatcher* as an opportunity to disrupt the existing conventions of world-building in the graphical adventure game genre. But creating a game whose greatest pleasures were built around unearthing its infinite world details rather than on solving puzzles or progressing the narrative meant questioning the very fundamentals on which the adventure game was based. At the time of *Snatcher*'s proposal, Kojima's superiors at Konami met the idea of imbuing a game with *sekaikan* with similar resistance to *Metal Gear*'s stealth action. According to Kojima, "I was told controls or gameplay were more important than the *sekaikan*. That's how it was internally, but I would get remarks like, 'What the hell do you mean the game's world? Who cares about that?'" (quoted in Mashita 1992, 103). Konami had released role-playing games with adventure elements, like the 1987 *Knightmare III: Shalom* for the MSX2, but *Snatcher* was its first attempt at building a true adventure game, and Kojima was insistent that deep world settings would distinguish it from its competitors. The desire to craft a rich world for players to explore would form one of his key beliefs for design: "My personal view is that—whether it's an adventure game or RPG or simulation—I would like to convey a strong *sekaikan* in my games from now on. Players can experience something here that they cannot in real life" (quoted in Mashita 1992, 104).

Snatcher's *sekaikan* is created through the accumulation of information found in its lore, dialogue, and environments, both in the game and its paratexts. Kojima personally researched and penned Neo Kobe's lore, much of which can be accessed via the Junker HQ's computer network, Gaudi (localized into Jordan for the Sega CD version), but can also be scrutinized in the game's mammoth 64-page instruction manual. Details include the formation, rules, and equipment of the junker; models and mechanical blueprints for various robots and vehicles, including a four-page breakdown of the construction of the snatchers; and a history of Neo Kobe itself, complete with a calendar for the year 2042 and statistical data cataloging the city's laws, demographics, economy, environment, climate, geography, geopolitics, sources of transportation and energy, and even its residents' leisure, sports (such as air surfing), and amusement (the robot musical stands out). Through the accumulation of these details, Neo Kobe transforms from an amorphous cyberpunk setting to one that seemingly reflects real-life, cosmopolitan, Asian cities and city-states such as Hong Kong and Singapore. Kojima and his team even incorporated into the game's package what Jonathan Gray (2010) has called an "entryway paratext" which preps or determines audiences entrance to a text (35): The *Snatcher* instruction manual begins with a short comic that goes into a bit of backstory between Gillian and his estranged wife, Jamie, and the world of Neo Kobe before the player has even picked up the controls.

Snatcher's interactive mechanics are a balance of investigative and shooting play, but its *sekaikan* is accessed most prominently in the design of its investigative portions. Much of the game is spent at the Junker HQ gathering information and going to different locations to investigate the building mystery. *Snatcher* utilizes a first-person perspective menu-based interface rather than the third-person point-and-click interface of games like *King's Quest*. This means that rather than investigate the details of the images, players must access the details of an action tree with Look, Investigate, Talk, Listen, and Move options (see Figure 3.1). Only certain combinations of actions will yield results; for example, players must first "investigate" an object or environment and then "look" at it to further scrutinize it. Once the various options have been exhausted, players are usually then confronted with an "action" first-person shooting sequence involving the snatchers or other enemy robots on a 3 x 3 tile grid. While these portions are meant to evoke the action sequences from the detective and buddy cop films of Kojima's youth, they are rigid and repetitive in their execution. On the other hand, the investigative portions offer the most variety in terms of options and outcomes. As *Snatcher* doesn't reflect the "hidden objects" puzzle ethos of Sierra Entertainment's adventure games, the game's affordances are focused on repeatedly

Figure 3.1 Example of the action tree in *Snatcher* (Sega CD: Konami 1994).

visiting areas, talking to people, and learning about details within the static images.

These affordances consist of a lot of repetitive action but varied results, as players are rarely presented with the exact same text-based responses or descriptions twice upon talking to any person or investigating any object. One extreme and comical example is when the player talks repeatedly to Mika Slayton, a receptionist at Junker HQ, who provides several different rejoinders to Gillian's attempts to ask her out on a date. Another example is a video phone that players can access when they go to Gillian's apartment to call his estranged wife, Jamie. Depending on when players call, they will access different conversations with Jamie, revealing new aspects of both her character and Gillian's as they try to rekindle the love they no longer can remember. Such seemingly spontaneous scenes are what Sebastian Domsch (2013) calls "event triggers" or actions that are performed by the player that "triggers a narratively relevant event that would not have occurred" without the player's action (41). Event triggers in games often occur spatially, though with *Snatcher*, the event triggers are textual-spatial, as they involve players navigating the space through text commands. Event triggers are also often employed for narrative purposes, "tricking" players into triggering story events while making them think the action occurred spontaneously. With *Snatcher*, this extends to even minor, "hidden" dialogues and events that require selecting commands repeatedly in various situations. Curious players can test the limits of the system, talking to characters for their responses in seemingly the most inappropriate moments that can trigger further conversations or events.

The amount of textual variation and event triggers revealed the dedication of the creators to think of multiple and exhaustive permutations of player interaction, fostering the idea of a living, actively changing world. This aspect was even advertised by Konami on the back of the game's box, touting its screenplay as "over 900 pages." The game's multiple outcomes for player inputs illustrate what Espen Aarseth (1997) has termed the "ergodic discourse" of adventure games, where narrative is revealed through the negotiation of a space between the game and the player. A typical adventure game is not played by being "read" once but "by being played over and over, as the way we reread a great and complex novel" (113–14). Only when the readers/players feel they have exhausted all possibilities in the event space will they put down the text. Thus, despite the action-oriented ad copy and cyberpunk trappings, the core mechanic of *Snatcher* is not shooting but investigation. Players are presented with a static environment and then are encouraged to survey and exhaust every permutation of that environment for additional "readings." This aspect of investigating environments *before* infiltration would also become a core component in the Metal Gear Solid franchise.

The dedication of its creators to pack these environments with copious details did not go unnoticed by fans and critics. One magazine wrote, "These details build the game's *sekaikan*, and there likely hasn't been an adventure game with such attention to *sekaikan*. There might not even be many RPGs that have gone so far" (Yamashita 1988, 3). Little of this information has any bearing on the game's story or mechanics but does create the feeling of Neo Kobe's reality that players can feel they are a part of. More importantly, much of this information is optional, allowing players to proceed with the game's story or to diverge into trivia collection depending on the experience they want at the moment. "Unlike a movie, where you look at the plot from a single angle, games are interactive," Kojima noted. "If there's one block in the game, we need to think about its design from all angles" (quoted in Mashita 1992, 104). This textual play differentiates *Snatcher* from digital comics—where players are merely pressing cues to progress the story—and keeps it in the realm of adventure games, where player interaction is necessary to complete puzzles or to piece together environmental cues.

Remediating Cinema/Anime

Kojima was determined to have more say over the development process than *Metal Gear* when he began designing *Snatcher* in 1987. Rather than leave tasks to others, Kojima said he made adventure games because he "wanted to do it all and control all the roles" (Kojima 2008, 92). He had a simplified scripting engine created so that he could manipulate the game's program, from the commands and flags to when animation or text displayed; basically, everything in the game except the sound, graphics, and programming. "It was a way to take back control from the programmers," said Kojima (Parkin 2012). The design docs for *Snatcher* (which was originally titled *Junker*) indicate that the engine Kojima created was heavy on "switch" commands, and the language allowed Kojima to precisely indicate the timing of when dialogue would appear or when music would cue (Westbrook 2011). It was the first time at Konami where Kojima would be able to directly regulate the game experience, and *Snatcher*'s eight-minute opening cut scene, complete with opening staff credits, loudly announces his cinematic ambitions from the start screen.

The development of *Snatcher* was intimately small, with many of the luxuries that kind of production system affords to exacting creators. At the beginning of the project, Kojima and character designer Tomiharu Kinoshita were the only two working together on models and layouts, a process that Kojima enjoyed: "It was like we were making a film or an anime" (Konami 1989, 3). Even at its largest, the team was about half the size of a typical Famicom game project, meaning the game's developers assumed multiple duties, could respond quickly to problems, and tested out many ideas without a lengthy approval process. This can be seen in the visual design process in particular: Kinoshita said he and mechanical designer Yoshihiko Ota initially "just drew and drew" approximately 300 character and mecha design sheets (Konami 1989, 4), indicating the level of freedom the small team had to pursue its own aesthetic choices and direction.

Snatcher stylistically remediates contemporary Japanese animation, particularly the type of darker "adult" anime that had become popular in the 1980s through video distribution and the niche otaku, or superfan, market. The game's presentation aimed for a cinematic quality that was advanced for graphical adventure games, incorporating visual references to both contemporary Hollywood action cinema and Japanese sci-fi animation. Satoshi Yoshioka, a character designer for the PC Engine port of *Snatcher*, said he was instructed to make the graphics "as 'cinematic' as possible" (Tieryas 2017). According to Yoshioka, the visual design of the game was heavily influenced by contemporary Hollywood science fiction and horror cinema such as *Blade Runner, The Terminator*, and *Alien*: "I made the graphics used in the game with a great deal of respect to [these films]. I was especially interested in the Hollywood SFX [special effects] at that time, and I tried to honor their spirit" (Tieryas 2017). These cinematic and animetic influences are all over the game's visual designs. The snatchers namesake is taken from *The Body Snatchers* (1955), a Cold War–inspired allegory by Jack Finney that has been adapted to film multiple times, though their appearance in the game is an almost direct copy of the T-800 cyborgs in James Cameron's *The Terminator*. Neo Kobe directly references Neo Tokyo in Katsuhiro Otomo's groundbreaking manga and anime *Akira* (1982–8), which also inspires much of the dystopic cityscape. And as Yoshioka states, *Blade Runner* figures into much of the game's visual design, from the neon noir color palette to the design of Gillian Seed, whose long trench coat and scruffy appearance are based on Rick Deckard (junkers are even referred to in the game as "runners").

Other characters are inspired by actors and actresses whom Kojima personally had an attachment to through watching them on television as a child. Jamie Seed is based on Lindsay Wagner, who played Jamie Sommers in the sci-fi television series *The Bionic Woman* (1976–8), and Randam Hajile is loosely based off of Sting's Feyd Rautha character in *Dune* (Lynch 1984). Certain areas of the game feature more characters from Kojima's memory, such as the seedy nightclub Outer Heaven, which is populated by a den of sci-fi and *tokusatsu* characters like the Xenomorph and Kamen Rider (see Figure 3.2). Even Kojima acknowledges the game skirts the line between homage and plagiarism. Referring to the anime miniseries *Gunbuster* (1988-89), which was a parody of and homage to robot anime created by Hideaki Anno and the fan-turned-pros at Gainax animation studio, Kojima stated, "*Snatcher* was pretty much the same way; there's a ton of references in the game that sort of skirt copyright laws" (Gifford 2009). The bricolage of these references, however, creates a visual scheme of its own that is less based on any single film or set of films, and more on the genres and types of characters Kojima and his staff were attracted to at the time. It is, indeed, not dissimilar to how Japanese animators, inspired by Star Wars films and Hollywood science fiction, created the body of works (including *Gunbuster*) that formed the bedrock of the "space opera" genre of the 1980s.

外に出る   注文する
見る   持物
調べる   メタルギア使う
呼ぶ

Figure 3.2 A nightclub scene in *Snatcher* (NEC PC Engine: Konami 1992).

Also similar to *Gunbuster* is the way that *Snatcher* becomes a work that expresses the storytelling desires of its creators beyond its initial parodic designs. The cinematic presentation of *Snatcher* acutely infects the game's narrative progression through manga-like storyboards and plotting. While paper prototypes are common during the initial planning stages, Kojima and his team created a three-tiered storyboarding process for how the game's story should be visualized to players. The first stage involved creating a "Pre-Storyboard" (*kikaku konté*), which loosely illustrated the general flow and direction of the script in each layout. The storyboards were revised repeatedly to dramatically present the scenario to the player. The second stage was the "Storyboarding" (*ékonté*) process, which accounted for the flow of the action upon inclusion of characters and backgrounds. The storyboards were checked and revised for their planning, characters, sound, and programming, becoming a "bible" for the developers. Finally, the "Drafting" (*shitagaki*) stage involved drawing in the details and colors, determining the lighting, instructing where to insert animation or SFX, and digitizing. This level of attention to narrative framing suggests Kojima wanted to emphasize the story, even if it meant in some instances to de-emphasize player interaction and agency. Thus, the storyboards used here are part of a larger design approach of switching back and forth between controlled, cinematic sequences that reveal narrative details, and more open-ended investigative play that allows for players to explore the world at their own leisure.

More specifically, all of this carefully planned direction of style and scenes had an important complementary design purpose: to involve the player *emotionally* in the investigative play of the mystery. The detailed process allowed Kojima to exert control over the tension of scenes and the gradual reveal of information, such as the sequence of shots that comprise Gillian's entrance into Neo Kobe City. The player is first presented with an establishing shot of the Neo Kobe skyline as the staff credits roll over them. This opening credit sequence is followed by alternating close-ups and medium shots of Gillian within the interior of his vehicle as it moves through the city, conveying his anxiety inside its tight confines. Finally, the sequence cuts to a wide shot of the Junker HQ building to indicate Gillian's arrival at his destination. The scene effectively lays out the atmosphere of Neo Kobe City, puts players into the position of Gillian as he is about to start a new job in a new place, and establishes the home base for the player's (and Gillian's) information gathering. The storyboards of this scene, presented in the game's instruction manual, show how instructions were layered at each step of the storyboarding process to convey a mood which players would feel before exploring the world on their own (see Figure 3.3).

This cinematic design extended beyond the development of the PC-8801 and MSX2 *Snatcher* and began a trend for Kojima and his teams to continually revise the game's experience when upgraded technology became available. Because of the difficulties in programming for the PC-8801 and MSX2 simultaneously, lack of experience with the staff, a condensed planning schedule, and a tight budget, production took over a year and a half (Kato 2014b). The game that finally shipped in 1988 was severely reduced from the six-chapter scenario that Kojima had originally conceived of down to two. The team stepped away from the game to work on *Metal Gear 2: Solid Snake*, but upon that game's release in 1990, they were reassigned to port *Snatcher* to NEC's PC Engine (the TurboGraphx-16 outside Japan and France). Rather than settle for a simple copy, Kojima and his team took the opportunity presented by the PC Engine's CD-ROM add-on to completely rework the game's graphics and enhance its audio, presenting the first instance where Kojima expanded upon the same game for upgraded hardware. He was

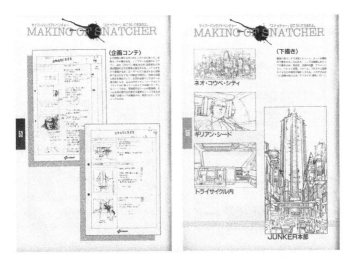

Figure 3.3 Storyboards for the opening prologue to *Snatcher*. On the left are the "pre-storyboards," while on the right are examples of "drafting" detail (NEC PC Engine: 1992).

also now officially credited as the game's "director" and not simply the creator of its "scenario" as in previous versions.

The port benefitted from the small team production as many of the same staff who worked on *Snatcher* could control how they updated the game's art and narrative. Yoshioka explained, "I could redesign the supporting roles like Chin Shu Oh relatively freely. So I designed them to suit my preference" (Tieryas 2017). All of the layouts were redrawn and recolored to fit the enhanced color palette of the PC Engine, and Yoshioka drew small portraits for each of the characters to appear next to the text when they were speaking. From a narrative standpoint, while Kojima couldn't finish his six-chapter opus, his team was able to add a concluding third act to wrap up the PC-8801 and MSX2's unfinished cliffhanger. This final act has few interactive segments and plays more like a digital comic, with little of the environmental investigation or gun-shooting sequences that were present in the first two acts. The third act foreshadows Kojima's tendency to build interactive components around long, cinematic cut scenes, such as those found in his Metal Gear Solid games, in which narrative is not subject to player alteration. Kojima was not unaware of the limitations he imposed, as many players apparently voiced their complaints to him, but restricting player agency in this last act was a conscious choice designed to impart the tragedy of the ending: "I wanted players in Act 3 to feel the frustration and sorrow of not being able to alter the fates of these characters" (Gekkan PC Engine 1993, 125). Kojima's approach to narrative construction is made clear in this early example, where player ability to shape the narrative or create multiple endings is avoided for the purpose of a clear message or theme that moves the player emotionally, an aspect of his game design that I will elaborate on later in the chapter.

This narrative control also includes that of the game's audio experience, which created new incentives for players. As Carl Therrien (2019) points out in his analysis of the PC Engine, while many of the console's games were advertised as "cinematic" experiences, most games had to be judicious with recorded voice and animation due to storage limitations. *Snatcher's* ludic economy, or reward mechanisms, "relied on the attractiveness of every new scene as an incentive for players to take on a series of complicated puzzles" (110). Kojima and his sound team amplified the emotional intensity of the game's many still-frame dialogue sequences to compensate for the game's lack of animated movement, and these performed dialogues also doubled as cut scene rewards for players to work toward. The Konami Kukeiha Club commissioned a full soundtrack for the PC Engine port, and Kojima spared no expense hiring top-quality voice talent from the Japanese animation industry, enlisting Yusaku Yura (*Saint Seiya* and *Chibi Maruko-chan*) as Gillian, Mami Koyama (*Magical Princess Minky Momo* and *Dr. Slump*) as Metal mk-II, Kaneto Shiozawa (*Fist of the North Star* and *Crayon Shinchan*) as Randam Hajile, and singer Kikuko Inoue (*Ranma ½* and *Ah! My Goddess*) as Jamie. All were established voice actors (*seiyu*), with numerous titles to their credit. Advertised in the instruction manual as "the largest recorded amount of dialogue" ever to appear in a game, the recording took place over a full day at the Avaco Creative Studio in Nishi-Waseda, with eight voice actors providing two and a half hours of dialogue for twenty-six different characters. This was an early example of the sort of celebrity casting that many adventure games would follow, from Jane Jensen's *Gabriel Knight* series of games to Sega's *Yakuza* franchise.[2]

Kojima directed the cast himself, starting a precedent where he would personally oversee the Japanese-language voice direction for all of his games. While the actors could use the layouts from the old game for Acts 1 and 2 to synch their dialogue, the recording was taken with only the script and character designs, with Kojima giving directions on the atmosphere of a scene or where characters were blocked. The resulting audio took up every last bit of storage capacity on the *Snatcher*

CD-ROM, to the point that the developers could not even squeeze in a ten-second music clip toward the end of production. But the finished product, along with the addition of a complete musical score, greatly enhanced the emotional impact of *Snatcher*'s complex story and its newly evocative illustrations. As one reviewer put it retrospectively, "*Snatcher* also has elements of a long-lost art form—the radio drama. Since so much of the game consists of still graphics, much of the emotion is conveyed through the voice acting and sound effects" (Kalata 2011). The reviewer here compares *Snatcher* to radio drama in its evocative use of sound and dialogue to compensate for a lack of character movement in animation. In fact, Kojima's use of distinctive sound production harkens back to other older media forms, including early Japanese TV anime. In describing Osamu Tezuka's 1963 TV anime *Tetsuwan Atomu*, Mushi Pro animator Sugii Gisaburo remarked that "the apparent cheapness was often reduced once sound was added" (quoted in Clements 2013, 121). Kojima's use of evocative sound design and voice acting similarly allowed *Snatcher*'s small amount of animation and its reliance on still drawings to resonate emotionally with players.

Snatcher's legacy goes beyond the quantifiable data. It did not sell well initially but was met with strong reviews. *MSX Magazine* gave it a total score of 119/150, with particularly high marks for its scenario, graphics, and value, and expressed a desire to play more: "Please make a sequel, Konami. Our readers are asking for it, too!" (MSX Magazine 1989, 27).[3] It finally found an audience upon its port to the PC Engine; while exact numbers are hard to find, according to Konami rep Yoshinori Sasaki, "it was a monster hit for a PC Engine game" (EGM 1995, 176). *Snatcher*'s cinematic style and deep *sekaikan* paired with an interactive investigative approach to the narrative would herald a number of other cinematic adventure games, from the stylish and politically minded "technothrillers" of Suda51's *The Silver Case* and *Killer 7*, to darker open-world, Western detective games such as Quantic Dream's *Heavy Rain* and Rockstar's *L.A. Noire*. *Snatcher* didn't have the same impact outside of Japan, largely owing to (1) its delayed release in Western territories in 1994, six years after its first release in Japan and (2) the going-defunct Sega CD/Mega CD add-on accessory to the Sega Genesis. Kojima had little to do with the Sega port and English localization, but the game largely retains many of the features of the PC Engine version, and reviews were mostly positive. Some incredibly so, like this one from a reviewer at *GameFan*: "Simply EVERYTHING about this game is totally perfect, from the beautiful graphics that haven't lost anything in the conversion from 512 colors to 64, to the music, which is actually

BETTER on the Sega-CD, to the flawless narration and voice acting" (Rox 1994, 46–7). Still, while the team was proud of their work, Kojima was largely dissatisfied that he was not able to complete the game he set out to do. He would attempt to correct this with his next adventure game, *Policenauts*.

Building Beyond and the "Multi-Process Scenario"

Upon completion of an RPG remake of *Snatcher* called *SD Snatcher* (Konami 1990) and *Metal Gear 2: Solid Snake*, Kojima was promoted to Konami's PSG (Product Management) Division as a division manager (*buchô*), taking on a more administrative role to oversee the production of several arcade and consumer games. "My job was to tell the teams, 'Do your damn work!' But I was jeered by all of the teams," said Kojima. He soon thereafter moved to Konami's Technical Research Lab, a building in the far west region of Kobe, researching the development of 3D polygonal technology. According to Kojima, while he could not work on any new titles, he implemented some of the research at the lab "bit by bit" into his next adventure game that would eventually become *Policenauts*: "I even completed the storyboards" ("Kojima Hideo" 2000, 71).

Toward the end of 1993, Kojima was moved to Konami's newly formed Development Division 5, in charge of a small team of about ten developers huddled in a small room. Some, such as sound producer Kazuki Muraoka, had entered Konami at around the same time as Kojima and worked with him on the original *Metal Gear* in 1987. Others, such as artist Yoji Shinkawa and programmers Noriaki Okamura and Kazunobu Uehara, entered the studio at roughly the time of the formation of Development Division 5 and joined Kojima's team. "We didn't greet each other in the morning, but we would casually ask each other, 'Want to grab some lunch?' or 'Let's go drinking tonight,'" said Kojima. "I was the boss, so there was no other work besides making games. It was bliss" ("Kojima Hideo" 2000, 72). Development Division 5 was the birthplace of the Kojima Clan (*Kojima-gumi*) that would work closely with Kojima on the Metal Gear Solid franchise for the Sony PlayStation. But before that, they began with Kojima's second graphical adventure game.

Policenauts' investigative play is similar in several ways to *Snatcher*, both in concept and execution. The game once again begins with sci-fi cinematic origins, trading *Snatcher's* cyberpunk setting for outer space.

Kojima has repeatedly written about how he and his generation "really admired astronauts," even cinematic ones like the astronauts in *Planet of the Apes* who "know so many things that we normally have no idea about." (Konami CP Department 1996a, 119). The story also reflects the contemporary popularity of buddy cop films, wherein the player once again assumes the role of a detective protagonist as he works to investigate a mystery alongside his former partner.

Playing detective had by this point become a central component not just of Kojima's procedural adaptations of detective fiction but of a design philosophy toward creating "simulated experiences." As Kojima explains:

> I think there are two types of games. One is where the container—whether its contemporary or a Western or sci-fi—is realistic, and you have the players freely explore and play in that container. The other is where the player takes on a specific role in a created world. The good point about the latter type is if, for example, you have a film or novel that has a courtroom setting, you can get the experience of being a lawyer even if you don't know difficult legal terminology that normal people wouldn't have any idea about. You can have that kind of simulated experience. In a film, the protag might say something you would never say. If you were told you have to suddenly be Jonathan Ingram and you were a typical salaryman, that's a tall order. If you make the container and tell people to play inside it, they'll take their reality in it with them. If you want to take people away from their everyday lives, it's necessary to give them a destiny to fulfill. (Saito 1996, 91)

Kojima here echoes some of his thoughts on "games as experiences" that he penned to Konami's employees several years earlier. *Snatcher* and *Policenauts* have aspects of free exploration for players, but they are designed more as procedural adaptations of cinematic genres, in this case, the detective and buddy cop genres. Thus, while *Policenauts* gives players some degree of freedom in how to proceed in the game, it is similar to *Snatcher* in that there is a single, developed story that the player cannot ultimately change. Its description by some reviewers as a "visual novel," or graphic narratives with branching paths, is incorrect. Visual novel creator Jiro Ishii describes this as the gap between "linear" and "nonlinear" adventure games with one key difference: "In linear adventure games, the player can die. There is a 'right answer' and a 'wrong answer,' and the structure of the game amounts to, 'Can you find the right answer and get the right ending?'" (Taitai 2013). Thus, while *Snatcher* and *Policenauts* might visually look like they are games that have a strong affinity with visual novels, their true legacy is in detective-based investigative games such as the *Phoenix Wright: Ace Attorney* (Capcom 2001) and *Professor Layton* (Level-5 2007) franchises. The stories are linear, do not possess branching paths, center on concrete protagonists and culprits, and are primarily organized around the player gathering information that will resolve the narrative mystery.

The presentation of *Policenauts'* graphical adventure differs from *Snatcher* in two important ways, though continues to emphasize *sekaikan* through environmental investigation. One significant shift is from a menu-based interface to a point-and-click one, in which the player can select objects with a cursor and click on them to reveal the data underneath. *Policenauts*, like *Snatcher*, is limited by affordances that do not quite match the ambitions of its creators' desire for a fully interactive environment. Kojima's workaround for this was to have an abundance of text to access in the environment: "Having text prepared for every place you investigate, and having that text change depending on the circumstances, I think really helps create the illusion that you are 'in' that world" (Shmuplations Ace Attorney). In a sense, Kojima and his team wanted players to feel like they were actively investigating environments in an anime film through the point-and-click interface, but since the affordances did not yet allow players to control avatars within these environments, their workaround was to *describe* the detail of each object in the environments so that players could visualize the new information even when they were not presented with a corresponding image.

This combination of object selection (input) and game feedback (output) was present in the "interactive cinema" of *Snatcher* as well, though uniquely personalized in *Policenauts*. Point-and-click interfaces are sometimes derided for forcing players to "pixel hunt" small, barely noticeable objects on screen to progress. To counter this frustrating tendency, Kojima and his team built a system that would sensitively react to players' individual inputs. Distinct from "multi-ending" visual novels, where players are given a large degree of freedom to customize the game's story, the creators of *Policenauts* opted for what they termed a "multi-process scenario" that "responds to minute player actions, words, and developments but does not affect the larger story or themes, allowing players to still actively appreciate the drama" (Saito 1996, 103). In practice, what this meant was that player inputs could slightly modify character and environmental responses based on their timing

Figure 3.4 Point-and-click interface used to explore Jonathan Ingram's office in *Policenauts* (Sony PlayStation: Konami 1996).

and order, adjusting the story's pace and progress to the player despite proceeding linearly. As such, *Policenauts* is customized to the player as they scour the environments for clues and additional information.

This is no more evident than in the opening sequence in Jonathan Ingram's office, where the player is immediately placed in the role of Jonathan as he waits for a client to arrive (see Figure 3.4). The player is given no details regarding his backstory and is encouraged to kill time by investigating the office. By clicking on any newspaper clipping, framed photograph, or inanimate object, Jonathan provides a narration that helps to piece together what happened to him and his current situation. Players are thus conditioned to investigative detective work even before being presented with a case. The client arrives and the narrative progresses once the player clicks on all objects in the scene, but what makes the investigation personalized is how the player seems to control its flow. Some objects, such as the flashing answering machine, can be clicked on multiple times for different messages that reveal to the player that Jonathan is largely unsuccessful as a P.I. Other objects will slightly alter his narration depending on the order in which they are clicked; looking at photographs of Jonathan's ex-wife Lorraine or LAPD partner Ed Brown, for example, will make him casually reference these characters in the narration of other objects. Despite the linearity of the game's narrative—clicking on all "important" objects is the only way to progress—players can observe that their individual choices have consequences as the game's descriptive text provides them with appropriate feedback. In this way, players do not simply act out the role of detective but actively feel like they are in the gumshoes of Jonathan Ingram as the game responds to their investigation. As will be made clear in the following chapter on Metal Gear Solid, the multi-process scenario is a good example of Kojima's approach to games as both emergent, interactive experiences and rich, satisfying stories. The combination of player interactivity with controlled storytelling on display here is a defining characteristic of all of Kojima's games, allowing players to feel like they are in control of how the game proceeds despite having little influence over the larger thematic or narrative structure of the game.

A second difference with *Snatcher* is the game's lack of a central database for accessing its deep *sekaikan*. Instead, its *sekaikan* is gradually revealed as you make your way through the game's many areas. Kojima once again wrote large amounts of data for Beyond, triggered through dialogues and in the environments. The game considers minute aspects of space habitation, from space-specific foods, products, and amusements to new forms of diseases, medical treatments, and industries that emerge to deal with these ailments. This level of detail struck even the award-winning film director Mamoru Oshii, who praised Kojima (somewhat backhandedly) that if films and games must choose between story and world, *Policenauts* is undoubtedly "a game that chose world over story" (Konami CP Department 1996a, 122). However, while the abundance of information can seem overwhelming, Kojima took care not to provide *too* much specific detail regarding the time or geography of Beyond: "We purposely left much of the world of Beyond vague because we wanted the player to imagine it. The only concrete place is the central pillar, and no other map is provided. It's conversely the depth of a 2D game" (Konami CP Department 1996b, 77). In providing key visual and narrative details but withholding others, Kojima and his team wanted players to bridge the gaps in the game's *sekaikan* with their own imagination. It would not be the last time that Kojima asked players to perform acts outside of the game that connected them to the game world.

The *sekaikan* was also not limited to the world of *Policenauts*, as Kojima attempted to connect its world to his previous games. *Snatcher* does this as well—a bar named Outer Heaven, your robot sidekick Metal Gear mk-II—though *Policenauts* has an even larger array of references to draw from. Characters from *Snatcher*, such as Jamie Seed and the informant Napoleon, make brief cameos in the background of environments. Artifacts referencing *Snatcher* also appear in random locations, such as a copy of the New Kobe Times (*Shin Kobe Shimbun*) found in Jonathan's office, or a *Snatcher* calendar that appears in a hospital room. While none of these details go so far to indicate that the worlds of *Snatcher* and *Policenauts* are the same, they do reward players who have played the worlds of Kojima, and such details can be found in Kojima's games going forward. Some examples from *Metal Gear Solid* include a clip from *Policenauts'* theme song that plays when booting up the game, posters and animated clips of *Policenauts* incorporated into various environments, and supporting character Meryl Silverburg (Kojima's favorite character), who becomes an important recurring character in the Metal Gear Solid franchise.

Riling Emotions, Raising Awareness

Like *Snatcher*, *Policenauts'* contemporary story was designed to create a significant emotional response in the player, and Kojima strained to give an additional sense of meaning and importance through a central theme that would enliven and enrich the gameplay. "What kind of story is going to make the gameplay come alive? Likewise, what kind of gameplay is necessary to advance the story?" asked Kojima. "I think 'game design' is the practical work of reconciling and combining these two elements in a game" (Game Hihyô 1996, 57). This is a crucial aspect for Kojima's games that took hold in *Policenauts*: the story is designed to enhance the player's emotional investment in the gameplay.

One way this is done is through getting players to identify with the feelings of the game's avatar-character, Jonathan Ingram. In her study of emotional design, Karen Isbister argues that players identify with avatars on levels of the "visceral, cognitive, social, and fantasy" (Isbister 2017, 11). As players control Jonathan (visceral), receive rewards and punishments (cognitive), and inhabit his persona (social), their identification with him grows exponentially (fantasy). This identification is effectively manipulated in *Policenauts'* many shooting sequences designed around climatic moments in the game's narrative. Getting players invested in the detective's personal struggle meant that their emotional investment would be greater when it came time to input quick actions. This cathartic play is evident in the care Kojima took to develop the main antagonist in the game, Redwood, who Jonathan repeatedly chases and engages in gun fights:

> What I really wanted to do with *Policenauts* was make the player feel what the characters feel. With Redwood, you know he's a bad

guy right from the start, and he does more and more bad things like kill your friends or partner to make you truly hate him. When you do pull the trigger, your feelings are at a boiling point. (Konami CP Department 1996b, 75)

This emotional response was also designed to get players to think about the consequences of their actions. Kojima felt that games needed to be more than play in order to have a greater societal impact: "If we don't feel something after putting the game down, I don't think the games industry will ever escape the realm of just being games" (Saito 1996, 93).

These factors led Kojima to create a story that drew heavily on contemporary events in Japan at the time. "Japan bashing," or anti-Japanese sentiment, was rampant in the United States in the 1980s toward Japan's economic miracle and its technological industries (see Thorsten 2012). *Policenauts'* Japanese antagonist—the pharmaceutical executive Tokugawa—mirrors villains in late 1980s to early 1990s Hollywood action films such as *Die Hard* and Ridley Scott's *Black Rain*, or Philip Kaufman's 1993 cop thriller *Rising Sun* that depicted corporate Japan in a negative light. But Kojima's own father was a pharmacist, and Tokugawa—whose company on Beyond acts as a front for illicit drug manufacturing—was also constructed as a criticism directed at the Japanese pharmaceutical industry. Kojima argued that what in the game is referred to as Tokugawa's "Japanese way of medicine" was actually representative of Japan's "truly awful" medical system, with problems including graft, golf-lobbying, and shady hospitals increasing profit margins through drug prescriptions (The PlayStation 1996, 155). The criticism of Japan's health care system is juxtaposed with the health issues that are present on Beyond's space colony and stem from complex global bioethical questions in the 1980s and 1990s. Many in Japan fiercely deliberated the parameters of brain death and organ transplants from brain-dead donors. These debates form the context for the game's portrayal of colony residents, many of whom suffer from organ failure and require transplants after living in space for their entire lives, and who are then supplied by a ring of organ traffickers. And the public discourse over space travel that resulted from Toyohiro Akiyama becoming the first Japanese person to go into space in 1990 also weighs heavily on the general discourse within the game's world, particularly its in-game news broadcasts.

Moreover, the sci-fi robots of *Snatcher* were replaced with a more tangible and realistic villain: "The game was designed with a modern enemy in mind after the fall of the Berlin Wall and the end of the Cold

War. Industrialists—and not the government—were the new elite and powerful enemies" (Konami CP Department 1996b, 78). This focus on the "enemy at home" would presage the more pointed critiques of powerful corporate institutions and their influence on society in the Metal Gear Solid series. In film-noir fashion, these sordid details contrast with the pristine space suburb that Beyond appears to be on the surface and the warmly nostalgic image of the Policenauts that recalls the Original Seven Project Mercury US space flight team of the late 1950s. As author Project Itoh has articulated, "Heroes. Suburbia. The Colony. What *Policenauts* depicts is an image of people's dreams that (only very recently) has been driven down by reality" (Itoh 2008).

Kojima wanted players "to receive these themes like a game of catch" and think seriously about the nature of space exploration and other social issues:

> I think it would be great if, upon finishing the game, players thought to themselves, "I'm going to study more about organ transplantation" or "I wonder what would happen to humans if they went to space," even if it was only for a week or so. Or conversely, if the game can affect how players live in a positive way. (Sega Saturn Magazine 1996, 200)

His inclusion of real-world social issues, contemporary themes, and, importantly, a desire to communicate a message to players with these themes can be seen as a forerunner to "games for change" that attempt to use games for social change by engaging with contemporary issues in meaningful ways. Indeed, there have been various games that examined geopolitical issues via strategy simulation well before *Policenauts*, from Mindscape's 1985 *Balance of Power* to Springboard's 1988 *Hidden Agenda*. Kojima has much in common with the amateur programmers in Soviet-era Czechoslovakia who were making subversive games that could express activist leanings by escaping state regulation and censorship (see Svelch 2018). What made *Policenauts* unique was its incorporation of these ideas in a commercial game, created by a major publisher and for a mainstream audience while using tools from similarly commercial cinema and anime. With *Policenauts*, Kojima began a pattern of writing timely stories cloaked in genre trappings, with the express purpose of providing commentary and prescriptive advice to players regarding contemporary affairs. I'll return to this idea in Chapters 4 and 5 with the Metal Gear Solid franchise and *Death Stranding*, but *Policenauts* demonstrates how Kojima early on encouraged this type of social consciousness in players.

Redesigning Beyond from Port to Port

Policenauts is a game that, once again, embodies Kojima's supervision of the game experience, showing the director's control not just in the design but in its continuous redesigns for various console platforms. Like *Snatcher*, the production of *Policenauts* was similarly intimate; Kojima has likened it to making an independent film due to the control over nearly every creative aspect it afforded him: "The game design, dialogue, ADV scripts which used the scripting language, storyboards, flags, even the art and sound, I did most of it myself" (Konami 2008). While it is an exaggeration to say that Kojima did all the art and sound, it is not an overstatement to say that he has never had more control over a game than on *Policenauts*. This is because Kojima did not just supervise the development of *Policenauts*; he oversaw every single port of the game to multiple platforms over a two-year period in what was a mad rush of system releases including the 3DO, Sony PlayStation, and Sega Saturn. With each port, Kojima supervised changes to the character designs or scripts to improve what the developers wanted to communicate. This was largely due to the different processing capabilities of each platform that Kojima and his team were porting the game to. The range of possibilities increased with each platform, and Kojima and his team took these opportunities to add to the game's narrative and audiovisual presentation. The character design for Jonathan Ingram, for example, became "a little rounder and younger looking" with the move from the PC-9821 version to the 3DO version to better contrast with his former comrades and convey how time has passed him by. Additional scenes were added, extraneous dialogue was cut, and some scenes were completely rewritten for dramatic impact. When Jonathan and Ed first are reunited in the PC-9821 version, for example, Jonathan pushes Ed into helping him with his investigation, but in the 3DO version, Ed is spurred into action after taking pity on Jonathan.

This redesign extended to the animation. While the PC-9821 version subcontracted animated sequences to the animation studio AIC, Kojima's team took many of the still images and added small computer graphic enhancements such as moving backgrounds, smoke effects, motion blur, white noise filters, and grain with each subsequent version. A young Yoji Shinkawa was the art director for the game, and he and his staff came up

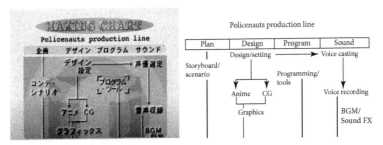

Figure 3.5 Production pipeline featured on *Policenauts: Private Collection* (Konami 1996).

with the novel idea of removing frames from the film, scanning them into a computer, and changing what they wanted in digital editing suites to save time from redrawing and recoloring the many cels. "It was a ton of work," he said, "even if you only see it for a second" (Saito 1996, 95). Indeed, Development Division 5 basically became an animation studio at one point. The structure for the game's development, visible in the extras included on the Sega Saturn port, looks more like an animation production pipeline, with segments of storyboarding, key-frame and in-between drawing, inking/coloring, and voice acting comprising the development flowchart (see Figure 3.5). The team added and tried new elements from port to port, to the point that, according to programmer Noriaki Okamura, "From the 9821 version to the present PS version, there are almost no original elements left" (Saito 1996, 94). The PlayStation port, for example, took advantage of the system's MDEC proprietary video compression unit, which allowed for higher-quality animation. And in the final port for the Sega Saturn, players could use the system's Virtua Gun peripheral for the shooting sequences, drawing players further into the role of the character through their own bodily performance of the interface.

The game's voice acting was but one aspect of several, indicating an even stronger dedication to cinematic audiovisual presentation, but one based, again, on Kojima's specific cinematic memories and affinities. The voice actors, some of whom returned from *Snatcher*, were specifically chosen by Kojima for their experience working in both television and feature-length films. *Policenauts* took the additional step of showing their names alongside the character's when the character first appears on-screen, a popular practice for films that air on Japanese broadcast television and which is part of a larger subtitling practice called "telop" that guide viewers by reiterating or explaining what is appearing on screen. Additional touches—such as summary screens which bring the player up to speed after loading a saved game—conveyed the experience that the player was participating in a weekly television series. There is also, once again, a litany of references to films both iconic and popular at the time. Nearly every significant character is based on a real-life figure, from the readily obvious actors Mel Gibson, Danny Glover, and Sean Connery to the more culturally specific, like the idol Karen Kirishima, or Masahiko Ueno, the former director of the Tokyo Medical Examiner's Office. The game's San Francisco-inspired setting also references many films set in the city, particularly the Steve McQueen action vehicle *Bullitt* and the Alfred Hitchcock thriller *Frenzy*. Even minor details of *Policenauts* were harvested from Kojima's scrapbook: a target that the crew took back with them from a Chicago shooting range was inserted into a shooting range in the game.

Policenauts did not just redesign the visual presentation; its small team culture iterated on the affordances of the scripting engine itself. Kojima's team saw the potential for *Snatcher*'s scripting engine of flag branching management. With the *Snatcher* port for the PC Engine, the team worked from a yacc,[4] improving the structures of descriptive systems and variables. This knowledge was implemented and augmented in *Policenauts* to coordinate different complex branches and repeating processes, essentially widening the range of dialogue possibilities far beyond those available in *Snatcher*. As production assistant Yoshikazu Matsuhana puts it, "While playing, you can ask the same person the same thing again and again, and each time, you can relish the deep experience of varying dialogue" (Saito 1996, 95).

The import of the scripting language's development was not lost on the programmers, who viewed their work as monumentally shifting the way Konami titles would be developed going forward. According to Okamura, "I might be exaggerating, but as we were making *Policenauts* as a software, I was strongly of the mind that we were making tech that would be essential to Konami, so we included things that we could use five or ten years down the road" (Saito 1996, 94). According to debugger and programmer Kazunobu Uehara, *Policenauts* should be considered the "origin" of the program design of KCE Japan West, a branch of Konami that would be headed by Kojima and core members of the Kojima Clan, which would go on to create multiple core franchises for Konami. Both *Snatcher* and *Policenauts'* emphasis on varied dialogue interactions and copious event triggers are reflected in the even more varied and interactive character actions of Konami's popular *Tokimeki Memorial* (1994) dating sim, which has spanned over fifty separate titles across twenty-five years and millions of sales and downloads. Each game features various avatars who hide a wealth of personal information of which only a fraction can be accessed in a single playthrough.[5] This type of replayable design can be found in more contemporary "roguelike" games like *Hades* (Supergiant Games 2020), where players unlock bits and pieces of richly acted story and character through repeated playthroughs. The language also had a significant impact on Kojima's subsequent action-adventure games as the program essentially became the GCL (Guarded Command Language) used in *Metal Gear Solid*'s many Codec radio conversations. So while Development Division 5 afforded Kojima creative control, it also significantly benefitted his programmers and Konami's bottom line. As Okamura put it: "*Policenauts* was for us programmers a big experiment lab" (Saito 1996, 94).

The Comedy of Reflexive Play

Policenauts never received an English-language release, but its many versions were met warmly by critics and players in Japan. The few English-language publications to review the game were once again enthusiastic for Kojima, writing Konami "has outdone themselves in everything from the beyond-beautiful music to the professional quality cinemas" (*GameFan* 1996, 15). Not all reviews of both *Snatcher* and *Policenauts* were positive, however; some, especially English-language critics, were uncomfortable with the games' odd mixture of drama and humor. One representative reviewer, for example, was perplexed by *Snatcher*'s constant subversion of its own seriousness. Particularly annoyed by the "characters' persistent and irritating habit of making references to the fact that it's a game," the reviewer argues: "For me to really immerse myself in a role-playing game, I need *some* suspension of disbelief. But that's impossible if I'm repeatedly being reminded that the whole thing's not real" (Dulin 1995, 69). Indeed, while the worldview and visuals of *Snatcher* and *Policenauts* are deep, complex, and cinematic, there are many instances where the developers seemingly break the spell of immersion they so labored to create. If we viewed these games through the lens of Huizinga's "magic circle," then Kojima and his team of mischievous developers would be "spoilsports" who break the spell of the sacred pact that players and programmers agree upon (Huizinga 1949, 11).

The reviewer essentially argues that Kojima and his team disrupt his "flow," what the psychologist Mihaly Csikszentmihalyi has termed "the state in which people are so involved in an activity that nothing else seems to matter" (Csikszentmihalyi 1990, 4). This would be to assume, mistakenly, that Kojima and his team were trying to recreate the experience of watching *Blade Runner* or a similar cinematic spectacle where viewers get so absorbed that they forget their surroundings. Rather, Kojima always viewed *Snatcher* and *Policenauts* as metagames that are subject to being played and played with; in his and his staff's estimation, players can never truly forget they are playing a game, and the game's design reflects this understanding. Some have labeled this Kojima's penchant for including "easter eggs," or secret messages and jokes that the developers hide in the game for players to find. But this would be to assume that there is a "true" game that is being interrupted by these jokes and surprises. The reality of *Snatcher*, *Policenauts*, and all of Kojima's games is that this subversion is so baked into its genetic makeup that it is not a diversion from the game but a fundamental design element of the game itself.

Interruption of player flow is, in fact, a common occurrence in the adventure game, as the genre is prone to intertextual referencing and self-referentiality. As early as *Zork*, part of the pleasure of the game was probing the limits of the text parser in a sort of "informal Turing test," where "players (and designers) delight in clever and unexpected responses to other useless actions" (Lebling, Blank, and Anderson 1979, 52). Such responses are not linked to the narrative or ostensible goals of the game but serve as diversions into humor. Krista Bonello Rutter Giappone (2015) argues that comic digressions serve to surprise and challenge the genre's predictable conventions by "making the player aware of their manipulation by the game, and her/his own expectations in relation to it." Such moments serve to mobilize players "*against* immersion, turning interaction into inter[upted/ing] action, rather than being a means towards the experience implied by immersion" (Giappone 2015). In this formulation, immersion in a game is not the goal; designers provide interruptions and digressions within the game, and players seek out and derive comedic pleasure from accessing them. These diversionary disruptions set up a dynamic between designer and player that draw attention to the limits and potentials of the medium.

If the core of Kojima and his team's aims is to progressively push the boundaries of the video game medium in terms of story, style, and mechanics for the purposes of creating change in players and their engagement with the world, then reflexively disrupting player immersion within the graphical adventure genre fits entirely within these aims. One can see this in the many funny side quests, events, and dialogues that players can trigger throughout the main story. As Kojima puts it:

> Rather than feel that you are walking on the rails of a story, games emphasize the activeness of the player. If at some point in the story, the player wants to stop and play around, that's fine. Actually, there needs to be sub-events where the player can play without regard to the story. The player must be the one to move the story forward.
> (quoted in Mashita 1992, 103)

To take *Snatcher* as an example, the game comprises many such diversions that break the spell of the drama, from ordering colorful local specialties from hawkers (Neo Kobe Pizza) to calling phone sex lines. Protagonist Gillian is equally playful, and designer Yoshioka drew a mix of expressions for him—surprise, exhaustion, joy, and embarrassment— that captured his comicality. "Gillian had an interesting mix of humor and seriousness. Kojima wanted to convey Gillian's witty and charming nature, even in some of the more intense moments, so that it would make him seem more 'human' in contrast to the robotic Snatchers," explains Yoshioka (Tieryas 2017).

Indeed, a common strategy in many popular boys' manga and anime of the 1980s was to humanize their cool heroes through their exhibition of a juvenile, lecherous side. This sense of sexually tinged humor permeates *Snatcher* and *Policenauts*, providing a stark contrast to the violence and grim topicality of the games' sci-fi plots. While Gillian and Jonathan exude cool exteriors like Rick Deckard or Martin Riggs, they equally as often display moments of lecherous perversion, like when Gillian has the option of renting a pornographic video when he investigates a video rental store. *Policenauts* is loaded with such moments, as Jonathan's dialogue with several different female service centers around his clumsy attempts at flirtation. One sequence on a spaceship involves not just ogling the shapely flight attendant but actively sexually harassing her by moving the cursor over parts of her body, clicking on them, and receiving a "bounce" effect; players who click enough times will find the flight attendant's helpful attitude change for the worse.

The inclusion of such scenes acknowledges and indulges the male-oriented playing demographic of the MSX2 and PC Engine, where "fan service" was both a ludic reward and marketing strategy.[6] Such female objectification is an aspect of Kojima's games that some have been critical of, particularly of the scantily clad Quiet in *Metal Gear Solid V: The*

Phantom Pain (Roberts 2016; Tamburro 2016), though Kojima's games will objectify male characters (Snake, Raiden, Vamp, and Sam Porter Bridges) almost as frequently. Such scenes of lust are also common in many male-oriented, *shōnen* manga and anime of the 1970s and 1980s from which Kojima has drawn inspiration, such as *Lupin III*'s Arsene Lupin, *Urusei Yatsura*'s Ataru Moroboshi, and, probably the most significant, *City Hunter*'s detective-like "sweeper" with a permanent erection, Ryo Saeba.[7] As Kojima became a household name and his games grew more gritty and realistic, such representations felt more out of place, though are characteristic of the late 1980s cultural context of which Kojima and his teams were and are very much a part and which Kojima continues to openly reference and cite. According to Kojima, the scenes were also apparently popular with *Policenauts* original PC audience: "The BCCH check-in girl is one of the more popular girls among the staff. In earlier versions of the game, players couldn't have as much fun talking with her, but from the Saturn version on, we were able to include requests from a lot of different fans" (Saito 1996, 35). Such behavior, incidentally, is also overtly discouraged narratively in similar ways to its manga/anime inspirations: if players choose to ignore their protestations, female characters will also react negatively to Jonathan for the rest of the game, and even random NPCs met in future interactions will become uncooperative or accuse him of being a pervert.

Kojima's sense of lewd comedy has other possible inspirations. One might be his upbringing and Konami's headquarters in the Kansai region of Kobe and Osaka, an area that produces a good number of the country's comedians due to a thriving stand-up comic (*manzai*) circuit and the presence of Japan's largest comedy talent agency Yoshimoto Kogyo. Another might be his cinematic upbringing, where he cites both *The Pink Panther* film series and the films of Alfred Hitchcock as a way to bring stress relief to moments of seriousness or tension: "That's why I put in gimmicks like cardboard boxes and alligator hats. Inspector Clouzot is a very serious character, but the gap between his attitude and actions is what is funny" (Kojima 2008, 59). The most reasonable explanation is that, like Kojima's game narratives, his games' comedic intentionality is a mix of influences from his film, TV, and manga consumption as a child.

What is also clear is that this comedy actually emerges from the two games' investigative mechanics: players "find" ways of undermining the game's seriousness of purpose through their own curious, investigative play. The humor that results is less dependent on well-timed acting or textual wordplay and, as Kojima explains, is unique to games in their ability to surprise the audience and make them laugh at themselves: "Games are an interactive media. If movies can make people laugh, then games must make players laugh at their own actions" (Kojima 2008, 58–9). This also means that Kojima and his team had little respect for what the "boundaries" should be for immersion and the various means to get players to laugh at their own expense. In *Snatcher*, a humorous blurring of game and reality occurs when the in-game environments include references from reality, but these references are frequently buried within the game and must be uncovered during the course of the game's investigative actions. Players who study the game's environments will see, for example, how the names of the game's developers appear on Neo Kobe City's buildings, while those who try to exhaust the Gaudi computer network will be able to access info on the game's characters and voice actors.[8] By acknowledging the artifice behind the game and, importantly, the player who is playing it, the game constantly keeps players guessing as to when the game's world moves between reality and fiction.

But this blurring of game and reality is not limited to the game's acknowledgment of reality. As both Metal Gear games blurred the lines of the magic circle through calling attention to the game design or asking players to find clues on the game's box art, *Snatcher* and *Policenauts* call attention to the various electronic interfaces that mediate between player and game. In one scene, for example, the player needs to find the computer passcode from a recently deceased victim. A note on his body says, "Search the House!" (*ie wo sagase!*). This might be interpreted as investigating the victim's house, or even the model home in his dining room. But, in the MSX/PC version, it's the clue to his password: the answer is hitting the Home key on the keyboard. An even more elaborate blurring occurs when investigating an abandoned warehouse. A faint ticking sound can be heard, and Metal Gear mk-II tells the player to turn up the volume on the PC/TV to hear it better. Upon further investigation, the player comes across a bomb that is ready to explode. Gillian and mk-II barely escape the warehouse before the bomb goes off, resulting in a deafening explosion. When Gillian complains that his ears hurt, mk-II tells the player it's their fault: "You shouldn't have left the volume up." Possibly the most preposterously wacky idea was one that was not actually implemented but was nevertheless proposed by Kojima to his superiors: an invisible "dying message" chemically imprinted onto the floppy disk that would become visible through the heat from the hard disk drive after several minutes of playing. Upon being "activated," the message would smell like "blood," forcing the player to eject the disk and see the message. Fortunately or unfortunately for Kojima, he "got yelled at for it and they didn't let [him] do it" (Gamefest 2012).

Policenauts' bomb-defusing sequence, a difficult series of puzzles set to the ticking timer of a bomb about to explode, is one of the most complex forms of this reflexive play that is realized through the combined efforts of Kojima and his team. In the sequence, Jonathan must first gently open the bomb's case, but the seriousness of the situation is undermined immediately when Ed says to "left click" to open the screwdriver and "right click" to close it. Ed is no longer talking to Jonathan in the game, but to the player outside the game world, his words effectively bridging the worlds of both. The event itself is unforgiving, likely resulting in several deaths for the player but always restarts with Jonathan and Ed referencing their own deaths (see Figure 3.6). Event programmer Hiromitsu Yamaguchi followed this by inserting a scene where Ed volunteers to help out if you die more than once; the computer takes over defusing the bomb, and just when the player thinks they've been granted a free pass, "Ed" immediately fails. Die enough, and the puzzle becomes ridiculously simple upon a restart ("Look at how easy the maze is. Anyone can do that"). In effect, the event defuses player stress by using the scripting engine to generate multiple responses from Jonathan and Ed. The event's brilliance is in its

ジョナサン
もう一度トライするぞ？

Figure 3.6 "Jonathan, let's try this one more time." Characters acknowledge the player's failure to defuse a bomb in *Policenauts* (Sony PlayStation: Konami 1996).

subversion of "failure," taking gaming's most stressful aspect and building a puzzle where the player wants to fail to see what the responses from the characters might be. The game's humor results from getting players to laugh at their own failure and encouraging them to try again and again. Kojima's reflexive distancing of the player is ultimately related to his games call to action. This type of reflexivity has parallels in theatrical traditions, most notably in Guy Debord's "situationist movement" and the "epic theatre" of Bertolt Brecht. Brecht used techniques that distanced the audience from the theatrical performance and prevented them from experiencing emotional catharsis, often by interrupting the action on the stage through sudden musical interjections, having actors directly address the audience, and even speaking stage directions out loud. Brecht's "defamiliarization effect" had the effect of making spectators aware of the artifice of the theater, spurring them to greater political reflection and toward advocating for actual social change (quoted in Brooker 1994, 193).

Starting with *Policenauts*, Kojima's games consistently ask the players to reflect upon real-life social issues, and the tendency of his games to draw the player out of the "magic circle" of immersion and to recognize the artifice of the game medium is similar with Brecht's call to political action. As Steven Conway (2010) argues, this sort of action is not merely a breaking of the fourth wall, as players are both spectators *and* performers, both implicated but also able to impact the action. When the game acknowledges our presence, it inverts our sense of control over technology and, by extension, our everyday lives. The comedy that results is due to an "enjoyment to be had in such breaks, a thrill in the unexpected autonomy of the technology, like the child who dreams his/her toys living their own secret lives when he/she is not watching" (148). In effect, by getting players to laugh at the game and themselves, Kojima highlights how the game—and the player—is not disconnected from a reality that still has many problems that will not fix themselves. What seems like a bit of fun is also Kojima's way of probing us to consider what are the edges of a game, and what happens when we go past them.

The Playful Spirit of the Kojima Clan

With *Policenauts*, Kojima's reputation as a designer was established, at least in his native Japan. One preview of the game not only remarked upon the fact that it was a "Kojima game" but even compared the director to native luminaries like Hayao Miyazaki for their abilities to generate "wonderfully realized and discrete *sekaikan*" (Yamashita 1994, 160). With the completion of the Sega Saturn port of *Policenauts* in 1996, Kojima was now an industry veteran of a decade. No longer needing to plead for his ideas to be heard by skeptical superiors, he was now the designer of multiple influential games. The emphasis of script-based gameplay allowed him to direct the pace and timing of the sound and images, to write the entirety of its narrative and dialogue, to intersperse interactive sequences which put the player inside experiences he appropriated from cinema, television, genre fiction, anime, and manga, and all of this in service of posing larger social questions to players to jolt them out of a sense of gaming complacency. The embrace of the graphical adventure game was particularly important for Kojima, as it was a perfect match for his sophisticated narrative and audiovisual aspirations. The control he maintained over his games was unique at Konami, and his authorship was fully recognized in the opening credits of *Policenauts*: this was now "A Hideo Kojima Game."

Kojima's influence also extends to the team he formed while working in small divisions at Konami: the beginnings of the Kojima Clan, which would eventually lead to the creation of a subsidiary studio at Konami, Kojima Productions. Encouraged by its director, the Kojima Clan showed little regard to what constituted the boundaries of the game space and, importantly, to the boundaries of game development. To the contrary, they seemed to delight in subverting player expectations and echoed their director's desire to create unique *taiken*. "How fun is it to make dramatic situations in games?" said Okamura. "I want to make this kind of game too. If I become a director, I want to make games where you 'experience' things" (Konami 2008). Much of the Clan's camaraderie was forged over years of close-knit development in this craft studio-like environment. Kumi Sato, a modeler for *Policenauts* and its female characters' "boob jiggle," said she was immensely proud of being part of the team: "Now, I work with over a hundred developers and there are people on the team I've never even spoken to. But I can count on one hand how large our team was at times for *Policenauts*, and we were able to impart our vision through that small team" (Konami 2008).

The hands-on development would benefit Kojima as he would go on to shepherd teams of over a hundred developers, on projects with significantly larger budgets and expectations at Konami. Where developers at large studios today are assigned to specific jobs and tasks, Kojima and his team were able to manage multiple roles and experiment to an unusual degree within the security and resources of a large studio. "I think we were born at just the right time," Kojima said. "We started with smaller games, so we had to do everything by ourselves" (Gifford 2009). Working on a small team at a large studio allowed Kojima to see all aspects of game development, utilize significant professional resources, and respond frequently to player desires, while also being able to iterate with the speed and confidence of an independent operation. These were tools that would continue to serve him as he embarked on his and Konami's largest franchise over the subsequent two decades.

Chapter 4

THE PROGRESSIVE FRANCHISE

KOJIPRO'S COLLECTIVE DESIGN IN *METAL GEAR SOLID*

While the Kojima Clan was busy working on *Policenauts*, Hideo Kojima himself was simultaneously working on his next project. Upon learning about the new console system from Sony codenamed the PSX, he was intrigued with the platform's ability to render sophisticated 3D polygonal graphics and store many hours of recorded video and audio via CD-ROM. He had already penned the project's story in cafes during his downtime, which would be mostly unchanged in the final version. He also enlisted Yoji Shinkawa, the rookie illustrator of Development Division 5, to create mock-ups of the mech key visuals. This work, and the work of the Kojima Clan, was interrupted by the Hanshin Earthquake in 1995. The devastating damage to the Hyogo region meant that the staff had to move from the now uninhabitable Kobe studio in Port Island. Many of the staff relocated to the Konami Computer Entertainment office in Osaka to work on the various console ports of *Policenauts*, but Kojima moved to head the recently created Konami Computer Entertainment Japan (KCEJ) office in the swanky digs of the Ebisu Garden Place in Tokyo (Kojima 1998b, 14–15). Here, Kojima began to work in earnest on the game that would cement him as a household name in international gaming discourse and also launch one of the best-selling and most critically acclaimed franchises in video game history: *Metal Gear Solid*.

Metal Gear Solid (hereafter *MGS*) continues from where *Metal Gear 2: Solid Snake* leaves off, putting players into the sneaking shoes of the genetically/technologically enhanced mercenary protagonist, Solid Snake. In the *MGS* series, the player character Snake must neutralize terrorist forces and avert a nuclear threat in a covert, one-man operation. Each game builds upon the last to create an expansive serial narrative that incorporates Cold War politics and histories over the course of increasingly detailed and spectacular iterations for multiple generations of the Sony PlayStation. These games have also led to many video game and transmedia spin-offs and extensions, creating one of Konami's most globally recognized and lucrative franchises, as well as serving as the inspiration for any number of similar "stealth game" series including *Hitman* (IO Interactive 2000–), *Tom Clancy's Splinter Cell* (Ubisoft 2002–), *Assassin's Creed* (Ubisoft 2007–), and *A Plague Tale* (Asobo Studio 2019–).

Figure 4.1 Back page of the 2000 Autumn edition of magazine *Konami Look* (Konami 2000).

During this period, Kojima also became more and more widely recognized within the gaming community as a visionary game creator. This was partly because of his prominent role in developing the MGS franchise but also due to Kojima becoming "authorized" within a moment of cultural transition for the video games industry. As Selim Krichane has argued, the English-language discourse of Kojima prominently increased following the release of *MGS*, with magazines and other media portraying Kojima as a unique artistic talent that could rival the sorts of auteurs found in the film or television industries (Krichane 2020). Kojima, with his vault of cinema knowledge and desire to be taken seriously as a director, was the ideal match for the gaming industry's appeal for artistic respect and cultural importance.

But this discourse was not just a product of the English-language media. As shown in Chapter 3, Konami and media outlets had promoted Kojima as a "director" as early as *Snatcher*, and the studio ramped up this promotion across the Japanese-language media discourse with the success of *MGS*. One of the most prominent examples of Konami's "directorization" of Kojima was on the back page of the Autumn 2000 edition of the company magazine *Konami Look* (Figure 4.1). The type reads:

There are many giants who are called directors around the world today, but in the world of games, there isn't one person who has an official company position and title of "director." Hideo Kojima was first hired as a "planner," but his love of movies as a college student led him to create games from a cinematic perspective upon entering the company. With *Policenauts*, *Metal Gear*, and *Snatcher*, he has garnered many fans of his games. Hideo Kojima is the first person at Konami to be granted the title of "director," and his games are known to his fans as "Hideo Kojima Games." Just as you can judge a film's worth by its film director, you can now judge a game's fun by its "director." (Konami Look 2000, 36)

It is instructive to see how the company attempted to use Kojima as a sign of artistic value following the success of *MGS*. Rather than subsume its designer as a cog in the system like in earlier eras, Kojima's presence at Konami became a way for the company to distinguish itself from other studios. It is tempting to conclude, as some writers have, that Kojima is simply a product of company promotion, and that his elevation has come at the expense of his teams. One representative study of this line of thought, for example, analyzed the credits of MGS games and found that an "inner circle" of developers typically works with Kojima, raising questions "on why and how the prominence of Kojima is maintained" (Freybe, Ramisch and Hoffman 2019, 16).

Such a question is a reasonable one, though also perhaps reveals the parochialism of game scholarship. Working with the same teams is not unique to games and is common in many entertainment industries, but this has not prevented film scholars from finding associations between the films of, say, director Howard Hawks despite frequent collaborations with writers like William Faulkner and Jules Furthman or actors like Cary Grant and Walter Brennan. Analyzing film or game credits for its staff's contributions can provide a sense of the scale of the production and the divisions of its labor but does not indicate how that labor interacts or is organized by the developers of a particular team. Considering several members with whom Kojima works are fairly consistent from game to game, this, in fact, allows us to better understand the particular role of Kojima within the MGS franchise. In the absence of ethnographic fieldwork in Konami or more detailed postmortems from the development team, analyzing the existing discourse behind the games from the production teams as chronicled through industrial self-disclosures can help map how the franchise was designed and developed. Such self-disclosures chronicled in making-ofs and interviews also contain their own level of spin and brand control, but analyzing the mostly Japanese-language discourse of the developers themselves grants a better understanding of the role Kojima played within his teams, as well as clarifies what the individual members of those teams were responsible for. Thus, I explore the design and discourse of not only Kojima's role in the MGS games but also that of the Kojima Clan, a mix of veteran and fresh-faced game developers that Kojima recruited into Konami's Development Division 5 or who joined his team upon the development of the MGS franchise (Figure 4.2).

As with previous Kojima adventure games like *Snatcher* and *Policenauts*, the innovations of the MGS franchise are similarly located in four areas of Kojima's progressive design:

- Contemporary geopolitical narratives
- Cinematically inspired storytelling
- Thematically linked gameplay
- Playful reflexive spaces

These various modes—narrative, visual, and gameplay—echo a "multimodal approach" to analyzing MGS, where "verbal and textual

Member	First Konami Title/Credits	Later KojiPro Credits
Yoshikazu Matsuhana	*Snatcher:* Assistant director, Program, Command interpreter	*MGS1-5:* Producer, Production manager, Supervisor
Kazuki Muraoka	*Snatcher:* Sound director, Sound program, Music	*MGS1-5:* Producer, Sound director, Editor
Kazunobu Uehara	*Policenauts:* Kernels, 3D Visual compression and processing, Effects scripts, Tools	*MGS1-3, MG Ac!d:* Program director, Supervisor *Boktai:* Technical supervisor
Yuji Korekado	*Policenauts:* Effects scripts, Script porting, Tools operator	*MGS1-5:* Lead programmer, Enemy AI *MG Rising, Survive:* Producer
Noriaki Okamura	*Policenauts:* Supervision, System design, Movie drivers, Captions, Voice synching, Tools, Film digitization	*MGS Portable Ops, Peace Walker, Survive:* Producer *Z.O.E.*, *Tokimeki Memorial Drama 1-2:* Writer and Director
Shinta Nojiri	*Policenauts:* Script porting, Tools operator	*MGS1-3:* Writer and Designer *MG Ghost Babel, Ac!d:* Director
Yoji Shinkawa	*Policenauts:* Mechanical design, CG director, Digital retouching, Textures, Display design, Packaging, Poster illustrations	*MGS1-5, Zone of the Enders 1- 2, Death Stranding:* Art director, Character Design, Mechanical design, Concept artist
Kumi Sato	*Policenauts:* Modeling, Textures, Wireframes, CG animation, Breast bouncing supervision	*MGS1-5, Zone of the Enders:* Animator, Cinematic artist
Tomokazu Fukushima	*Metal Gear Solid:* Writer, Script, Flag management	*MGS2-3, Ghost Babel, Ac!d:* Writer, Setting research
Shuyo Murata	*Zone of the Enders:* Writer	*MGS2-5, Death Stranding:* Writer, Research *Zone of the Enders 2:* Director

Figure 4.2 Recurring members of the Kojima Clan, when they joined, and what they later became responsible for within Kojima Productions.

cues combine with filmic elements and highly specific gameplay strategies" (Stamenkovic et al. 2017, 22). In short, Kojima's direction of the MGS series continues his synthetic approach to game design, employing the narrative and audiovisual tools of cinema and long-form fiction, the interactive components of rule-based systems, and theatrical devices that reflexively disrupt the game medium in order to impart anti-war messages and meanings to the player. In this chapter, I examine these aspects of Kojima's progressive game design of the MGS franchise, specifically the first four games Kojima directed that focus on the escapades of Solid Snake and introduce the legend of Big Boss produced for the Sony PlayStation 1, 2, and 3: *Metal Gear Solid, Metal Gear Solid 2: Sons of Liberty* (2001), *Metal Gear Solid 3: Snake Eater* (2004), and *Metal Gear Solid 4: Guns of the Patriots* (2008) (hereafter *MGS1, MGS2, MGS3,* and *MGS4*).

Any one of these games could be the subject of a book-length study and, indeed, such books of and on the franchise exist (see Burch and Burch 2015, Wolfe 2018, or Brusseaux, Courcier and Kanafi 2018). In this chapter, I instead look at the franchise holistically, arguing that Kojima and his team continued to exert a similar type of control over game development despite increasing budgets and blockbuster franchise expectations. I use each of the four sections in this chapter to tackle one game in the MGS franchise as an example of one of the four aspects of Kojima's progressive design, showing how Kojima's methods for supervising game plans and scripts with his 2D graphical adventure games for the MSX2 were adapted in the move to the three-dimensional spaces of the Sony PlayStation.

Progressive Franchise Design

Kojima's insistence on planning, writing, and directing so many of the "canonical" games of the MGS franchise allowed him to maintain a personal control of the series despite the increasingly large staff that developed each game. This in turn allowed him and his team to keep the franchise fresh and disrupt conventions of video game franchises by continually investigating relevant social issues and themes, incorporating cinematic trends, reinventing core gameplay concepts, and interrogating the established divide between the worlds of the player and the game. Thus, while my mapping of the MGS franchise is in some ways emblematic of the development of a commercial game franchise at a Japanese studio from the late 1990s to the late 2000s, I simultaneously argue that Kojima was able to buck conventional studio practices in pursuit of an idiosyncratic franchise approach that relied on his and his teams' personal narrative/audiovisual tastes and, importantly, his continued desire to impart a socially relevant message to players through emergent play.

Each of the MGS games balances Kojima's desire for narrative control and meaningful play (deep thematic stories and cinematic style) with more interactive elements (stealth-based systems and reflexive spaces) with the move to three-dimensional spaces. Kojima's design in the MGS franchise is a combination of structured and unstructured play elements. On the face of it, his games are what Jesper Juul (2002) has called games of "progression," where "the player has to perform a predefined set of actions in order to complete the game" (324). These games often focus on role-playing and adventure elements rigidly designed around moving a story forward, which dovetails with Kojima's insistence on building his games around stories. However, the play experience of the MGS games most frequently revolves around systems of "emergence," where a game is "specified as a small number of rules that combine and yield large numbers of game variations" (Juul 2002, 324). Games of emergence—such as competitive games including board or fighting games—emphasize unstructured play that can result in divergent play experiences.

For all the ink spilled here and elsewhere on Kojima's stories and world-building, he argues that the "connective tissue" of his games is its emergent game properties:

> If you aren't enveloped in the action of walking or shooting, you will quit playing. I really value that aspect of games. When I make games, the story is the beginning and end, and in the middle I fill it with many events and game elements. When those elements are connected on a time axis, the game really becomes a story. (Konami 1998, 5)

Story and *sekaikan*, or world-building, is a way to make those elements meaningful, but Kojima argues that the systems and mechanics themselves need to be fun for players to continue. Each MGS is structured in essentially the same way as Kojima's adventure games, in that narrative exposition and cut scenes alternate with opportunities to interact with the game's environments. Kojima has confirmed this in interviews, where he argues that *"Metal Gear Solid* is pretty much the same as *Snatcher* and *Policenauts*, even if the method of unraveling the story is different. The themes I want players to feel are the same whether the story is unraveled by action-based gameplay or by navigating through menus" (Thearkhound 2019). As Kojima realized with *Policenauts*, however, these themes can find greater emotional resonance with more interactive action sequences, since players can "empathize more if there is some action-based gameplay" (Thearkhound 2019). Thus, with the move away from puzzle- and menu-based gameplay of his adventure games, Kojima's MGS games present players with increasingly open three-dimensional spaces and characters that they are able to control and connect with in diverse ways. And though these interactive portions are bookended by lengthy narrative cut scenes, what distinguishes the MGS franchise from other AAA franchises is that the stealth-based systems and narratives frequently complement one another: the systems are *informed* by the concepts of the narratives, which change with each successive game.

Such an approach of radical system reconstruction is unusual for most game sequels or franchises. As one critic puts it, "Often, the follow-up to a successful video game is less a sequel than a software iteration" (Suellentrop 2010). Each successive game in a popular game franchise typically refines rather than reinvents the core mechanics and visual aesthetic of the previous game, for to deviate too much from a successful formula means to risk alienating the franchise's existing player base. This can be seen in the subtle iteration most prominently displayed in sports game franchises like ESPN's *Madden* and 2KSports' *NBA2K* or, conversely, Konami's *Winning Eleven* and *Power Pros* franchises; while each game updates the previous game with more detailed physical profiles, responsive AI, and revised team and player data, the mechanics of the games are only marginally altered, and the rules of the games only change to reflect the actual professional sports leagues. There are of course exceptions, such as the radical innovations in Nintendo's core *Super Mario Bros.* platformers. More frequently, war game franchises (e.g., the *Call of Duty* series), action-adventure game franchises (e.g., the *Uncharted* series), and role-playing game franchises (e.g., the *Dragon Quest* series) update their games with new time periods, locations, characters, equipment, and narratives but do not typically redefine what made previous games successful or interrogate the logics on which those worlds are constructed. The play of the game, moreover, does not always conform to the larger themes of the narrative as played out in the exposition, cut scenes, or environments, focusing instead on refining mechanics of previous games in the franchise that players are already familiar with.[1]

This is not the case with the MGS franchise. While the core mechanics and stealth gameplay of each MGS remain the same, Kojima sought to radically question the purpose of the game sequel and the player's complicit role in its often formulaic perpetuation through marked changes in successive games. With each reinvention, the Kojima Clan introduced narrative and gameplay elements which complemented one another and reinforced larger themes and messages. While the Kojima Clan posed the question of what are the boundaries of video games with their adventure titles for the MSX and PC Engine, with the MGS franchise they posed a different question: What are the boundaries of a video game *franchise*? Each game in the MGS franchise builds off its predecessors not simply in small mechanical or audiovisual improvements, but in the larger narratives and themes shaped by contemporary issues; environments and characters that demand greater player scrutiny; and the increasingly flexible rules and systems of the gameplay itself. Throughout this process, Kojima subverts players' expectations of what a game sequel should be by interrogating their expected sources of ludic control and pleasure.

Plot: Thematic Connections, Interactive Narrative, and Serial Relevance

Kojima has written or cowritten the script for every MGS game which he directed, and the process for these games has been similar across the franchise. He starts with a "plot," or script, for each MGS through a distinct theme that references real-world concerns. It is a method that, as detailed in the previous chapter, started with *Policenauts*. In the planning docs for *MGS1*, Kojima articulated an "anti-nuke and anti-war concept": at the center of the game's conflict was the risk posed by the global proliferation of nuclear weapons ("the greatest fear of the 20th century") in order to instill in players "an improved consciousness towards violence and war" (Kojima 1998a, 147). These themes of anti-violence and using nonviolent means to solve problems run throughout the entire MGS series, all of which feature nuclear threats in the form of mechanical weapons. Each game argues against the use and proliferation of nuclear weapons via narratives that show the human and political consequences of such weapons in the postwar global order, as well as gameplay (which will be examined later) that encourages players to only pursue violent solutions as a last resort.

Each MGS also features a secondary theme that draws more specifically upon contemporary social and technological issues. Like his script for *Policenauts*, Kojima created a story with *MGS1* that revolved around modern geopolitical events intertwined with American political history and ideology. Specifically, he emphasized the theme of "gene" to refer to the game's exploration of the bioethics of genetic manipulation and the idea of "escaping your genetic destiny" (Kojima 1998a, 147). This was likely a reflection of Kojima's concerns about the Human Genome Project, an international science effort launched in 1990 and concluded in 2003 that mapped the entire DNA sequence of the human genome (Kolata 2013). While the project was instrumental in helping researchers treat diseases such as cancer and diabetes, it also was accompanied by concerns that employers or insurance companies could use the information to discriminate against individuals (Greely 1993, 264–5). Similar debates over bioethics played out in public over the cloning of Dolly the Sheep, the first mammal cloned from an adult somatic cell in 1996 (Hutchinson 2019, 157–62). These concerns are reflected in the plot for *MGS1*, where US operative Solid Snake is sent to a nuclear waste disposal facility on an Alaskan Island codenamed Shadow Moses. His mission is to rescue two hostages from FOXHOUND, a renegade special forces unit, and ascertain whether they have the capability of launching a nuclear strike. As Snake infiltrates Shadow Moses, he uncovers that the island is not only a front for a nuclear weapons development complex but that the government has been creating genetically modified super-soldiers through lab experiments. The leader of the renegade FOXHOUND unit is Solid Snake's cloned brother, Liquid Snake, who is also a proponent of Richard Dawkins' "Selfish Gene theory" and believes that a person's fate is determined by their genetic code. Kojima's story thus merges intertwining interests in Cold War politics: the continuing problem of nuclear arms disarmament with ethical and legal issues that could result from authorities having unfettered access to personal genetic information.

This concept-theme pair of nukes and genetics directs much of the narrative and provides players with guided motivations while also continuing with Kojima's prior desires to impart a greater meaning to players and make them reflect upon larger social issues and problems. With *MGS1*, Kojima strongly wanted games to be more than toys, a perspective still dominant in Japan, and become tools for potential social and individual change, an idea that he expounds upon at length:

> "To be of benefit" is a quality I feel is lacking in games today, so I aim to create games that have some positive elements embedded that can hopefully move players emotionally, or make them think about their friends or parents, or gain an interest in the problem of nuclear arms. *Metal Gear Solid* has an anti-war and anti-nuke theme, and while players can hurt others during the course of the game, I wanted to tell them such actions are ultimately wrong. I feel recent games are missing this. (Konami 1998, 5)

Kojima's comments echo those of his experience design in *Policenauts*, where the goal of the narrative is to involve players both emotionally and intellectually. Players become emotionally invested in the game's characters and world and then are encouraged to reflect upon its problems, which have parallels in the real world. Kojima was worried "that the decoding of the human genome would lead us down a mistaken path in the 21st century much how nuclear weapons did in the 20th century" (Muraoka 1998, 35). With *MGS1*, Kojima dramatizes this debacle with a story featuring genetically modified soldiers at the mercy of the US government. But he also provides a counterargument in Snake's (and the player's) ability to overcome their destiny, a message that was intended to resonate with players' own insecurities. "If a child of unathletic parents who hates sports tells his parents he doesn't want to participate in the sports festival, his parents might go, 'Well, he's my kid, after all,'" said Kojima. "But it'd be great if that kid plays *Metal Gear Solid* and thinks to himself, maybe I'll give the sports festival a shot" (Konami 1998, 5). Kojima's touching words here embody previous desires to make games reflect society and have players consider how to address its problems. As the threat of nuclear war fades from collective memory and the possible abuses of gene therapy and genetic manipulation emerge, concerns over the loss of individual control in an increasingly information-dense society remain. With *MGS1*, Kojima implores players consider that their nationality, environment, or genetic code does not make them prisoners to their fates. If they become actively aware of history, politics, and their own sense of agency, there is potential for personal or collective resistance even on a small scale.

A vital strategy that Kojima uses to deliver this information to players is via exposition, a tool of linear media such as novels or films where the reader-spectator is given information through narration or character dialogue. A chunk of *MGS1*'s thematic narrative is delivered to the player via scripted cut scenes, many of which are noninteractive and often didactically emphasize the themes of the narrative. Far more of this exposition, however, is accessed by the player through the "Codec," a nanomachine radio communications system built into the small bones of Snake's ear. Similar to the transceiver screen in *Metal Gear 2*, these conversations in *MGS1* are fully voiced and occur between the player character Snake and various supporting characters on a separate screen interface (see Figure 4.3). Snake's bosses, Colonel Roy Campbell, and Dr. Naomi Hunter, for example, will use the Codec to call Snake to deliver important information about the missions in the game's story in lieu of cut scenes. But what makes the Codec unique compared to military or space combat games where players receive mission briefings or instructions is the fact that the player/Solid Snake can actively use it to call for support during the course of the game. Because of this optionality, many of the Codec conversations must be *discovered* by players themselves. For example, when players acquire new weapons, they can contact weapons expert Nastasha Romanenko, who will provide information about the newly acquired equipment and its potential use in the game. As these conversations with NPCs

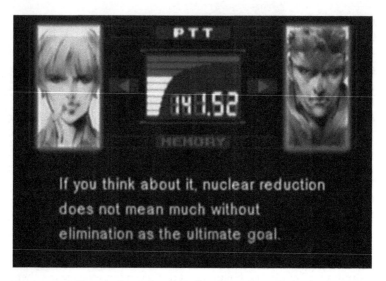

If you think about it, nuclear reduction does not mean much without elimination as the ultimate goal.

Figure 4.3 Pulling up the Codec and calling Nastasha in certain areas of *Metal Gear Solid* (Konami 1998) can trigger discussions of nuclear proliferation.

are completely optional, players can adjust the experience to their own gameplay style. Those who want a more action-oriented pace can skip the Codec conversations almost entirely, while those who want to know more about the world, enemies, and environments can access the Codec for more detailed information.

The Codec, like the computer terminal in *Snatcher*, acts as an interactive database into the *sekaikan* of *MGS1*'s world. It merges the scripting system of Kojima's adventure games with immersive 3D environments to reveal deeper human characteristics of NPCs. Conversations with NPCs will vary not only depending on the location or equipment but also on how and how often players interact with the environment. Much of this conversation is not required to progress within the game but deeply develops the player character Snake's understanding of the game's characters and world. One review of the franchise calls the Codec its "life-pumping heart" because it "lets moments of human warmth and character seep into what are supposed to be lone-wolf sneaking missions" (Edge Staff 2015). Contacting one NPC allows the player to save the game file with her, but with each save, she will provide an ancient Chinese proverb or quote from a popular movie. Some of this is connected to advise for progressing in the game, but much of it comes across more like casual film geek rapport.

Romanenko is a completely optional supporting character but is also a repository for Cold War history and the dangers of nuclear arms and energy manufacturing. Players who speak to her enough will see how she and her family were exposed to radiation from the Chernobyl nuclear accident, giving her character a gravitas and connection to the story that goes otherwise unnoticed. Players can call characters multiple times in succession to receive different responses, testing the limits of what the writers have programmed. Calling up NPCs following certain actions will also reveal different emotional responses. Using the Codec while in the ladies' restroom will result in furious responses from female NPCs; if you hurt or kill too many dogs in one area, every NPC will react negatively to your cruelty. In this way, using the Codec allows NPCs to exhibit a range of emotions and even reinforce the themes of the game. If waiting is the core mechanic of MGS, then "calling" is a secondary, nearly equally important mechanic that is designed to reward player curiosity in the game's world.

Kojima writes the script for all of the MGS games, from the cut scenes to much of the mandatory Codec conversations, though he has been assisted by two writers—Tomokazu Fukushima and Shûyo Murata—for most of the optional Codec conversations. Fukushima joined the Kojima Clan in July 1997, but his initial contributions were limited due to joining the production of *MGS1* only a year from its release. According to Kojima, he "helped with the voiceover script and contributed words like 'patricide' [*chichigoroshi*] and 'cowardice and blind courage' [*kyôda to banyû*] in some of the game's harsher dialogue" (Kojima 1998a, 156). By *MGS2*, however, Fukushima and Kojima shared more of the writing duties where, according to Fukushima, "Director [Kojima] was largely responsible for the real-time cut scenes and mandatory radio calls, while I was in charge of the optional radio calls" (Kojima 2002, 56). Kojima and Fukushima worked out a system where Kojima would write the rough script and Fukushima would edit it in chunks on shared computer files on which both could see and work. In total, the two created about 2,500 files, covering the many cut scenes and Codec dialogues within the game and weaving the game's many themes into the story and characters. This division of labor affords Kojima control of much of the construction of the main story and cinematic presentation, while Fukushima or Murata contribute to the game's deep *sekaikan* and lore. These optional dialogues also allow the writers to go "off course" when characters mouth more personal permutations on film or music, essentially giving us a line into the interests and concerns of the developers by proxy.

This describes the process for writing the script for *MGS1* (and its sequel), but another aspect that makes the MGS franchise unique from other action game franchises is its continuing storyline that attempts to tackle changing contemporary social conflicts. No single MGS possesses the same themes or even the exact same principal player character as each of the games deals with an evolving world adapting to changing sociopolitical issues and rapid technological progress. The fact that Kojima writes each of these games has been described as a blessing and a curse, as outlets have criticized his "preposterous plot twists" or "leaden dialogue" that suffers in translation (Schreier 2015; McCarthy 2008). But the benefit of this consistent authorship is the creation of a sprawling narrative with intertwined themes that spans multiple titles, allowing the franchise to tackle ever more complex and controversial global conflicts. Each successive game can be enjoyed without having played its predecessor, though players would find their play experience richer through connecting various threads from previous games.

MGS2 demonstrates this tapestry as its themes build upon *MGS1*'s ideas. The game's concept explores a different threat to the world—the ability to control the flow of information on the internet—as well as a new theme: "memes" or what cultural information we choose to pass on to the next generation. It also upends conventions of protagonist continuity in an action game sequel: players do not get to control Snake for much of the game, instead controlling the younger and considerably less experienced Raiden. Some players voiced their frustration at the complex plotting and bait and switch of its popular hero from *MGS1*, though this change, too, reflected Kojima's desire to tie the player more concretely to the world with a hero that better represented their more vulnerable status. While all sequels introduce some degree of creative innovation (Tschang 2007), Kojima's insistence on introducing new themes and characters is rooted in the idea that the MGS franchise is connected to the larger world. Players should be challenged with fresh ideas, relate to different perspectives, and master changing systems because the world will always have new problems that cannot be solved with the same solutions.

It is this embrace of controversy and trust in the sophistication of its slightly older playing demographic that also sets the MGS franchise apart from other army or combat franchises that are in thrall to the US military: its sustained critique of the post–Cold War unipolar hegemony of the United States. This criticism is particularly directed at America's foreign policy and how it is endlessly fueled by what former US president Dwight D. Eisenhower has termed its "military industrial complex" (MIC), or the symbiotic relationship between government-backed military and defense contractors/corporations. *MGS1* addresses this problem directly, with a postscript that appears on screen before the end credits:

> In the 1980s, over 60,000 nuclear warheads existed in the world at any given time. Their total destructive power came to 1 million times that of the Hiroshima A-bomb. In January 1993, America and Russia signed START2 and agreed to reduce their deployed strategic nuclear warheads to 3,000–3,500 by December 31, 2000. However, as of 1998, 26,000 nuclear warheads still exist in the world.

This statement once again ties *MGS1*'s narrative to real-world events, in this case, the lack of urgency in curbing nuclear weapons proliferation at the time of the game's release while implicitly blaming the United States (and Russia) for not honoring its treaty commitments.

Though the MGS franchise was not conceived as a multipart narrative, each game builds upon the last to create a semifictional universe that shows the havoc created by the MIC, an alternate history of American foreign diplomacy and intervention that simultaneously references existing historical events and figures alongside futuristic technologies and weaponry. In *MGS2*, Kojima articulates in his game planning doc that the "evil" players fight against is the American government or, more specifically, "the festering discharge that has built up within the democratic state of America over the years" (Kojima 1998b, 37). In *MGS3*, the US government uses and discards its heroic soldiers for its own political gain, while in *MGS4*, the MIC has created an environment outside America's shores that is perpetually in warfare. This critique is more oblique in *MGS4*, where the United States is not named directly, though the imagery of warfare in the Middle East conjures the recent US invasion of Iraq in 2003. Kojima would return to a more direct critique of the United States through history in other games set in the 1970s and 1980s, commenting specifically on American tactics abroad—from fomenting coups and propping up dictatorships in South America to waterboarding terrorist suspects in Guantanamo Bay—for the purpose of coercing governments or extracting information for their own gain. Cumulatively, they are a damning critique of how America (and, to a lesser extent, other Cold War powers) uses new technologies, arms, and covert espionage to exert its influence and maintain power throughout the world. While Kojima's sharp criticism is concentrated on America's global hegemony, some scholars have also questioned whether this criticism avoids addressing the role of Japan in the Second World War and Cold War politics in the postwar global order (see Hutchinson 2019, 213–17 and Moore 2017, 68–74). Nevertheless, Kojima asks players to question their own heroic role in the narrative, as well as—for many MGS fans in the United States—their own government's "heroic" role in international affairs.

Style: Mixed Influences, Cinematic Cut Scenes, and Archival Footage

Perhaps the most well-known association with the MGS franchise is its fidelity to a cinematic presentation. While this is not always accurate—many of the games for portable systems like the Nintendo Game Boy and Sony PlayStation Portable emphasized a mixed range of media such as graphic novels and radio drama—the games that Kojima directed for the Sony PlayStations have become synonymous with cinematic spectacle. There is nary a review of the series or profile of MGS that does not emphasize the franchise's cinematic presentation or contain a phrase like Kojima being a "pioneer in the integration of cinematic techniques into video games" (Taiyoung 2012, 348). This is in some ways expected as Konami has promoted the cinematic quality of "Kojima's games" from as early as *Snatcher*, and Kojima himself has advertised his bona fides as a cineaste through his own film reviews in magazines and comments on social media. Calling any game "cinematic," however, is a vague descriptor, as cinema itself is multimodal and composed of many different, often wildly opposing audiovisual styles. Will Brooker has argued, for example, that most games are more influenced by art cinema than Hollywood due to their reliance not on flashy montage but rather on the continuous camera of the first- and third-person shooters (Brooker 2009, 128). Indeed, one of the hallmarks of Kojima's direction of the MGS franchise is the wide array of audiovisual influences that are incorporated from game to game. It is more accurate to say that Kojima and his team are influenced by cinematic production methods and filmic/televisual genre references that the hardware allows rather than any particular cinematic style. As Kojima puts it, "We want to make something with good direction, story, and human drama. That might be called cinematic, but we're not trying to create cinema; rather, we're aiming for entertainment that is similar to cinema's effect" (Konami 1998, 5). In this section, through a brief mapping of the audiovisual production of *MGS2*, I unpack what these methods are and how they are incorporated into the franchise's audiovisual representation.

We can first see a mix of influences in the third-person shooter (TPS) and first-person shooter (FPS) camera perspectives in the MGS series. The perspective of every MGS is mostly from the TPS perspective, where a camera floats omnisciently behind the player character Snake and follows his movements through the environment. Later games in the series allow the player to control this camera, but with *MGS1*, there were greater restrictions that allowed Kojima to "direct" the action between three different omniscient camera perspectives: a top-down view similar to the MSX2 games which tracks the player's movement, more dynamic camera angles that change depending on the area or if the player character pushes their body up against a wall, and a static first-person view that the player can pull up (see Figure 4.4). This mix of a "curated view" alongside player freedom allowed *MGS1* to become "a transition stage between the arcade feel of the 8-bit originals and the much more detailed simulation of *MGS2* onwards" (Stanton 2015a). *MGS2* retains this mix of TPS perspectives, though reduces dynamic angles in favor of allowing players to switch to a (FPS) perspective when targeting enemies or scouring the environment. The FPS perspective in *MGS2* betrays its artifice by revealing details in the environment filtered through a film camera such as water drops, dust particles, and lens flares. Such a perspective evokes audiovisual representation in sports simulations, as the "primary point of reference is television coverage of the sport, rather than the experience of the sport itself" (King and Krzywinska 2006, 136). Similarly in the MGS series, the camera

Figure 4.4 Dynamic camera angle in *Metal Gear Solid* (Konami 1998) imposed to direct the drama within the environment.

captures the view of an action or espionage film or TV series, with many of the gritty audiovisual conventions of those genres.

Character designs also reveal a similar mix of visual references and influences. Kojima works on character designs for every MGS game with Yoji Shinkawa, an illustrator who joined the Kojima Clan upon entering Konami, and has been the character (and mecha) designer for the MGS franchise ever since. Shinkawa's designs are similar to those of his Konami adventure games and a match for Kojima's own visual and genre interests: Hollywood action cinema and Japanese science fiction. As documented in Chapter 2, Solid Snake's appearance in both Metal Gear games for the MSX2 borrowed from characters in action films like *The Terminator* and *Mad Max*, while the eponymous bipedal walking tank Metal Gear is clearly inspired by mecha, or giant robot, anime. This blend of influences is preserved in the move to more original character designs for *MGS1*. Solid Snake is given a sleek new physique and visage that, according to Shinkawa, is still inspired by Hollywood stars such as Jean-Claude Van Damme and Christopher Walken (Hodgson 1998, 142). Meanwhile, enemy characters such as the paranormal Psycho Mantis, the cyborg ninja Gray Fox, and the now completely motorized walking mech Metal Gear REX are nods to staples in sci-fi anime and *kaiju*, or monster, films such as the Gojira/Godzilla franchise.

These dual influences are even more pronounced in *MGS2*. Emotional characters and marine settings are the backdrop to a romance-heavy plot inspired by James Cameron's 2000 blockbuster film, *Titanic*, but in a world populated by vampire-like villains and amphibious flying mechs. Shinkawa's designs are essential in merging two opposing visual forces: the realism of existing American military tech and institutions with fantastical and science fictional ideas inspired by Japanese popular fiction artists such as Yoshiaki Kawajiri (*Vampire Hunter D*) and Yoshitaka Amano (*Final Fantasy*). Shinkawa adopts multiple methods in creating a template of designs, using detailed pencil sketches for character perspectives, watercolor paintings to flesh out emotions, and even material models for vehicles and the titular mech Metal Gear Ray. For every character, Shinkawa and Kojima discuss the basic idea and description of the character before Shinkawa comes up with his own interpretation. If Kojima has a problem, then Shinkawa goes back to the drawing board, and this back and forth continues until Kojima gives his approval. In many cases, this dialogue creates new ideas that become part of the gameplay or narrative. It was Shinkawa who came up with the idea of equipping Solidus Snake, the principal villain of *MGS2*, with a powered robotic suit and twin katana blades because he "always personally like powered suits" (Kojima 2002, 37). On the other hand, Shinkawa's designs could also inspire ideas from Kojima. Upon adding a cybernetic prosthetic to the design for Revolver Ocelot, a returning villain from *MGS1* whose hand is severed, Kojima ran with it: "One day, he just told me, 'That's Liquid [Snake's] arm' (laugh). I guess that's more interesting so I'm fine with it" (Kojima 2002, 41).

These characters are then mapped into 3D modeling computer programs for incorporation into the 3D environments of the game and, uniquely, used in the real-time cut scenes. Many games at the time used full-motion video cut scenes composed by computer graphic animation departments or studios. The quality of these scenes is very high but can create a gap between the visual experience of the cut scenes versus the game diegesis. It also can mean important storytelling is completely outsourced to those not involved with the studio or even the game's development. Kojima knew his team could not compete with top Hollywood CGI but still insisted on doing the cut scenes with his team:

> I didn't want to outsource the cut scenes to an animation studio because that's the juiciest part; just sending off the storyboards to someone else is too sad. We want to do the detailed bits like adjusting the camera work or lens, but we don't have the time or ability to make it such great quality. So the compromise is the in-game cut scenes featuring polygonal characters and environments. (Konami 1998, 5)

The Kojima Clan used the in-game engine to direct the cut scenes in *MGS1*, a practice they continued in every subsequent MGS game. Like Kojima's previous adventures games, *MGS2*'s cut scenes were all storyboarded, but in this case, they were also scanned into a computer, a process 3DCG director Takashi Mizutani termed "web-boarding" (*web-konté*, a play on the word *ekonté*, or "picture continuity") (Kojima 2002, 100). Mizutani and 2DCG director Juntaro Saito created a system where anyone on the team could click on a panel and see what assets and techniques—from characters and environments to camera angles and blocking—would be required to stage the scene. Kojima and Mizutani worked together over several weeks to direct the motion capture of these scenes with real actors, with the footage then mapped onto 3DCG character models and superimposed on digital environments.

Doing so allowed Kojima and his team to create strong visual and spatial continuity between interactive gameplay and linear narrative, maintain control over how cut scenes would develop the narrative, and as a bonus, cut down on loading times when the game transitioned between gameplay and story. Using the in-game engine to render cut scenes thus allowed the team to collaboratively overcome the game's technical limitations and create immersion through visual consistency and efficiency.

The resulting scenes are edited in a way that reflects not only the limits of the platform technology at the time but also contemporary action cinema techniques and talents from Hollywood and Japan. Characters in *MGS1* have lower polygonal counts in their faces, so the cut scenes are mostly composed of shots that are typically no more than five seconds in length, and rapid montage is often employed to avoid images that linger on static avatars. But as the technology and reputation of the PlayStation progressed, so did the forms of expression that the developers could choose to emphasize in the cut scenes. *MGS2*, benefitting from the increased visual processing power of the Sony PlayStation 2, could utilize longer shots to display the expressive bodies of its more detailed avatars. Though the game continues to employ rapid montage for action sequences, it also incorporates techniques from films popular at the time, such as slow-motion sequences inspired by nineties sci-fi thrillers such as Mamoru Oshii's *Ghost in the Shell* and the Wachowskis' *The Matrix*. The success of *MGS1* also allowed the developers to recruit talent from within the film industries. The thematically linked opening credits, for example, are designed by Kyle Cooper (*Seven* and *Iron Man*). Mizutani also stated that the crew benefitted greatly from working on a separate game with Ryuhei Kitamura (*Azumi* and *The Midnight Meat Train*). Kitamura's taste for gravity-defying camera angles and elaborate stunts also makes its way into the more extravagant set pieces and choreography of *MGS2*.

This hybrid cinematic influence in cut scenes also extends to their aural components, primarily in their voice acting and music. Kojima and sound director Kazuki Muraoka recruited sound designer Tak Ogawa (*Back to the Future* and *Miami Vice*) for sound effects and composer Harry Gregson-Williams to do the score for the game's cut scenes upon hearing his music in the action film *The Replacement Killers* (Fuqua 1998). According to Muraoka, one aspect that attracted them to the composer was his ability to produce quality sound despite a low budget: "The film didn't spend a lot of money on its music. There wasn't even a live orchestra, but the dynamism of the percussion really stood out and impressed us" (Kojima 2002, 122). Working without footage was a new experience for the film composer, but Kojima and producer Rina Muranaka worked out a system where Kojima would email the composer some directions of how he wanted the music to be used in the game ("Do you think you could send me 30 seconds of 'sneaky?'") and Gregson-Williams would reply with more precise musical descriptions ("So very down-tempo and tense and spare"). In this way, the three built a picture of how the music would be deployed in the game (Yarwood 2021).

This collaborative process is also on display in the game's voiceover work: Kojima once again directed veteran voice actors from the anime industry (Akio Otsuka, Kikuko Inoue, and Kenyu Horiuchi), making it a point to have as much of the cast in the booth at the same time in a process he called *hippariai* or "tug of war," where the actors can bring out unexpected emotions or interpretations of the dialogue by listening and bouncing off of one another (Kojima 2002, 126). Popular *seiyu*, or voice actors, in Japan are very busy, often booked for multiple productions during the course of the week or recording their sessions alone to fit their schedules. With little time to prepare for each recording session, many *seiyu* will often see their lines for the first time the day they arrive at the sound studio. This leads to a standardization of quality within the animation industry, with *seiyu* often hired for their established personalities rather than being asked to adapt to the role or world. Kojima sought to avoid this predictability by leaving the direction in the booth to the sound director, while talking with the cast before recording sessions and after during drinking parties about their roles.[2]

An important secondary component of the Konami-produced scenes is Kojima's incorporation of real archival footage from newsreels and documentary film. These clips are interspersed between the computer-generated segments and often play without sound while a character will narrate an important piece of dialogue. These scenes essentially remove players from the game world and insert images from the real world, functioning as a cut scene within a cut scene. Such techniques serve to blend real and game histories, a narrative device that Kojima had in fact used in his early Metal Gear games for the MSX, though not in the actual game itself. Due to the technological limitations of the system, photographic archival images of soldiers and the battlefield were incorporated into an alternate historical chronology outlined in the instruction manual of *Metal Gear 2*. With the MSX, Kojima increased the *sekaikan* of his game through its paratexts when the system's affordances would not allow it.

In *MGS1*, much of this footage is a mix of black-and-white newsreel and color news documentary of nuclear missile tests, waste storage facilities, lab settings, military operations, and, repeatedly, the atomic bombing of Hiroshima. Rachael Hutchinson argues that the use of historical footage in *MGS1* is similar to that of director Kinji Fukasaku's *Battles Without Honor or Humanity* (*Jingi Naki Tatakai*, 1973), which used mixed-media methods to contrast warring Hiroshima yakuza gangs with the political-military violence of postwar American occupation. Like Fukasaku's films, Kojima's interweaving of black-and-white film brings home the "enormity of what happened to Japan in 1945," while the color footage "has the feel of journalistic reportage, giving the player an inside view of a largely hidden industry" (Hutchinson 2019, 180). Similar live-action footage is inserted into the cut scenes in *MGS2*, though the material mostly comprises live and TV news clips of shots of New York, the backdrop of the game, at the turn of the century (see Figure 4.5). Kojima implicates the player character Snake into the real world, connecting the game's fictional villains and environments into serious concerns about America and its present place in the information age. Juxtaposed against "live" modern computer graphics in the cut scenes, this grainy archival footage reinforces the real-world histories and issues on which the MGS franchise is based while providing players with the feeling that they are "accessing" clandestine information that is underreported by mass media.

Despite the audiovisual design considerations behind these cut scenes, they are not without their detractors. Game designer Richard Rouse (2005) has criticized the overuse of cut scenes in games, taking players from an "active role in the proceedings" to a more "passive" role where they "sit back and watch instead" (208). The number and duration

Figure 4.5 Archival footage interspersed into cut scenes in *Metal Gear Solid 2: Sons of Liberty* (Konami 2001).

of cut scenes in the MGS franchise lengthened with every game in its first decade, culminating in a backlash with critics and audiences, with one negative review of *MGS4* calling it a "collection of movies interspersed with interactive segments" that is "in some ways barely a game at all" (Schiesel 2008).[3] Others have criticized the occasionally overwritten and on-the-nose dialogue of the characters as "silly" and "ridiculously weird" (Gamespy 2003). As James Newman points out, however, lengthy cut scenes have multiple important functions. They establish the motivations of the player character and introduce the setting, location, and atmosphere of the world. They also orient the player within this world with practical guidance and suggestions, from controlling avatars and using weapons to navigating menu and interface options. These two aspects suggest that cut scenes actually demand a high level of engagement from the player, as someone not paying attention to the information provided in the cut scene might not be able to navigate the gameplay as effectively. Most importantly for the themes of the MGS franchise, cut scenes can act as spaces that provide players with a break from the action. Like other games, these scenes can simply be a rewarding intermission from more tense and stressful moments, but with the MGS games, these breaks can create a "critical, self-reflective space in which action and performance may be scrutinized," encouraging players to "(re)construct or make sense of their experience, positioning themselves within a personal journey or quest" (Newman 2004, 89–90). Such a function of cut scenes is especially important in the context of *MGS2* as players are encouraged to put themselves into the player character Snake's (or Raiden's) shoes and question their role as a mercenary avatar and puppet of the US government.

For better and worse, the intensive incorporation of cut scenes to progress narrative has become a standard with commercial action and adventure games, and the MGS franchise plays no small part in influencing other games to take a heavily cinematic approach. Adventure games such as Quantic Dream's *Heavy Rain* and *Detroit: Become Human*, Dontnod Entertainment's *Life is Strange* series, and Supermassive Games' *Until Dawn* all feature glossy cinematic production values in what are essentially branching interactive dramas with varying cut scenes triggered by player decisions. Perhaps no game studio has been more inspired by a cinematic approach than Naughty Dog, creators of the *Uncharted* and *The Last of Us* franchises. *The Last of Us* (2013), in particular, is heavily inspired by MGS, with cut scenes that feature high-quality voice acting and character modeling based on real locations and actors. *The Last of Us* is also heavily influenced by the stealth mechanics and gameplay of the MGS franchise, the subject of the next section.

Systems: Conceptual Gameplay in Environments, Avatars, and Interfaces

The gameplay of the MGS series continues the novel emphasis on nonviolent stealth gameplay of the Metal Gear games for the MSX2. As described by Derek Noon and Nick Dyer-Witheford (2010), the franchise emphasizes "unobserved movement, subterfuge, camouflage, evasion, trickery, and out-smarting enemies, not just shooting everything that moves" (78). The games encourage this type of gameplay by punishing players who are discovered with overwhelming situations that might deplete their health, forcing them to hide while enemies disengage at best and kill them at worst. The thrill of the games is in avoiding the enemies carefully enough in order to not suffer the punishments that discovery entails. As explained in Chapter 2, this is an example of the franchise's "procedural rhetoric" that implicitly argues for nonviolent play, where anti-war narrative themes are complemented by stealth gameplay that encourages players to avoid aggressive conflict. In other words, players do only not passively receive the game's themes from its cut scenes, which may or may not conform to the actual actions performed by the player character, but also actively work to perform those themes within the game's missions and environments. While this basic idea of nonviolent play is preserved in every MGS, each successive game introduces additional themes which add to the complexity of the narrative and are complemented by the increased range of affordances in the gameplay. With the MGS series, the procedural rhetoric of each game also expands to tackle the additional themes within the narrative, and the hallmark of the MGS franchise's gameplay is that its systems are reconstructed with each game so that its narrative themes and gameplay align.

This approach to thematically aligned gameplay is an idea that Kojima talks about extensively, most notably in a keynote address at the 2009 Game Developers Conference, where he explains how his teams challenge player complacency through the constant reinvention of existing stealth systems. In his address, he highlights two key approaches to the "solid game design" of the Metal Gear and MGS games. The first is creating new stealth mechanics as better technology allows for a greater range of affordances, such as in *MGS1* and *MGS2*. The increased processing and storage capacity of the Sony PlayStation compared to the MSX, for example, allowed the team to add 3D camera angles, prerecorded video footage and voice acting, and first-person avatar perspectives to the narrative and gameplay elements of *Metal Gear 2: Solid Snake*. This was the impetus for the sequel's "solid," which referred not only to the titular hero of *Metal Gear 2* but also to the new solidity that could be found in 3D polygonal models. The same approach applies to *MGS2*, as the additional processing power of the PlayStation 2 allowed for a heightened "realism" in the enemy AI—where enemies appear in greater numbers and can cooperate in teams—and environments, where the game could generate real-time physical elements, shadows, lighting, and weather effects. New platform tech allowed Kojima and his team to create additional assets and more detailed environments that expanded the scope and difficulty of stealth gameplay.

A second approach applies to increasing the depth of previous games' stealth mechanics for existing technology, such as in *Metal Gear 2* for the MSX2, by focusing on the addition of new rules and systems. This was achieved by expanding the patrol ranges of enemy NPCs, including new interfaces such as the radar map, and creating more diverse movements for Solid Snake such as a crawl action. Kojima's deeper familiarity with the MSX2 allowed him and his team to improve the sequel's gameplay without having access to additional processing capability from a new platform. Such an approach is also evident in the development of *MGS3*, the focus of this section. Following *MGS2*, Kojima and his team were tasked with developing a sequel on the same PlayStation 2 hardware, but Kojima's refusal to make a traditional sequel meant that the game would depart from its predecessor without having the benefit of improved platform tech. The game would have to be reworked from the ground up, but Kojima now had a team and design process in place that would tap the experience of his colleagues.

The systems design of *MGS3* reflects some of the challenges Kojima faced with the game sequel and its associated growth in scale. As the games got bigger, so did the teams, going from the twenty or so Kojima Clan developers on *MGS1* to nearly 200 by *MGS4*. With the shift to the PlayStation and its expanded processing and memory capabilities, Kojima initially maintained a strong supervisory role through writing extensive "debugging sheets." He would consistently scribble out feedback and points of refinement on notecards for various aspects of the game to the team. The sheets address everything from game balance to camera angles to the placement of items in environments. Kojima wrote over 10,000 such sheets for *MGS1*, signaling that his supervision of the game's system continued despite the move to 3D spaces and increased game capacity (Kojima 1998a, 158). It's a process he continued to use on subsequent games in the franchise.

With the shift to larger teams and games, however, Kojima also acknowledged that their construction would need to be more collaborative. Beginning with *MGS2*, Kojima and his longtime lead scripter (and later producer) Yoshikazu Matsuhana mapped how the narrative and systems interacted through a working document called a "scriptment," a term coined by film director James Cameron used to describe a written work that essentially has a level of detail and dialogue somewhere in-between a treatment and a script (Cohen 2008, 82). Kojima's scriptment, however, was a neologism that he describes like a working game bible: "It's basically the game from beginning to end, with notes about what happens throughout the game, what happens to the character, and whether there are sounds that he makes or sounds in the environment" (Bramwell 2004). The scriptment combined narrative exposition, a dialogue script, and brief descriptions of sequences of gameplay that would then become fleshed out through the contributions of other sections of the team. While featuring the plot summary, character bios, and basic gameplay elements common to game design docs like John Carmack's "Doom Bible," Kojima's scriptment was an ongoing process revolving around detailed settings that could be fleshed out and expanded upon as new ideas emerged from Kojima or the rest of the team.

A large part of this collaborative scriptment was an acknowledgment by Kojima that he would need to adjust his method of game direction for larger teams. Kojima's management of ever-expanding systems and gameplay became less controlling, keeping a fundamental theme in mind but allowing teams that specialize in environments or enemy AI to take greater ownership over their particular areas of expertise. Despite this increased workflow, according to Matsuhana, he would "absolutely talk to all of the staff every day, no matter how many were involved in development" and could still "see" the entire team (Kojima 2002, 27). What this "vision" meant in practice is that while Kojima could not be as hands-on with each aspect of the game, he could still *oversee* development and check in frequently with sections responsible for individual aspects of the game. He would then solicit ideas from different departments and reject or include the ones he thought would improve the overall experience.

This type of development management and studio organization is not unique to Konami, though even within the industry, Kojima

Productions possessed a special status under a company so large. As Casey O'Donnell (2014) has argued drawing from actor-network theory, even within a single company multiple development studios can exist alongside, compete with, and possess different design practices from one another. There is often "minimal collaboration" between studios, and different studios have "different practices, systems, technologies, processes, and internal cultures" (178). It is useful to view such teams as discrete networks comprising various "nodes" that include not only human developers but even various "nonhuman actants," such as the coding languages, platform technologies, or design concepts that must be worked with and through.

Though Kojima maintained the position of a strong central node in the network that each node reported to through both his scriptment and debugging sheets, each node in the network could contribute independently for a kind of distributed agency. Kojima's role as the central node was to provide guidance to various departments, connecting the game's systems back to the themes of the main narrative. Through a persistent feedback loop, developers would create additions or alterations to the systems which Kojima then approved or asked for further refinement. This system naturally could result in disagreements within the team, as programmer (and later producer) Yuji Korekado describes in a documentary interview promoting *MGS4*. While Kojima as a director might ask for refinements to the game's narrative or gameplay, Korekado explains that the programmers' prerogative is to "stabilize" the game's mechanics or other performance issues: "We need to go back and forth to find the best middle ground." Korekado's comments here show how commercial game development is a process of negotiation, with the director/designer and programmer compromising on what is desired and what can be realistically implemented without triggering a string of bugs, glitches, or significant release delays.

As the previous two sections explained the design of the narrative exposition and cinematic style/dialogue of the MGS franchise, this section will look at the rule-based systems that comprise the franchise's stealth gameplay. This gameplay is broken down into three interrelated components: environments, avatars, and interfaces. Every Kojima-directed game in the MGS franchise considers how these three components—each of which will be explained in detail—inform one another to create an approach to stealth gameplay that mirrors and reinforces the game's narrative themes. Unlike the more rigid narrative and cut scene delivery, however, Kojima emphasizes flexibility in how players interact with these three components. As he explains it, "Take the equation '1+1=2'. For me, if the answer is 2, then '3−1=2' is just as valid. In *Metal Gear*, for instance, I always prepared at least 3 different ways to solve a problem" (Shmuplations Zone of Enders). This flexibility in player interaction is core to how Kojima and his team approach the procedural systems of MGS, as it allows players to freely explore multiple options to a problem, destination, or encounter.

Environments: Fieldwork and Immersion

MGS3 is a game that departs from previous games in the series by setting its story in the Cold War era of the 1960s. Where most sequels iterate with upgraded weaponry and equipment, *MGS3* goes in the opposite direction, stripping the player character of much of the technology that they had become accustomed to in previous games. Equally as important to the era shift is the environmental diegesis, where urban areas and military installations have been swapped for the dense foliage of swamps and jungles. And the game once again presents a change in perspective, this time by casting as the player character the principal antagonist of the Metal Gear series, Big Boss, who at this point in time is still a very green soldier codenamed Naked Snake who must navigate unfamiliar Russian terrain to take out a nuclear superweapon. He must also assassinate The Boss, a legendary American soldier and defector to the Soviet Union who also happens to be his former mentor. Snake must channel his inner predator to immerse himself in the jungles while hunting for food, gathering information, and hiding from and stalking enemies.

Each MGS title features the player character Snake (or Raiden) navigating a series of increasingly open environments to complete a mission objective. The construction of these environments involves fieldwork, as core members of the development team visit specific locations while taking detailed notes and location photography in order to visualize similar areas in game form. A form of this field research was conducted for *Metal Gear 2*, where the team played war games in the nearby mountains, though the purpose was less about understanding environments and more about recreating enemy behaviors. This fieldwork, chronicled through extensive Konami-produced press coverage of game profiles and special features inserts, has the dual function of providing the team with audiovisual assets to construct the game's settings while promoting the dedication of the development staff toward environmental fidelity and the reproduction of "authenticity." Booklets included in special limited editions for *MGS1* and *MGS2*, for example, showcase developers visiting key locations in the United States, such as Fort Irwin in Los Angeles, New York's Wall Street, and other facilities like containerships and sewage disposal plants in order to recreate the look of objects and the feel of environments within the game. *MGS3* is set in the rainforests of the former Soviet Union, so Kojima took his team to Amami Oshima and Yakushima, two island ecoregions in southern Japan known for their lush evergreen forests and vegetation. A group of 120 developers stayed there for five days, taking in the idea of jungle survival specific to their own job functions. Sound designers recorded the noises of wildlife, art designers recorded footage of the scenery and foliage, and level designers "walked deep into the forest to experience the feeling of despair" (Konami 2005b, 70).

This despair was understandable: compared to the smooth textures and clean structures of the previous MGS games, the rainforest setting would be a significant imaginative challenge for the developers. Environmental design in every MGS presents a puzzle for developers to solve in how to render complex and ambitious environments with limited technology. Where the perspective for these environments began with a 2D top-down view in the MSX2 games, in the transition to 3D polygonal graphics, Kojima needed a way to reconceptualize what had been 2D maps and spaces into a three-dimensional space. Initially, he did this literally, building "sets" of the game with Lego bricks and then shooting these areas with a digital camera that fed images to a PC. This made the sets not simply models but an active analog guide for his team to understand perspective and movement within 3D spaces. *MGS2* partly continued this analog process, though also introduced a computer program called VRS that digitized sample areas and allowed team members to experiment with segments of the game. The increased processing capabilities of the PlayStation 2 allowed for much greater detail within the environments, to the point that players could target and shoot individual bottles off bar counters.

MGS3 presented a conundrum to level designers: how to render much larger open environments with the same level of immersive interaction as *MGS2*. The compromise was to shift the game's frames generated per second from sixty to thirty, sacrificing graphical detail for size, scale, and variation. According to lead background artist Mineshi Kimura, this also saved the team a great deal of labor: "You could say that half of the entire workload was erased by eliminating the seams of the textures" (Konami 2005b, 71). To compensate for the diminished detail, the design team implemented a number of weather effects: rain, snow, fog, fire, and their extended effects on the natural environment. Despite the fact that the game's environments are split up into discrete maps, each of these maps could comprise over 100 meters in game size, replicating the feel and variety of the forests of Yakushima, and allowing for a greater range of strategies on the part of the player to progress in the game's world. Further adding to the feeling of an immersive jungle environment was the addition of various wildlife— from frogs and snakes to crocs and goats—that change to match the shifting geographical features of the game. What makes this flora and fauna more than simple background color is the fact that the player character Snake must kill and eat them during the course of the game to restore stamina. Thus, a visual feature of the environment becomes a crucial form of interaction for players to scrutinize in order to survive.

The larger environments allow *MGS3* to respond to some of the design limitations of the first two *MGS* games, which were similar in some ways to the puzzle-like design of the MSX2 games. For example, as Anthony Burch (2015) observes in *MGS1*, soldiers can track the player character Snake if he leaves his footprints in the snow, but as virtually no other areas in the game feature the same geography, learning this fact of the game does not benefit the player in learning how to interact with the game's rule-based systems. Each environment will often introduce an element that is exclusive to that environment and no others; this allows the game to continually present fresh challenges to the player but can create situations that do not always build upon lessons or skills learned earlier in the game.

MGS3, on the other hand, has a firm design stance that emphasizes affordances which are consistently utilized in the rest of the game: players are predators and should scrutinize each environment for its interactive components. Bats, rabbits, and beehives are all sources of energy, and grass, swamps, boulders, trees, overhangs, and ridges can all double as cover. In one area, for example, the player character Snake must cross a bridge being patrolled by three guards (see Figure 4.6). Further, Snake can utilize features of the environment to accomplish the goal of crossing the bridge and progressing to the next area. Players can shoot down a beehive hanging on a tree branch over one of the soldiers, making him run away in fear; they can hang off the side of the bridge and sneak past the other guards; they can shoot the rope of the bridge to throw the guards off balance so that they fall off; or they can go in guns blazing and take out the guards as violently as possible. The final option is the most difficult one, so the area's inclusion of multiple environmental features has the function of reinforcing the themes of nonviolent play, encouraging players to use other skills like patience, observation, and ingenuity to

Figure 4.6 Scouring the jungle environment in *Metal Gear Solid 3: Snake Eater* (Konami 2004) for optimal ways to proceed.

progress. This also allows the player to conserve ammo and health for the few encounters in the game that cannot be solved with these skills and must require brute strength. This idea of thoughtful environmental consideration is weaved throughout the game, where players encounter features of areas that can have a lasting effect on later areas. Taking out a parked helicopter in one area will allow the player to progress easier in a later stage, while blowing up supply or munitions shacks will create weakened or hungry soldiers on later patrol routes. Both activities are not necessarily explained to the player, thus rewarding player curiosity, but they also attract the attention of nearby guards, meaning players must calculate the risk versus reward in exchanging present danger for future safety.

Beyond reinforcing anti-war/violence themes for players who don't want to die and have to restart the game, the stealth-based areas also work to reinforce the larger secondary themes of each narrative. In one area of *MGS1*, for example, Snake enters a facility filled with dismantled nuclear warheads that prevents the player from using any of his weapons for fear of causing a plutonium leak. Another area similarly works to align the player with Snake's confusion: the player must traverse the same area repeatedly in order to acquire codes that will shut down Metal Gear, only to find out that they were being deceived by the FOXHOUND terrorists and were working to arm the weapon the entire time. This pairing of narrative misdirection and mechanical limitation functions as an example of what Hutchinson has called the series' "rerouting" of player agency, "deepening the player's

identification with Snake through their shared frustration and belief"
(Hutchinson 2019, 218). These environmental limitations also work
to align player emotions with the specific anti-nuke and "free will"
themes of *MGS1*. As Snake is instructed by his superiors not to use his
weapons, the player's frustration at suddenly being deprived of a useful
game mechanic mirrors Snake's own disgust at the irresponsibility of
the American government for stockpiling dangerous nuclear materials.

One environment in *MGS3* pairs narrative themes of anti-violence/
war particularly well with mechanics of limitation in order to evoke
player annoyance and reflection: the river of death. This area comes late
in the game after the player character Naked Snake has encountered
or avoided many enemies. It begins with a cut scene of Snake wading
waist-deep through a river, a burning mangrove forming a tunnel
overhead. The scene conjures dystopian images of war, particularly
the jungles of the Vietnam War as it has been represented in films
like Francis Ford Coppola's *Apocalypse Now* or Oliver Stone's *Platoon*.
Suddenly, The Sorrow—a psychic boss character who can communicate
with the dead—appears before Snake, telling him, "Now you will know
the sorrow of those whose lives you've ended." At this point, the player
regains control of Snake and continues up the river, but now The Sorrow
and ghostly figures hover in front of and move toward the player. Each
ghost represents an enemy the player has killed in the course of the
game, and touching them will result in the loss of Snake's health.

The area thus acts as a direct commentary on the player's level of
violent play in the game to that point. Players who have proceeded
stealthily through the game are rewarded with a shorter time of
completion, but players who have killed many enemies are punished
with a very time-consuming path filled with up to 100 ghosts of fallen
soldiers and more than ten minutes of repetitive, difficult gameplay.
While the cut scenes that precede this area certainly communicate
themes of anti-war/violence through the dialogue and aesthetic
that recalls anti-war films, the design of the environment and the
manipulation of rewards and punishments for players as they progress
through it conveys these themes even more forcefully, as players must
reflect upon the consequences of their violent ludic actions. Kojima also
points out in a commentary track of the *Metal Gear Solid 3 Extreme Box
DVD* how the scene evokes aspects of Japanese cultural and religious
beliefs, from its allegorical representation of the Sanzu-no kawa, or
"river of three paths" for the dead, to the inclusion of animal ghosts like
snakes, fish, and birds that reflect Buddhist tenets of placing animals on
a similar moral plane as humans (Hutchinson 2019, 221–2). Though

Snake must kill and eat animals in the game in order to restore health and survive in the game's jungle environment, players are not absolved of their predatory play.

Avatars: Enemies and Player Characters

The Kojima Clan did not just spend their time photographing locations and recording animal sounds in the forests of Yakushima and Amami Oshima. Like their war games with the MSX2 titles, the development team spent two days undergoing military simulation training, led by military consultant and SWAT team trainer Motosada Mori. Mori helped conduct military sims with staff for previous MGS games in order to help them understand enemy behaviors and movement patterns. With *MGS2*, this evolved to incorporate more elaborate enemy movement, with soldiers moving in teams to investigate sounds, clear rooms, or engage with the player character. Mori had the developers act out situations in the corridors of Konami's offices to mimic real SWAT teams, and professional actors were then motion captured to incorporate these details onto enemy movement within the game. Mori's military sims for *MGS3*'s survival environment involved staff donning camouflaged attire, tracking each other's movements in the forest, and sustaining on instant ramen. He himself even snuck up and "killed" each member of the staff in their sleep. Similar to the war stories of camping out in forests for audiovisual assets in the game's environmental design, such anecdotes are useful in understanding the role of "experience" in promoting design elements in the MGS franchise. Whether they were necessary to improve the enemy AI of *MGS3* or not, the team took pains with each game to one-up the previous installment in terms of "experiencing" the movement and behavior of enemy avatars, and Konami took full advantage of these efforts to promote the game's attempts at increased realism.

Of course, realistic enemy behavior is not exclusive to the MGS franchise, and many war games display enemy avatars that respond to player behavior. What perhaps distinguishes the enemy soldiers of MGS from such games is their exaggerated reactions to noncombat situations. Yuji Korekado, a lead programmer for the Kojima Clan in charge of enemy soldier AI for MGS, remarked that he felt the goal of the franchise's AI was to turn enemies into "comedians" (*geinin*). By programming enemies to react to not just attacks, but well-placed "girly magazines" or obviously distracting sounds, players could derive amusement from manipulating enemies left and right. Once the soldiers find Snake, they then engage in a kind of slapstick routine, chasing him around while shouting, "What are you doing?!" Korekado claims that, contrary to popular belief, programming smart enemy AI is easy: "What we were aiming for is a fun AI that players will want to mess with" (Nikkan Spa 2013). In short, despite all the attention paid to the realistic enemy AI of MGS, the franchise's *un*realistic enemy behaviors are just as important in facilitating flexible, emergent, and simply funny gameplay. The enemies of MGS are less extremely realistic than extremely flexible, capable of reacting to a wide range of player provocations in ways that encourage players to experiment and test the limits of their engagement.

As this enemy AI became more responsive and expansive, so too did the abilities of the player character Snake. Enemies in *MGS3* not only move in teams but—compared to *MGS1*—are also endowed with enhanced physical capabilities such as a greater number of combat moves and, importantly, a much wider field of vision to almost realistic levels. If not properly concealed, players can be spotted by enemies even in the distance, resulting in enemies slowly investigating the area for the players' whereabouts. To balance this more sensitive and varied enemy behavior, Mori and the developers worked together to introduce a more sophisticated physical engagement system called Close-Quarters Combat (CQC for short). Modeled on real-life physical confrontation tactics that are "characterized by sudden violence at close range" (Military Wikia), CQC in *MGS3* involves a system where the player character Snake can sneak up on enemies and grab them, leading to several other options depending on the button pushed or the direction in which a joystick is moved. A long push of the CQC (Circle) button quickly slits the enemy's throat, moving the left analog stick slams the enemy to the ground, and pressing in on the same analog stick interrogates the enemy for information.

The CQC system allowed the player to subdue enemies in nonlethal ways but also was effective in more closely tying the player to the emotional state of Snake. As the story is set in the 1960s, forcing the player character Snake to rely on more hand-based combat conveyed this shift in period while simultaneously reinforcing one of the core themes of the game that "we are all products of the time." The player is similarly shaped by the restricted affordances the designers incorporated to simulate the past era and more primitive setting. The CQC system is also surprisingly effective at conveying the feeling of panic and chaos in the heat of battle. The system was modeled on the pressure-sensitive analog buttons of the PlayStation 2, meaning that players can execute actions based on the strength in which they pushed the buttons. More complex actions such as interrogations require players to master pushing multiple buttons at different strengths at once, and enemies struggling to break free from the player's hold will make the controller vibrate. Players who grab enemies with the intent to interrogate and subdue could end up inadvertently killing them, especially if they are suddenly discovered. While the rewards of interrogation can be useful, players must be willing to endure the stress of being discovered or possibly dealing a lethal blow to their enemy captive. The CQC system thus expresses the fine line between life and death under conditions of scarcity and duress but also underlines the difficulty of using nonlethal stealth activity in tense situations that discourage it.

Not every enemy in the MGS series can be dealt with in the same way, and the boss characters express the pinnacle of enemy AI for each game. A carryover from the colorful characters of the MSX2 games, the boss characters in MGS meet Snake at pivotal moments in the game as principal villains. They are given heavy narrative incorporation, replete with backstories and monologues that express their individual personalities and motivations to oppose Snake or the US government. They also function as progress hurdles that test the player's aptitude in the game's mechanics, featuring more sophisticated movement, health meters, and ability to deal heavy damage compared to the typical enemy soldier. Their eccentric forms and attributes, inspired by the villains from weekly *tokusatsu* television programs of Kojima's youth, also give them a flamboyance in contrast to enemy combatants in war games. Each is equipped with unique fighting skills, such as increased agility, superpowered weaponry, or even fantastical abilities such as telekinesis (see Figure 4.7). The player character Snake must quickly decipher the patterns of the boss's movements and attacks and deliver opportunistic strikes in order to proceed in the game.

The boss characters in *MGS3* are some of the more complex in the franchise, though the battle with The End—an old but supernaturally skilled sniper—particularly reflects the game's themes of survival and being a part of the environment. Unlike in other boss encounters in the game, which emphasize quick reflexes in confined environments (Revolver Ocelet, The Fear, Col. Volgin), the player can approach the battle with The End in several different ways that involve stealth and deception. The battle with The End takes place across three different maps, and in each map, the old sniper targets players as they move across them. The player character Snake can take cover and, using the first-person perspective of a sniper rifle, scan the area for a rustle of

Figure 4.7 Ex-astronaut, pyromaniac boss character The Fury in *Metal Gear Solid 3: Snake Eater* (Konami 2004).

leaves or a glint of the enemy's weapon before taking a precise shot. This method can conceivably take hours, as The End will relocate to another map, forcing Snake to search him out and snipe him repeatedly before his health runs out. Another, more aggressive option involves Snake identifying The End's hideout and attacking him directly; with each attack, The End will dart away, using a number of feints and ambushes to catch Snake off guard. However, because he needs to stop to catch his breath, Snake can eventually corner him. Snake can even opt for a pure stealth option, slowly using cover to sneak up on The End from behind and holding him up for his ammo and clothes. These emergent mechanics do not just apply to the stage where the player character directly engages The End; earlier in the game, The End briefly appears in a wheelchair during an interactive cut scene, and a well-placed gunshot from long range can kill him instantly, circumventing the lengthy battle entirely. A final outlandish solution displays Kojima's continued regard of the entire game system as part of the game design: by changing the clock on the PlayStation 2 to one week ahead, the player can age The End into a death of old age, essentially employing the game console itself to "kill" The End. The boss battle with The End showcases the extreme flexibility in which players can achieve objectives while once again echoing the survival themes of the game's story and environments both within and outside of the diegesis.

At the center of these engagements is the avatar controlled by the player, the legendary Solid or Naked Snake. Beginning with the

MSX2 games, Snake was modeled after genre cinema stars, and this design ethos extended to the MGS series, where Snake's character was a combination of stars from spy, martial arts, and action films, particularly Kurt Russell's Snake Plisskin in John Carpenter's 1981 action film, *Escape from New York*. What makes Snake the controllable avatar seem superhuman is the fact that the player is presented with a host of affordances and perspectives that eclipse all of the enemies in the game. Compared to the enemy soldiers, the player can toggle between multiple weapons and gadgets and is presented with several different perspectives to view the action—first-person, third-person, and bird's eye view—giving Snake a vast advantage. The player character Snake can still move faster, see farther, and react quicker than the enemy AI, even as it grows more sophisticated with each game in the series, due to multiple tools and views of the action at their disposal. Only the boss characters contain more abilities than Snake as they can move faster, shoot more precisely, or are equipped with more weapons than Snake. This is why the battles with them are so thrilling, though players still have a host of superior affordances at their disposal: the ability to heal, hide, or move outside of predictable routes.

But while Snake is a protagonist who fits many stereotypical aspects of an American action hero in total control—chiseled physique, proficiency with weapons, flirtatious banter with women, courage under fire—he also narratively undermines many of these aspects, particularly as the series progresses. In *MGS1*, the narrative reveals that Snake is actually a clone of a legendary war hero created by the US government, one of hundreds harvested by faceless technocrats to form an army of super-soldiers. By Snake's final adventure in *MGS4*, his body has grown old, and his spirit disillusioned through an accelerated aging process, a deterioration displayed through the design of his frequently fatigued animation and cynical dialogue. In this sense, Snake comes to symbolize the elite but war-weary veteran, still capable of superhuman feats, but psychologically scarred from the inhumanity of battle. He is an "anti-action hero," whose steely exterior hides an internal humanity and vulnerability that represents the physical and psychological toll of the soldier of fortune (Hartzheim 2016, 180).[4]

The game's complex control systems work to tie the player to Snake the character, but what implicates the player in Snake's emotional state is that the narrative is equally complex, with many convoluted plot turns, twists, and sequences that remove control from the player character Snake and ultimately lead to player frustration. This frustration is most palpable in *MGS2*, where Snake is removed as an avatar of identification for the majority of the game and replaced with the novice and emotional Raiden, an avatar that seemingly undermines the player's desire for mastery and control at every turn.[5] As Tanner Higgin (2010) argues, this was by design, where feelings of frustration were built into the game's narrative so that "players are initiated into *MGS2*'s logics of control and affect" (252). The frustration of Snake mirrors the player's, both of whom are made to feel helpless through regimes of control, whether they be the architects of war (the Patriots) or the game (Kojima and his team of developers).

This convergence of frustrated player and character emotional states is possibly the most important mechanism by which Snake functions as an anti-action hero and can be seen in the final confrontation in *MGS3* between Naked Snake and his beloved former mentor, The Boss, a difficult battle with an opponent skilled in both stealth and close-quarters combat. At the end of the battle, the Boss lies defeated, and Snake must kill her to complete his mission. The camera cuts to a bird's eye view and slowly pans back as it waits for Snake to pull the trigger. The game forces players to press the button that will kill The Boss, putting them into the head and hands of Snake. On one level, this action makes the player complicit in Snake's actions, echoing what one critic wrote of the experience: "By forcing the player to take that final shot, even when there is no other choice, the question of 'what if' permanently remains" (Stanton 2015b). On another level, this removal of player agency mirrors Snake's own loss of agency as he must kill someone dear to him to fulfill his mission. The Boss's death is powerful and frustrating because of the player's complicity and how it echoes the game's setting-specific themes of being forced by circumstances into a situation beyond one's control. In the end, we are "products of the time."

Interfaces: Menus and Management

Mechanics of stealth are not just limited to controlling Snake in the game's diegetic environments. A secondary element of the game's systems requires players to manage nondiegetic interfaces of the game in order to access additional information or equipment. Some of these interfaces are overlaid on the diegetic environment, and some of them must be accessed via a separate screen. An example of the former are the health and stamina bars that display the player character Snake's status in *MGS3*, a collection of on-screen components that is otherwise known as a heads-up display or HUD (Wilson 2006). Players must monitor the HUD in order to see if they are in danger of failing the game. Health bars are a common element in many action games, though MGS involves them in subtle ways that connect you to the player character Snake. In *MGS3*, your physical health bar is low to start the game, signifying your status as a young and inexperienced soldier. The health bar increases after completing each boss battle and by the end of the game, your health bar is the same level as The Boss, displaying your growth throughout the course of the game and implying that you are now her equal. Conversely, as an aged soldier in *MGS4*, your stamina bar is replaced with a psyche bar, which depletes when Snake experiences the stress of battle or, comically, a slight about his age from a supporting character during a cut scene or conversation.

Separate screen interfaces comprise menus that the player accesses to acquire information. These can be classified as "meta-representation" interfaces, as they visualize information to the player that is not spatially represented in the game world (Fagerholt and Lorentzon 2009, 51–2). Meta-representation interfaces in MGS often mediate the game diegesis. An example of this type of interface is obviously the Codec (see Figure 4.2), where players open up a separate screen that contains a digital readout, boxes for character animations (with static or animated artwork of the character speaking), and a window that comprises the bottom half of the screen displaying the conversation text. As described earlier, the Codec is accessed periodically throughout as audio cut scenes that progress the narrative, or as hints or background information regarding the game's enemies or environments. If the narrative needs additional information, or the player needs help progressing past an area, the Codec can be used to fill in these knowledge gaps.

Both HUD and meta-representation interfaces in MGS must be actively managed for players to blend into their environments and avoid enemies entirely. One conspicuous example is the Soliton radar, a square display in the top right of the HUD that not only maps the immediate area's environment but also reveals the location of enemies (represented as white dots). A holdover from the reactive radar in *Metal Gear 2*, the Soliton radar allows players to adjust to the top-down, isometric perspectives of the new 3D environments by presenting them with additional information not privy to the game's enemies such as "vision cones," triangular shapes emitting from the radar's enemy dots that reflect the enemy's field and direction of vision. But the radar also presents a design flaw in that players can use it to override the perspective of the environment itself. In practice, this results in "players' attention being constantly pulled and pushed from the Soliton radar to the environment and back again" in order to monitor enemy movements and avoid triggering an alert phase (Ash 2015, 100).

MGS3 removed the Soliton radar interface, forcing the player character Snake to rely much more on paying attention to the diegetic environment, but as its removal makes avoiding enemies considerably more difficult, Kojima and his team took advantage of the jungle settings and constructed a secondary meta-representation interface that allows Snake to equip camouflage and blend into the environment. Players must access a menu screen that provides a list of camo that matches the texture and color of the environment. A camo percentage replaces the Soliton radar in the HUD to tell players how well they are blending into the environment and remain out of the vision cones of enemy soldiers; high percentages indicate strong immersion with the environment, while low percentages indicate the player can be spotted even from far distances. Other menus also apply to feeding or healing Snake if he is low on stamina or severely injured. These examples also show how interfaces can act as a complement to the larger narrative themes of the game. The removal of the Soliton radar coincides with the pared-down tech of the older era and the dense trappings of the jungle setting, forcing the player to rely more on "instincts" than technology.

While the idea of camouflage is a novel one that adds variety and tension to the traditional gameplay, particularly the hunting and stalking themes of the game's setting, in practice the accessing of camo involves careful management, as players must leave the game diegesis to access the appropriate wardrobe from the nondiegetic camo selection screen (see Figure 4.8). As the terrain frequently changes, this can result in constantly switching back and forth between the camo menu and the main screen. Such a process is common to the MGS series, where menu and equipment management is a primary aspect of the gameplay. In *MGS1* and *MGS2*, this management comprises various gadgetry; in *MGS3*, this revolves around food, rations, and camouflage; in *MGS4*, this involves unlocking and equipping a slew of sophisticated weapons. In later games of the franchise, these menu options extend to managing not just Snake but entire offshore military installations that act as a headquarters for a growing army operation. Whether conducting maintenance on the body of the player character Snake or the facilities of Mother Base, management thus grows to become a core mechanic of the franchise as it expands its narrative scope and player affordances.

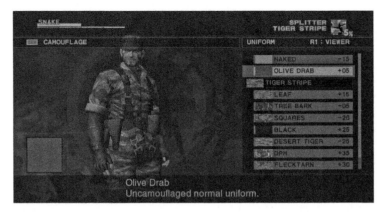

Figure 4.8 Camouflage select screen in *Metal Gear Solid 3: Snake Eater* (Konami 2004). High percentages indicate how well Snake is hidden from the view of enemies.

How this management ties in with the franchise's larger themes of nonviolence is in its ironic deployment: the further that the player character Snake progresses in the game, the more he is presented with greater options for combat and lethal weapons. As Martin Roth (2017) argues, the games "carry an admiration for weapons and war with them—the broad arsenal of deadly firearms available and the general setup of the protagonist as a one-man army attest to this" (163). While the use of wanton violence is still punished through alerts that call in soldier reinforcements, the allure of trying new weapons out on unsuspecting soldiers becomes increasingly enticing. As the player is presented with more and better options for violence, the challenge to resist their use becomes greater and greater. It is this very ability to resist this temptation in favor of nonviolent means, however, that gives play in the MGS series a moral character. Hutchinson (2019) argues that choosing to play violently or not "places more emphasis on the player's own violent or non-violent actions, deepening the ethical or moral judgement implied by the designer" (220). Making players conscious of this choice also creates the potential for players to become aware of the consequences of those actions. By flexibly letting players wield/ build weapons of violence or not, the games' foreground the deleterious aspects of their use while encouraging players to search for other methods of resolution. At the same time, allowing players to accept or reject the franchise's anti-war themes gives their own play a sense of moral agency, as they must grapple with the burden of choice.

There is also one final interface that encourages the player's moral behavior toward a nonviolent direction: a ranking system, which appears upon players' completion of the game and evaluates their performance. The ranking is based on factors related to their time of completion, number of saves, and, crucially, how many enemies they avoided and killed, with the highest rank of "Big Boss" being rewarded to players who do not kill or are discovered by a single enemy. The ranking system is a logical appeal that argues nonviolence is "not a path for the weak" but a "difficult, time-consuming and ultimately rewarding approach which requires a great deal of training and restraint" (Stamenkovic et al. 2017, 16). Through this final interface that concludes the game, mastery is defined through nonviolent play, and players are encouraged to achieve it through total pacifism.

Reflexivity: Repetition and Reflection

While the simulation systems of MGS deeply immerse players into the emotions and environment of the player character Snake, each of the games in the series also breaks this immersion through reflexive means that draw attention to the medium of the game itself. As discussed in the previous chapter, this reflexivity in Kojima's games has often been the subject of criticism for taking players out of the diegetic flow of the game, even if it actually serves the purpose of expanding the players' world into the environment of the game. The MGS series takes this reflexivity in creative directions, involving more than just the instruction manuals and game packages of the MSX2 games. Each game intentionally incorporates multiple features of nondiegetic media forms, platforms, and paratexts to further link, expand, and blur the game's diegetic environment with nondiegetic spaces.

The most prominent nondiegetic feature the MGS games incorporate is the technology the player uses to play the game. As indicated in previous chapters, Kojima early on viewed games as a synthetic medium that differentiated it from cinema. This meant viewing the hardware itself as an extension of the game, and previous games included situations where players needed to press computer keys that were not part of the interface in order to solve puzzles. With his first game totally designed for a game console (and not a personal computer), Kojima incorporated the Sony PlayStation console and controllers as a solution to solving difficult in-game encounters. This is most clearly demonstrated in the infamous boss fight with Psycho Mantis in *MGS1*.

Prior to the fight, Psycho Mantis "reads your mind" through accessing saved data logs on the player's memory card in order to demonstrate his telekinetic abilities. Players who have not saved very much are called "somewhat reckless" by Psycho Mantis, and if players have save files from other Konami games, he will comment on those games or genres ("You like Castlevania, don't you?").[6] In order to further demonstrate how his powers extend from the game world, Psycho Mantis tells players to place their controller on the floor so he can make it move through the "power of his will alone," and the haptic feedback of the DualShock controller is used to make it vibrate seconds later. The fight with Psycho Mantis is the real test of the player's abilities, as he can seemingly read the player's mind in battle by dodging Snake's every attack. To thwart his powers and be able to land attacks that cause damage, the player must physically remove their controller from the port and plug it into another port. While there are ways to win the battle with Psycho Mantis without touching the console, Kojima designs the encounter to reward players who think of the game beyond the screen.

Consideration of the technological apparatus is not limited to the console, and MGS frequently mimics the affordances of other technological mediums. For example, in the midst of the fight with Psycho Mantis, the action suddenly cuts to a black "VIDEO" screen as if the PlayStation had been disconnected from the TV port. Instead of "VIDEO," however, the bright green message in the upper-right corner reads, "HIDEO." Such a moment suggests that even the television screen can be manipulated by the game designers, pitting the player against the system itself. *MGS2* is rife with such situations, considering its story and protagonist Raiden has been trained on military simulations from *MGS1*. At one point in the game, Snake's adviser, Col. Roy Campbell, is revealed to be an AI construct. As it malfunctions, it repeatedly calls players on the Codec to tell them, "You have played the game for a long time" and to "Turn off the game console right now!" During an intense fight sequence shortly after, the screen suddenly scales down to reveal the "Mission Failed" screen that plays when the player character Snake dies. But upon closer examination, this is a trick similar to the Psycho Mantis "Video/Hideo" screen, as the "game over" screen reads "Fission Mailed" and players can continue controlling their avatars in the scaled-down screen. While players are not likely to be deceived by the game's provocations to turn off or reset the console, these interruptions to the game diegesis provide yet another obstacle for players to contend with during harried moments of gameplay, conveying a sense of the designer conspiring with the console system against the player.

As these examples indicate, the solutions to these obstacles are far removed from the experience of typical games, which nearly always encourage the player to resolve problems within the game's diegesis. They also are unique in the ways that Kojima, as the games' designer, uses these moments to insert his presence into the game action. This of course could be in part due to sheer hubris, but both the presence of the designer and the appeals to nondiegetic play have a deeper, more important function: to encourage the player to have a dialogue with the designers and explore the limits of their design.

On one level, such reflexive play can comment on the themes of the game itself, such as the social consequences of technological reliance and information manipulation present in *MGS2*. As Steven Conway (2010) argues, the ways in which the game attempts to remove control from the player suggests the game—and technological systems—can always "threaten to autonomously implode. The user is left helpless, seemingly at the mercy of technology gone (literally) mad" (150). Such a feeling of helplessness, in fact, would affect Kojima directly in July 2022 following the assassination of former prime minister Shinzo Abe in Nara. Shortly after the attack, users on the social media platform 4chan jokingly shared pictures comparing the actual shooter to Kojima. The posts went viral, being retweeted by politicians and reported on by news channels in Greece and Iran, before eventually being recognized as false. The designer became the subject (or victim) of his design, as Kojima's predictions in *MGS2* of info manipulation in the era of digital communications ironically played out in the spread of his own fake news.

On another level, Kojima and the designers of MGS ask players to explore aspects of games that go beyond the scope of traditional diegetic gameplay. Roth has usefully described these playful moments between player and designer as "states of exception," where the player must "observe, think and experiment with the environment repeatedly and beyond conventional, instrumental knowledge of the game (system)" (2017, 169). This approach results in "stimulating conflicts," in which the games allow players to choose both freedom and frustration (170). In doing so, the designers permit players to indulge in a wider range of possible actions and experiences of play. This concept of exploring ideological concepts through reflexive, boundary-expanding play is what can be called the *MGS* games' "ideology through reflexivity" (Hutchinson 2019, 208).

What these various perspectives emphasize is how the MGS franchise frequently foregrounds the material conditions of play in order to comment on the relationship between technology and the player. This idea is particularly visible in *MGS4*, the penultimate game in the Solid Snake arc and the most self-reflexive game in the entire MGS series. In concluding Solid Snake's arc, Kojima and his team constructed not only a polished new world for the narrative but also referenced player experiences of the franchise's decade-plus of existence. *MGS4* is set five years after *MGS2*, in a future where the global economy is dominated by private military companies (PMCs) staffed with super-soldiers regulated by nanomachines. Solid Snake is thrust into one last mission to a nameless Middle Eastern warzone to assassinate Liquid Snake, but his clone body has rapidly aged; though he is only forty-two, he looks like he is in his seventies. This premise is the setup for a series of twists and turns that evoke or revisit scenes and locations from previous MGS games. This complexity extends beyond the plot to *MGS4*'s referencing and commenting upon previous games' characters, audiovisual elements, and even the hardware that they ran on. The result of this meta-commentary is an ideological critique of the games industry and a deconstruction of the game sequel's perpetual repetition.

As the world of *MGS4* is set in a future of endless military engagements sustained by a pervasive AI system, a similar repetition is also reflected in the narrative and gameplay. Characters such as Meryl and Eva return, while others such as Raiden, Johnny Sasaki, and Liquid Ocelot are an assemblage of parts and ideas from previous games (Ninja/Gray Fox, Otacon, and Liquid Snake/Revolver Ocelot, respectively). The boss characters of *MGS4*, an all-female troupe called the Beauty and the Beast Unit, are too composed of elements of bosses from previous games. Screaming Mantis is a textbook example, as her name is borrowed from Psycho Mantis (*MGS1*), personality from The Fear and The Pain (*MGS3*), and fighting abilities from Psycho Mantis, Vamp (*MGS2*), and The Sorrow (*MGS3*). The battle with her evokes the reflexive aspects of the fight with Psycho Mantis, as Screaming Mantis will not only black out the screen but will also apparently "reset" the game, which causes the screen to appear to restart and display the Konami logo for several seconds before returning to the battle. Support will even call Snake on his Codec to supply him with "hints" such as swapping his controller to a different port before acknowledging in the game that the new PlayStation 3 hardware has wireless controllers.

These callbacks to previous games draw attention not only to the player or the platform but to the franchise's penchant for incorporating reflexive devices into the game diegesis. They also highlight the derivation that has become inherent to the games industry, where studios and players recycle the same experiences with marginally altered trimmings. This idea is made explicit in *MGS4* through its recycling of assets, such as the many "reused" environments from tanker settings that borrow from *MGS2* to jungle environments that evoke *MGS3*. The setting for *MGS1*, Shadow Moses, is physically reprised in *MGS4* as a location that the player character Snake must revisit, though the facility is decrepit and unmanned sentries now patrol the area in scripted routes that recall the limited sights and ranges of soldiers from the early games. Various nondiegetic devices are once again directly acknowledged—positioning the camera in a certain direction will trigger comments from Snake ("Overhead view—just like old times!")—while the ending theme to *MGS1* both plays upon entering the facility and is even credited on-screen via text that describes the song info (see Figure 4.9). As Snake moves through Shadow Moses, visual and aural flashbacks are triggered that play scenes of dialogue from *MGS1* ("A surveillance camera?"). Such flashbacks are littered throughout the game in cut scenes, where players can press buttons to trigger bursts of scenes from previous games—with the same older graphical representation—as if jogging Snake's (and the player's) memory. Some of these moments can even be explored, such as a "dream" Snake has of infiltrating Shadow Moses that reprises one of the early stages from *MGS1*. As character tropes are recombined and

Figure 4.9 Snake returns to Shadow Moses in *Metal Gear Solid 4: Guns of the Patriots* (Konami 2008) to the tune of the Metal Gear Solid ending theme: "The Best Is Yet to Come."

repeated, game environments are thus similarly recycled, reused, and even replayed.

Kojima has said in interviews that the inclusion of these older game assets in *MGS4* was intended as a service to the "people who love the Metal Gear series." As a capstone to two decades of Metal Gear titles, he hoped that players would "think about what you were doing ten years ago" and "look back to your life, to yourself" (Garratt 2007). Such "fan service" is typical for franchise titles, where longtime players are rewarded for their knowledge of previous titles, and Kojima's games have always included intertextual "easter eggs" from older games. Snake's return to Shadow Moses is a return to the memories of the game for the player, and both Snake and the player are placed in a similar position of nostalgic memory recollection—Snake for his old missions and players for their own experiences playing the game ten years earlier. Each player's experience in the recycled Shadow Moses conjures up individual play experiences from the past, personalizing Snake and the franchise for each player.

However, Kojima cautions this sentiment for *MGS4* by simultaneously asking players to "go beyond [these elements] in the future as well" (Garratt 2007). Snake's aged status reflects this passage of time for the player in an exaggerated but meaningful way; Snake, like the player, has changed, and revisiting the same areas in the same way as the past is no longer possible for both. As the rusted and abandoned interiors indicate, it also may no longer be desirable. Snake, for one, is no longer the svelte hero of previous games, and while he controls far better than the first PlayStation games, he also must stop periodically to catch his breath or stretch his stiff back. This means that Snake has more limited affordances compared to the past, and players must try to account for his limitations within their own play. James Paul Gee calls this the "player's story," where players become a "kind of person" depending on how they choose to play (and replay) Snake in *MGS4*: "It is not his goals or mine alone that determine how 'we play,' but the both of us together determine how we play" (Gee 2009). Kojima's inclusion of fan service in *MGS4* thus takes on additional meaning; the incorporation of familiar assets can lead players to wax nostalgia but also reflect on how they have been shaped by the inherent repetition in both games and game franchises.

Snake and game franchises like MGS are similarly shaped and constricted by the games that comprise them. This idea is heavily explored through the extensive reflexivity in *MGS4* but also in its promotional surround as various paratexts also reflect the weight of past burdens in creating something new. The Japanese promotional poster for *MGS4* features Old Snake, though in an image different from typical action games or other games in the franchise where Snake is portrayed heroically. Snake is arched back, with an expression that looks like he is screaming in pain. The tagline for the game is "Dissolve" (*chiru*), and it is featured at the top of the poster over Snake's body. The lower half of Snake's own body reflects this tagline, as it dissolves to reveal hundreds of smaller silhouettes of game items, weapons, and avatars. Kojima has explained that the image conveys Snake leaving behind his "DNA" in the form of all of his experiences. But one can also read this image as Snake, like most heroes of game franchises, being burdened from the characters, affordances, and experiences of past games in the franchise. And as "a game character is doomed to repeat himself," so too are designers of game franchises due to player and industry expectations to replicate previously successful formulas (Stanton 2015c).

This struggle and desire to innovate is also articulated in the making-of featurette that is packaged with the special edition of the game. Titled "Hideo Kojima's Gene," the thirty-six-minute documentary was created as a promotion for both *MGS4* and Kojima Productions (hereafter KojiPro), a subsidiary of Konami formed in 2005 that was headed by Kojima and composed of members of the Kojima Clan. During its production, *MGS4* became the focus of KojiPro with over 200 members working on the title, and the making-of featurette extends the reflexivity of the games into the production spaces of the designers. The documentary likens Kojima to Snake, leading a team of comrades as they struggle to finish the game and meet increasingly lofty expectations for the franchise during the last months of the game's production, the so-called "crunch" period of development. Several scenes feature Kojima playing through the game like a quality assurance tester, writing comments on notecards for staff to then implement, and visiting each department to personally relay his feedback. Members of KojiPro are portrayed as equally dedicated to their leader, though occasionally overwhelmed at the last-minute revisions that might compromise the stability of the game's code. Kojima and his team work together to find a middle ground to improve the game while sticking to the release date, showcasing both their dedication to artistic quality and fan/industry expectations. Despite the volume of work, several staff members express their enjoyment of the process toward the end of development. Various developers are interviewed to show how they can exercise their "power" through incrementally improving the game in the final stages of production, empowered by their leader's work ethic and penchant for perfectionist polishing to "try anything." The documentary concludes with Kojima saying he'd like to step aside and pass on the series to a new generation of creators who will "inherit the genes of MGS."

The documentary has an authoring function, most obviously emphasizing the series authors such as Kojima and KojiPro as protectors of its continued quality. At numerous points, staff members are remarked to have worked on past games in the series or even earlier on titles like *Policenauts*. *MGS4* is thus shown to be part of a legacy of excellence, created by the same core staff as earlier critical and commercial successes despite ballooning development teams, costs, and volume of work. The documentary also importantly reveals the desire for KojiPro to continue a dialogue with players through their games. Kojima and his staff are shown to create games out of a mix of obsession, professionalism, and sheer enjoyment. The developers of KojiPro reveal their own passion and attention through the inclusion of personal touches and authorial signatures despite the ostensible creative restrictions that result from increasingly commercial work. These portrayals mythologize KojiPro in the eyes of players and confirm their status as more than simple Konami employees. Despite the numerous changes that the franchise has faced in its growth, *MGS4* is positioned as a successor to the craft sensibility of Kojima's adventure games for the MSX and PC Engine as a domain that still is attempting to innovate and experiment even within the strictures of AAA commercial games. The documentary thus reaffirms the decades-long discourse of KojiPro pushing the boundaries of games and their continued narrative, aesthetic, and technological evolution.

Conclusion

The *MGS4* making-of documentary is a good point to end my analysis of the design of the MGS franchise, as it loops back to the opening of this chapter to tie together both Konami's efforts at promoting Kojima the director and KojiPro's continual foregrounding of reinvention over iteration in their construction of each game of the MGS franchise. If it seems like this chapter gradually moves away from Kojima to address how other developers or paratexts shaped the MGS franchise, this is partly by design. As the franchise grew in popularity, it also grew in the size of its development teams and budgets. Kojima's personal control over the series mirrored his own growth from a designer to a director to a producer to a vice president role at Konami Studios. Tasked with ever more responsibilities, Kojima could no longer have the same influence over every aspect of game development as his early adventure games. Beginning with *MGS2*, his role gradually transitioned to a supervisor who oversaw different departments, allowing those departments to find solutions to problems and avenues for creative expression while providing feedback throughout development.

Despite this abdication of total control, Kojima still exerts an immense influence over each of the MGS games due to his continued writing of the game's narratives and cut scenes, heavy input on character design, and insistence on creating systems that mirror the game's narrative themes, carryovers from the small team ethos of his MSX2 and PC Engine adventure games. His supervision of dialogue in Codec conversations and writing of cut scenes ensures that each MGS reflects contemporary social issues and concerns and encourages players to find solutions to change them. His own taste in film and other media forms influences the games' cinematic aesthetics and helps shape their stylistic characteristics. His insistence that each game's systems are continually reworked to complement these thematic and audiovisual changes also demonstrates his desire to make players not just receive but actually interact with these ideas to feel and inhabit their emotional dimensions, whether they remove control from the players or force them to consider the morality of using violence. Each game brings these real-world contexts into the players' environment through "fan service" and reflexive calls to materials, platforms, or paratexts of the game, asking players to consider their own histories as fans of the MGS franchise. Though the MGS games are longer, bigger, and more demanding than ever, Kojima still attempts to have personal dialogues with players through these reflexive affordances.

But while MGS displays Kojima's individual idiosyncrasies, the popular attention they have received has allowed the creative contributions of individual departments to be revealed in various industrial disclosures. What these disclosures reveal is how KojiPro absorbed and internalized Kojima's design practices, working within and affirming the structures and limitations of commercial studio game development while simultaneously attempting to disrupt them. Stephanie Boluk and Patrick LeMieux (2017) sum up this approach nicely in their assertion that "*Metal Gear* has not operated like a game as much as it has been a platform, simultaneously enabling and disabling certain possibilities" (139). This spirit of affirmation and disruption, enabling and disabling, can be thought of as an extension of the adventure games the Kojima Clan/KojiPro created for the MSX2 as demonstrated in the previous chapter. While each MGS emphasizes the stealth mechanics of "tactical espionage action," they also incorporate radical changes to the environments, enemy AI, player character avatars, and menu interfaces that create drastically varying gameplay experiences. This distributed agency occurs across different departmental nodes, operating collectively under Kojima's aegis but also acting within their own individual creative directions. This means that Kojima once again had to rely on talented programmers and artists to realize his ambitious ideas with the development of the MGS franchise, but unlike with *Metal Gear*, he was now at the top of the food chain instead of the bottom—the central node in MGS's developmental network—and able to command more resources, manpower, and creative leeway from Konami. Importantly, Kojima's elevated position reflected not just his own growth within the company but also greater buy-in and understanding from like-minded colleagues who had developed games alongside him for many years and who had become the arbiters for his progressive design practices.

Chapter 5

LIVE OPS

BUILDING CONNECTIONS IN OPEN WORLDS

The release of *MGS4* brought the story of Solid Snake to a close and was a conclusion of sorts to the direction that the MGS franchise had taken via its four canonical games (and many spin-offs) on the Sony PlayStation consoles. While Hideo Kojima reinvented the franchise through new gameplay systems in each game, some were also met with criticism for increasingly convoluted storylines and linear structures. *MGS4*, in particular, divided players and critics; some welcomed Kojima's commentary on the military-industrial complex and contemporary wars in the Middle East, while others thought it was a "frustrating, fractured game" with a "movie-to-game ratio of approaching something more like 80/20" (Welsh 2008; Kohler 2008). *MGS4* featured some of the most complex environments in the entire series, particularly early in the game, but often ushered players through these environments while leaving less space for repeated exploration. Other areas and missions involved less flexible mechanics, such as tracking a mole through a foggy city, or heavily limited gameplay, such as escaping pursuers via an on-rails motorcycle. *MGS4* also featured Kojima's penchant for cinematic cut scenes, though longer and comprising more of the game's playtime than ever before.[1] This heavy reliance on cinematic storytelling should be placed in the context of *MGS4* being the climax of a series spanning at least four different games (more if one includes the MSX Metal Gear titles), similar to how the final chapter added to the PC Engine port of *Snatcher* resolved many of the mysteries in the PC-8801/MSX version of the game despite its lack of interactive components. Nonetheless, in tying the many narrative and thematic threads of the franchise together in *MGS4*, the experience was more cinematically bloated and less interactive than its predecessors, particularly the simulation-like survival mechanics of *MGS3*.

Kojima had designed and directed at least one new MGS game for every Sony PlayStation console, indulging in the expanded scope of audiovisual representation and ludic affordances introduced with each system. But following the release of *MGS2*, Kojima also began producing and directing several games for a range of portable platforms. While these games do not tend to derive the same amount of attention and discussion as Kojima's opuses for the Sony PlayStation consoles, they actually contributed a great deal of new ideas to Kojima's progressive design practices. As the games were produced for systems with more limited processing capabilities, they could not rely on extensive cut scenes or realistic forms of representation to captivate players. The mobile nature of the platforms also meant that they were less conducive to lengthy narrative exposition or uninterrupted missions. Due to these restrictions, Kojima's games for these platforms rely less on the cinematic bombast that had come to characterize the MGS franchise and instead reflect the systems' emphasis on liveness and customization to player styles and needs. These elements, moreover, would inform the games for Kojima Productions when the studio returned to making more simulation-like games for the Sony PlayStation 4 (hereafter PS4) both at and after Kojima's employment at Konami.

In this chapter I examine the changes to KojiPro's design processes and emphases following *MGS4*. While Kojima from this point continues to emphasize the sociopolitically informed narratives and mixed-media aesthetics of his adventure game predecessors, he also embraces new thematic mechanics and reflexive spaces centered on greater degrees of player choice. He takes cues from contemporary online games to emphasize how players are connected to environments beyond their control and how they must adapt to changes in their surroundings and communities to make progress. At the same time, with the move back to the PlayStation, his games are designed around massive open world environments that allow players to explore areas with greater degrees of freedom. The result is that KojiPro's games post-*MGS4* still incorporate many of the thematic and audiovisual interests of Kojima and his teams since the early MSX days of development but with a striking shift in the role of the players—and player communities—in shaping the direction of that experience.

In this chapter, I introduce two design concepts in KojiPro's portable and open world games which emphasize player agency: simulation and asynchronous sociality. I begin with KojiPro's portable games to show how the studio's games for mobile platforms are designed around aspects of flexibility and customizability to players' specific environments.

I will then show how these design choices were carried over into open world games for the Sony PS4, particularly *Death Stranding*, Kojima's first game for his independent game studio after leaving Konami. *Death Stranding* marks an evolution in Kojima's design in its incorporation of asynchronous multiplayer gameplay, combining mechanics of simulation and sociality in an interdependent cycle. Despite this, *Death Stranding* simultaneously exhibits all of the characteristics of the progressive design featured in Kojima's adventure and stealth-action games for Konami. In striking out on his own, Kojima's game design continues to bear strong influences from his many years at Konami, including his desire to break from genre conventions and to create game experiences that push the boundaries of what players can control.

Portable Ops

As stated in Chapter 2, Kojima took on greater management duties at Konami shortly before the release of *Policenauts*. Beginning with several spin-offs for the *Tokimeki Memorial* franchise, he served as a producer for a number of diverse games while directing titles for the MGS franchise, from ports of arcade rhythm games like *Beatmania* to mecha action titles like *Zone of the Enders*. While many KojiPro staff supervised these games, it is difficult to discern Kojima's specific imprint considering his more limited role in their design and direction, even if the titles share some of the same progressive design practices.[2] There is one title, however, where Kojima had a much larger role in the initial proposal: *Boktai: The Sun Is in Your Hands* (Konami 2003).

Boktai was initially set to be designed and directed by Kojima before he was pulled away to direct *MGS3*, but the concept of the game is based off of his original proposals. Players take on the role of Django, a vampire hunter who creeps through post-apocalyptic ruins to purify the undead. The game's narrative features several of Kojima's personal influences. On a cinematic level, players must drag coffins of the undead from the crypts into the sunlight, paying homage to the actions of Franco Nero's ex-Union protagonist in Sergio Corbucci's 1966 spaghetti western, *Django*. Kojima in interviews has also remarked upon the importance of the game's central motif of the "sun" as one with outsized importance to his generation growing up in the 1950s and 1960s. Books featuring beach-going delinquents such as Shintaro Ishihara's 1955 novel *Season of the Sun*, films like Rene Clements' sun-soaked thriller *Purple Noon*, and even monuments like Taro Okamoto's famous Tower of the Sun art

Figure 5.1 *Boktai*'s UV light-sensing game cartridge.

sculpture constructed for the 1970 Osaka World Exposition brightly captured the popular imagination (Shmuplations Boktai). But the sun is more than simply a motif for the game's story. *Boktai* was designed for the Game Boy Advance to take advantage of the console's portability, and as Konami had some experience producing medical devices equipped with special sensors, the game's cartridge was fitted with a transparent sensor that responded only to UV radiation (see Figure 5.1). The game's central gimmick was that the light-powered weapon of the player character Django could respond to exposure to direct sunlight, and without it, players would have a much more difficult time progressing through the game by being forced to forage for rare light crystals dispersed sporadically in the ruins.

Hence, *Boktai* was the unique portable game that was punitive for players who did not play it portably or at least outside of their rooms. This fits in with Kojima's other progressive design rules of reflexively blurring the lines between game and physical spaces, drawing players' environments into the logic of the game's world and creating a more personalized game experience. According to Kojima, he wanted to imbue *Boktai* with the unique elements attached to each player's environment: "Their country of residence, the geography, the seasons, where they play, the time of day, their posture. Depending on these things, a play style emerges that adheres to their lifestyle" (Kojima 2020). Certain areas or bosses depended on having access to sunlight, meaning players were forced to watch weather reports or wait for poor weather conditions to clear in order to complete objectives. Players could get around this restriction by using a blue light to charge Django's gun, but even this hack was considered by the designers, who built in an "overheating" mechanism that would render Django temporarily weaponless if too much heat was applied from an artificial source.

Central to this idea of turning the environment into a game mechanic, albeit a chaotic one, was the concept of "liveness." Players could not merely retrace the steps of the designer but had to account for the unpredictability of independent environmental agents outside of their control. This idea stands in somewhat of a contrast to Kojima's games in the MGS franchise and its emphasis on mastery of the game's environments. Though *Boktai* is still a linear single-player game, Kojima argued that this "live" experience" is similar to multiplayer online games, which force players to acknowledge the will and agency of others: "Yes, the creators have laid down a framework, but the experience is unpredictable and changes depending on who you play with. I wanted to bring that 'live' fun to portable games, and create something where the environment, and even the very gameplay changes as you walk around" (Shmuplations Boktai). As the experience of playing *Boktai* could greatly differ depending on these environmental qualities, Kojima and his team wanted to encourage players to reflect on current ecological conditions and to be "grateful for the sun," a theme that is reflected in the post-apocalyptic setting where the solar system is on the brink of collapse. *Boktai*'s forcing players out of their rooms was also a sly commentary on the growing media coverage of *hikikomori*, or "shut ins," who refused to venture outside of their homes due to various social anxieties (Kondo 2001; Watts 2002). Where Kojima in past games referenced contemporary social issues in order to encourage players to think and engage with them, Kojima's solution to the *hikikomori* problem was more direct: draw players outside of their self-imposed bubbles and force them to engage with the world around them.

While the game did not come close to the sales of the MGS franchise, players responded favorably to this unique dynamic of playing games outside. For one reviewer, "*Boktai* offered the perfect excuse to get out and see more of San Francisco," as he played the game in sunny areas around downtown, Golden Gate Park, and Japantown (Parish 2013). *Boktai* was not a game that involved other players, but by forcing players outside of familiar spaces, it ensured that players would acknowledge the planetary "other" that consists of mother nature and its surroundings. One can argue that *Boktai* anticipated the "location-based game design" of titles such as Niantic's *Ingress* and *Pokémon GO* in the structuring of movement through physical spaces (Takahashi 2015). Kojima and his team would emphasize this element of outdoor "liveness" in other portable games for the MGS franchise, ever cognizant to the itinerant and ephemeral nature of play on such systems. Beginning with *Metal Gear: Ghost Babel* (Konami 2000) for the Game Boy Color, Kojima produced seven portable titles for the MGS franchise. Most of these titles were designed and directed by other Konami developers, drawing on the MGS lore for more experimental concepts. However, one of these games, *Metal Gear Solid: Peace Walker* (Konami 2010), was written, designed, and directed by Kojima himself.

Kojima has said in interviews he did not intend to direct *Peace Walker*, but "with the game being set in Costa Rica, and the theme being nuclear deterrence, the younger developers were having trouble" (Niizumi 2009). While *Peace Walker* continues the anti-nuke themes and brings back characters featured in *MGS3*, it radically breaks from the MGS franchise in its emphasis on customization and cooperation. *Peace Walker* builds upon ideas and systems introduced in other portable Metal Gear games, shifting from the grand environments of the Metal Gear Solid console titles to the mission-based progression that is featured in *Ghost Babel* and *Metal Gear Solid: Portable Ops* (Konami 2006).

Inspired in part by Capcom's *Monster Hunter* series, Nintendo's *Pokémon* franchise, and the city builder *SimCity* franchise, *Peace Walker* wears many role-playing design influences on its sleeve (Kollar 2010). While the basic concept of stealth and avoidance of enemies still takes precedence, players now proceed through smaller maps with objectives to collect treasures and defeat large bosses. The mech-powered bosses are, like those found in *Monster Hunter* (Capcom 2004), large and formidable, requiring ample stamina, patience, and skill to defeat, and Snake must equip different weapons and upgrade attributes in order to take them on most effectively. Aside from treasures, the missions also feature both hostages that can be rescued and soldiers that can be "recruited" through the game's amusing fulton surface-to-air recovery mechanic, a self-inflating balloon that whisks away screaming targets when attached. These human targets also have their own attributes, becoming members of your "party" in a way that is not dissimilar to how one catches creatures in any of the *Pokémon* games. What structures this play, however, is the game's city-building component: the rewards from these missions are then reflected in the game's "Mother Base," an offshore plant which Big Boss/Snake uses to build his mercenary army. While not nearly as complex as *SimCity* (Maxis 1989), overseeing the construction and expansion of Mother Base becomes a secondary game that emphasizes similar kinds of interface management and resource allocation.

Peace Walker also encourages greater customization of the narrative on the part of the player. The MGS franchise has always emphasized exploration of environments and rewarded curious play, though the narrative itself was nonnegotiable in its linear delivery outside of the optional accessing of Codec dialogue. Moving to the Sony PlayStation Portable reoriented Kojima and his team away from lengthy cinematic cut scenes and linear narratives into a structure that allows players to dictate the pace in which they proceed through *Peace Walker*'s narrative. While there is still a linear narrative featuring Big Boss and his comrades (told through dynamic motion comics) much of this plot and backstory are delivered via "cassette tapes," items which can be found during missions that can be listened to after the mission is complete. These tapes don't have the playful appeal of accessing hidden Codec dialogues scattered throughout the game, though they do have greater verisimilitude in that they reveal story/lore in breaks between the game action, rather than from a pause screen within it (see Figure 5.2). They can also reveal clues and hints regarding how to proceed in

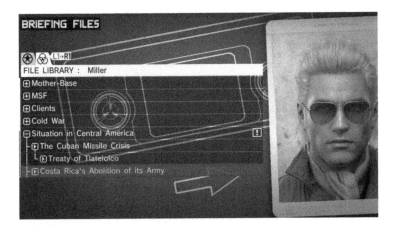

Figure 5.2 *Metal Gear Solid: Peace Walker*'s (Konami 2010) briefing files are a mix of game hints and radio dramas.

maps, providing a similar function to the Codec. Though *Peace Walker* favors immediacy over narrative, by separating the fields of action and information gathering, the game allows players to flexibly explore the game's *sekaikan* at their own pace and interest. Moreover, there is a significant amount of replayability in the game compared to previous MGS titles: once the main story is completed, the game continues but remixes/rearranges enemies and area layouts. Players who finish the story but are now seasoned in the game's mechanics can continue to play the game for these new structures.

Finally, *Peace Walker* also encourages players to cooperate with one another in order to complete mission objectives that they would not be able to do alone. This, too, was a response to the increased popularity of online social and multiplayer gaming throughout the 2000s, though Kojima insisted upon a more analog form of multiplayer similar to *Monster Hunter* and *Pokémon* that stressed in-person interaction by having players connect to each other's PSPs while in the same room. Kojima argued that players prioritized individual gain over helping others in most co-op games at the time. While maybe less convenient than connecting to strangers online, making players connect to one another in the same space ensured that they must know one another beforehand and, thus, would more likely want to work together, rather than against one another. *Peace Walker's* multiplayer breaks from the more popular fighting and shooting games of the period, emphasizing cooperation and "sharing" over competition. As Kojima put it, "I want players to feel the joy of helping each other out [. . .]. Even if one player is dying or weaker, they can help each other. We want to express the strength of friendship through that" (Totilo 2009).

This sharing/helping play manifests itself in several ways. Environments, for one, become easier to navigate as players can reach inaccessible areas, work together to flank enemies, and act as "spotters" when their partner's vision is obscured. The player's margin for error also increases, as players can share ammo, rations, or equipment with each other, and even "perform CPR" on fallen comrades to revive them. Finally, players can adjust to their partner's level of skill by "snaking in" and tethering themselves to another player. This allows the attached player to easily follow their partner, shoot on the move, or simply take a break and step away from the game while their partner continues with the mission. The comic emblem of MGS, the cardboard box, symbolizes this multifarious synergy as players can engage with various health and attack functions while humorously sneaking around inside of the "Love Box" together.

Simulation Ops

Peace Walker became a trial run of sorts for *Metal Gear Solid V: The Phantom Pain* (hereafter *MGSV*), which continued with the customizable innovations—mission-based structure, co-op play, heavy character and base upgrades—introduced in *Peace Walker*. While the MGS franchise gradually moved toward more simulation mechanics beginning with *MGS2*, the games were still structured linearly through cinematic narratives and progress hurdles contained within the environments (primarily through door locks and keycards). *MGSV*'s even more flexible structure opened up the MGS franchise and Kojima's progressive design into a direction that allowed players a greater degree of freedom engaging in the franchise's customary stealth gameplay through open world environments. With *MGSV*, KojiPro further deemphasized linear narrative and placed greater emphasis on the mechanics of simulation.

Gonzalo Frasca (2003) argues that in contrast to many forms of linear media, which excel in representation, games are a medium that explores distinct rhetorical possibilities via simulation. According to Frasca, "to simulate is to model a (source) system through a different system which maintains (for somebody) some of the behaviors of the original system" (223). These behaviors are of central importance in Frasca's definition, for simulations place greater emphasis on the behaviors or systems (inputs and outputs, rules, and outcomes) of the game instead of its audiovisual presentation. Frasca calls designers of simulations "simauthors," who "educate their simulations: they teach them some rules and may have an idea of how they might behave in the future, but they can never be sure of the exact final sequence of events and result" (229). Reflecting on Jesper Juul's framing of game types in the previous chapter, simulation games are much more games of "emergence" than "progression." While they might provide a narrative structure, their appeal is in encouraging players to find enjoyment in the rules and structures of the game. Pure games of emergence have no "end" in a traditional sense in that they are designed to be bound primarily by the interests and creativity of the players.

This open-ended play is expressed within the spatial orientation of simulations. Unlike games that revolve around goals that players achieve, actions that players master, events that players progress through, or characters that players embody, simulations are designed around complex and interactive spaces. Simulation is best understood as the relation the player has to space, what Espen Aarseth (2001) has called the "defining element" of computer games as they are "essentially concerned with spatial representation and negotiation" (154). Such spaces can be designed to limit or liberate player actions, creating "an environment for experimentation" (Frasca 2003, 225). At their most open, these environments become playgrounds for player experimentation, from urban sandboxes like the Grand Theft Auto franchise and city-building sims like the Tropico series to procedurally generated terrains like Mojang's *Minecraft*.

While *MGSV* still features a linear story and photorealistic graphics on par with any of its MGS predecessors, KojiPro's design shift from restricted to "open world" environments set in 1980s Afghanistan and Zaire makes it the most simulation-like game in the entire MGS franchise. According to game designer John Harris, open world games, as the term connotes, have players freely explore large worlds: "What all of these games share is the seeking of new, interesting regions at whatever time the player deems fit. No force forces the player's motion into new areas. There's no auto-scroll, and there are no artificial level barriers" (Harris 2007). For many games, such as massive multiplayer role-playing games (MMORPGs), open world game design means players spend hours exploring vast terrains, towns, and dungeons defeating enemies and collecting treasures. *MGSV* presents a hybrid approach: players choose objectives from a mission select screen, and then the player character Snake is deployed via helicopter into a specific area of the open world map. Once players complete the objective, they have the option of continuing to explore the game map or being airlifted back to base. Kojima's hand is still present directing the missions and set pieces; his name and the names of other developers appear across the screen as Snake choppers into each mission like the credits for a television episode. But his approach here is more "simauthor" than "narrauthor," as when the mission is complete, and even during the mission, players have the option to go "off rails" and partake in significant diversions.

These diversions are largely related to the density of the environments, which contain multiple moving components that add to the ostensible verisimilitude of the stealth experience. Similar to *MGS3*, Snake is equipped with fewer digital gadgets (though far more analog ones) and must rely on reading the body language and movements of enemy sentries when attempting to complete objectives. Unlike most sandbox simulation games, the environments themselves are designed with a startling lack of impediments for flexible player input. In the words of one reviewer of the game, "This is integrity of design: the idea that everything in a world is a physical presence that reacts as it should, rather than a solid 3D shape that's basically wallpaper" (Stanton 2015d). Nearly every structure in the game can be entered and utilized, creating a wide range of strategies for missions. The environments also are subject to real-time effects, such as weather and temporal changes, meaning that sneaking around in a sandstorm or through the cover of night necessitates a very different strategy than trying to complete such missions on a clear, bright day. Players are invited to attempt the same missions in varying conditions, scour the layouts, memorize enemy patrol paths, and then test how different combinations of these elements react to diverse stimuli. The range of options in completing a mission means that crossing a bridge or abducting a hostage can be an entirely different experience based on the player's style of play. The environments, moreover, are littered with objects—flora, fauna, wildlife, weapons, and sentries—that can be fultoned out and "collected" in a similar way to the base-building mechanics of *Peace Walker*. This combination of large environments, reactive objects and avatars, and range of player affordances means that players can either complete stealth missions smoothly like James Bond, create havoc through traps and decoys, or diverge entirely from the "mission" to fulton out exotic species.

The environment's flexibility is matched by the player character Snake, who is also given an absurd range of affordances to manipulate it. These affordances speak to the increased agency of players to interact with the game's more open-ended gameplay according to their own preference. Snake can access various types of equipment (guns, decoys, smoke grenades) but also several heads-up displays (binoculars, maps, "reflex mode") that provide the player with multiple forms of vision and information inaccessible to enemies. In her ideological reading of the game, Soraya Murray (2018) calls these visual references a "quintessential twenty-first century multiplex management strategy" (193) where players are trained not to view these existing landscapes as places where people and culture live, but as spaces to be "exploited and disciplined by Snake and his Diamond Dogs" (197). This "predatory" vision also extends to the game's base-building system, which applies simulation aspects to character and army management. Where *Peace Walker* was simply a series of menus, the Mother Base in *MGSV* is a collection of areas that is both managed and traversed by Snake. As players collect more resources from the maps, Mother Base becomes a visible catalog of their achievement, recording their progress in the game through arboretums, zoos, and entire floating military installations manned by Snake's private army, whose morale he boosts with his legendary presence. As Mother Base grows, however, its micromanagement becomes increasingly complex, and the initial feeling of achievement gradually feels compulsory as more personnel must be delegated to different departments or deployed to territories to amass resources. The proud monument to player glory transforms into a "bureaucratic orientation of management and collection" that must be maintained and grown for its own sake (184).

The bureaucratic systems of *MGSV*, however, are not presented without commentary, and at their most persuasive, they present options for players to subvert their dehumanizing tendencies. One such example is in the base-building multiplayer component, where players can invade each other's Mother Bases. As players must actively manage their base's personnel, artillery, and facilities to stave off attacks, they are also presented with the option to develop nuclear weapons. In keeping with the logic of nuclear proliferation during the Cold War, the description of nuclear weapons in the game emphasizes their destructive energy and political power: "The most powerful weapon of mass destruction humanity has ever created, nuclear weapons employ the tremendous energy released by nuclear fission. Merely possessing one make its owner a threat and has the effect of deterring retaliation from rivals." The development of nuclear weapons has some benefits and considerable drawbacks; players receive special trophies for possessing and disposing of nuclear weapons, opposing players are discouraged or prevented from invading their bases, and the offensive and defensive stats of the players increase. On the downside, the weapons cost large amounts of money and resources to develop, restrict players from invading other player's bases in turn, and penalize the player with 50,000 "Demon Points," a metric in the game that evaluates the player's moral or immoral actions. The considerable trouble required to develop and possess nuclear weapons reveals the designers' intentions, which are in line with the anti-war and anti-nuke positions of previous games.

But the multiplayer component also revealed how player choice could effect powerful change in the game's world, as players also had the option of deactivating their nukes and trusting other players to do the same. Doing so would give the player no real tactical advantage and on its surface might seem like a purely symbolic gesture that would likely result in the player getting bombarded by hostile enemy assaults. But players did so anyway, using a combination of social media forums and a fan-generated "Nuke Watcher" to disarm their own nuclear weapons or infiltrate other players' bases to decommission their nukes. Total nuclear disarmament was acknowledged in the game world for the PS3 version of *MGSV* via a cut scene that triggered and played on

Figure 5.3 Cut scene in *Metal Gear Solid V: The Phantom Pain* (Konami 2015) where total global nuclear disarmament is achieved.

July 27, 2020 (Sheridan 2020). In the cut scene, Snake and his comrades celebrate the decommissioning of the last nuclear weapon and pledge to protect the new nuke-free world order (Figure 5.3). KojiPro included this option amid a backdrop of increasing militarism in the twenty-first century, with countries around the world scrambling to produce nuclear weapons. A coda following the cut scene quotes the words of former US president Barack Obama in 2009: "Our efforts to contain these dangers are centered on a global non-proliferation regime, but as more people and nations break the rules, we could reach the point where the center cannot hold." This increased militarism was even reflected in Japan in 2014, where reinterpretation of Article 9 of the Japanese Constitution allowed its Self-Defense Forces to exercise the right of "collective self-defense" and engage in military activities outside of the nation's borders (Martin 2014). All of this military context is reflected in Kojima's development of *MGV*'s multiplay.

In light of this real-life global rearmament, the virtual decommissioning of nukes might seem insignificant, especially as players began creating new nuclear weapons in *MGSV* again soon after the last nuke was eliminated. However, even if disarmament obviously cannot translate to direct results in real life, Kojima's experience design demands that players engage the possibility. As Kojima put it: "If we can't disarm ourselves in the real world, at least the fictional game world offers mankind, the creators of nuclear weapons, the unparalleled 'experience' of making the conscious choice to create a nuclear free world. Through this experience, players will come to understand what it really means to take a stand against war and nuclear weapons" (Kojima 2017). Such a stance reflects what Rachael Hutchinson (2019) describes as a "parallel with in-game and real-world 'experience,' the collapsing of which gives meaning to gameplay" (228). As players showed they could (fleetingly) resist the game's design to stockpile weapons by decommissioning them instead, they validated the designers' faith that they could come together for a common pacifist goal. Importantly, this goal was achieved not through events and narratives solely within the game but through player organization and action outside of it. In the words of Kojima, *MGSV* passes the "baton to the player—who was previously bound to Snake," and in doing so, brings the "legend full circle" (Kikuchi 2016). Through experimenting with both the spaces of the simulation and the real world, players collectively joined Snake as "heroes" for a common cause.

Repairing Disconnection in Death Stranding

Following the release of *MGSV*, Kojima left Konami Entertainment in a highly publicized falling out between the two parties (Ashcraft 2015; Greenbaum 2021). After his departure, he used his industry contacts to start his own proprietary studio, Kojima Productions, with an exclusive deal with Sony Entertainment for his first independent game: *Death Stranding*. The live and customizable play of open world co-op games merged with Kojima's progressive design to form a hybrid experience of narrative and simulation in *Death Stranding*. While the experience is in some ways similar to MGS in its focus on a "lone wolf" protagonist, it is in service of a radically different set of themes and mechanics. Instead of casting the player character as a legendary hero and master of military tactics, *Death Stranding* casts players in the role of a delivery porter with a much more limited arsenal of affordances.

While the experience of *Death Stranding* might be quite different from previous Kojima adventure games that place the player in the role of a detective or mercenary, the central design of the game is firmly in the tradition of KojiPro's progressive ethos of merging a socially relevant narrative with thematically reflective mechanics. *Death Stranding* builds upon the multiplayer components of KojiPro's portable and open world games, where collective play worked as additions to the core gameplay, for an experience that revolves around the absolute necessity of collective play. Playing with others significantly transforms the experience of the game and reinforces its narrative themes but also actively imagines an alternate space of productive play that allows for an experimental approach to collective action. In addressing core geopolitical conflicts in the contemporary moment, KojiPro once again combined genre fiction, mixed-media aesthetics, and integrated environments and systems to get players to think through the narrative's themes of connection and actively work with avatars of change both in and outside of the game world.

Thematic Narratives

Like his previous games, Kojima began the planning of *Death Stranding* around a central theme which, in this case, revolved around the theme of "connection." Kojima said he wrote the script for *Death Stranding* as a commentary on what he believed at the time to be a sense of divisiveness in countries around the world: "President Trump right now is building a wall [...] Then you have Brexit, where the UK is trying to leave the EU, and it feels like there are lots of walls and people thinking only about themselves in the world" (Powell 2019). Kojima believed Trump's campaign of "making America great again" and Brexit, wherein the citizens of the UK voted to withdraw from the European Union and the European Atomic Energy Commission in 2016, represented an era of extreme "individualism" that was playing itself out across culture off and online. "The internet can directly connect players, certainly," he explained. "But some people use the anonymity that affords to say hurtful things to people without a second thought. Even in games we get online to pick up guns and shoot at each other" (Kikuchi and Hayashi 2019). Here, Kojima alludes to the negative environments created on social media platforms in the mid-2010s, which some argued were a "toxic mirror" to the rest of society (Simmons 2016). The world and story of *Death Stranding* were conceived with this global context of divisive politics and culture in mind.

Of course, Kojima does not represent any politicians directly in the game. To do so would alienate possible playing audiences but also would be an easy and overly simplistic representation of larger systemic issues, which is why Kojima has always used genre fiction to allegorize them. To reflect this theme of disconnection and isolation, the game begins in an post-apocalyptic America that has suffered a cataclysm known as the "Death Stranding." Following a mass extinction event, spectral beings called BTs ("Beached Things") that are trapped between a state of living and death roam the landscape. Their presence triggers acidic rain called Timefall, which ages and eventually deteriorates anything it touches, and huge explosions called Voidouts. Both Timefall and Voidouts have devastated the nation's infrastructure and driven most of the remaining population underground into colonies called Knot Cities. These shelters are all that remain of the new United Cities of America (UCA), which protect people not only from the effects of BTs but also human predators like terrorists and mules (cargo thieves).

Each of the Knot Cities relies on delivery companies for supplies, and the player controls one of these deliverymen—Sam Porter Bridges—on an expedition across the broken UCA as he seeks to reconnect the disparate Knot Cities to a central energy and information grid called a Chiral Network. Sam and other porters are equipped with BBs ("Bridge Babies"), unborn fetuses placed in an artificial pod to replicate the womb of their "stillmother." As BBs are also in a state between life and death, they are able to detect BTs and help porters navigate the vast landscape if they are hooked up to them. The BB's pod is attached to Sam as he works to "reconnect America" and help rebuild its broken networks and infrastructures.

In some ways, *Death Stranding* is a response to Benedict Anderson's concept of the nation as an "imagined community," or the idea that a community is formed from the imagined bond between its citizens. Anderson argues that nations are imagined communities because "members of even the smallest nation will never know most of their fellow members, meet them, or even hear of them, yet in the minds of each lives the image of their communion" (Anderson 1983, 6). This imagined bond is completely severed in *Death Stranding*, as the people of the United States no longer imagine themselves as part of a collective. The game's themes are a reflection not just of the United States but of the increasing populism that had grown in nations around the world in the late 2010s, from the United States to Europe to parts of East Asia, where isolationism and xenophobia became increasingly tied to national identity. Imagining the nation is not enough to sustain it when its people increasingly do not trust their fellow countrymen. America in *Death Stranding* is a symbol of this dysfunction, and the player character Sam must make the country "whole" again by rebuilding its institutions and international standing, which have corroded from fear and suspicion. The theme of the game, then, is simple and direct: without strong and tangible bonds, the collective cannot sustain. Players must correspondingly rebuild the country's material infrastructure, which has crumbled due to public neglect and environmental decay, and reconnect the country's citizens, who have isolated due to literal and figurative toxicity.

Death Stranding's story is set in a fictional future America and continues with Kojima's scripts that are critical of the United States and its various efforts at information and population control in the twentieth and twenty-first century. But saving America in *Death Stranding* becomes a larger allegory for saving the world, an idea that would take on an additional poignance and uncanny prescience in the face of the Covid-19 pandemic, where the entire planet was paralyzed by an infectious coronavirus that killed millions and hospitalized tens of millions more. People isolated in their homes to protect themselves from the virus or to obey national lockdown directives while relying on public servants and delivery services for basic living supplies. Several media outlets made the claim that Kojima and *Death Stranding* had predicted the future, where delivery and social media services were relied on to connect people in a world that no longer allowed the same physical connections as in the past (Nakamura 2020; Schnabel 2020). The reality was that Kojima was precisely commenting on the isolation of the present, which the pandemic simply amplified.

Mixed-Media Aesthetics

The audiovisual elements of *Death Stranding* reflect these themes of connection through KojiPro's penchant for stylistic multimodality. The game continues with the style of representation that had developed during the MGS franchise, combining photorealistic graphics with extensive cinematic cut scenes. As MGS was one of the franchises that had pushed the games industry toward ever more realistic forms of graphical representation, this preference was no longer stylistically exceptional, but *Death Stranding* shows how Kojima and his team continue to use mixed-media aesthetics to convey narrative information. Players experience the narrative through reading emails, listening to Codec-like transceiver broadcasts, and hearing musical cues—particularly an array of popular music artists like Low Roar and Silent Poets—while they are delivering packages or during breaks in the action. Each of these forms is used for their own sources of information such as backstory, mission hints, and directives and to complement in-game sequences. Though cut scenes are still a dominant mode of delivering narrative material, a great deal of the game's narrative is, like *Peace Walker* and *MGSV*, relayed not through cut scenes but via an array of text and audio-based media items and devices acquired throughout the game's world and then accessed through menus outside of the game world.

The character designs also reflect a convergence between cinema and games that harken back to Kojima's early games for the MSX, when character visages were produced from real-life celebrity likenesses. While the character designs for *Death Stranding* are still created by Yoji Shinkawa, who left Konami with Kojima, they are based around the motion-captured images of celebrity actors and actresses such as Norman Reedus, Mads Mikkelson, Lea Seydoux, and Lindsay Wagner (see Figure 5.4). Many of these figures connect to some aspect of Kojima's personal tastes. Mikkelson and Seydoux, for example, played leading roles in James Bond films, while Wagner makes a repeat cameo due to Kojima's idolatry of *Bionic Woman* as a child. Others, such as Guillermo del Toro and Nicholas Winding Refn, are cast as characters in the game despite minimal acting experience due to their personal friendship with Kojima. Del Toro collaborated with Kojima on the horror game *P.T.*, a "playable teaser" for Konami's *Silent Hill* franchise that ended up being cancelled.[3] Refn, on the other hand, reciprocated Kojima's invitation to appear as a character in *Death Stranding* by casting Kojima as a sword-wielding Yakuza character in his miniseries *Too Young to Die Old* (2019). Even several minor characters that appear throughout the game world have some personal connection to Kojima, such as Geoff Keighley, the executive producer and host of The Game Awards who has

Figure 5.4 Character modeled after comedian Conan O'Brien, who visited the offices of Kojima Productions during the making of *Death Stranding* (Kojima Productions 2019).

supported Kojima and spoken publicly of their friendship throughout the years (Barnett 2020). In the game's Japanese version, moreover, the characters are still voiced by several voice actors with whom Kojima has worked since his Konami days, such as Akio Otsuka, Kikuko Inoue, and Nana Mizuki. In this way, while *Death Stranding* reflects larger trends in the games industry toward incorporating celebrity talent, Kojima's insistence on casting actors and nonactors to whom he has some personal connection reflects the game's themes of direct connection on the production level.

The environments of *Death Stranding* also have a significance in communicating themes of new beginnings and reconnections. The game's use of the Decima engine, itself originally constructed for and "recycled" from Guerilla Games' *Horizon Zero Dawn* franchise, is used to construct sprawling, open world environments. These environments are dynamic and can be altered through major environmental effects. Two of these effects—Timefall and Voidouts—have clear parallels with atomic bombs and their resulting fallout, connecting to past Kojima anti-nuclear themes and creating a nightmarish scenario where nuclear holocaust can occur at any moment. An interesting wrinkle is that once a location has experienced a Voidout, it is also purged of the BTs that previously haunted it. This allows players to traverse these renewed areas without any longer having to face the threat of Timefall or BTs. While not in any way endorsing nuclear holocaust and environmental disaster, *Death Stranding*'s dynamic environments evoke apocalyptic fiction such as *Dune* and *Nausicaa of the Valley of the Wind* in their depictions of planetary resilience in the face of human-induced climate devastation.

Interestingly, while the barren and open landscapes that comprise *Death Stranding*'s environments are ostensibly representative of the former United States, there are no visual signifiers of past American civilization similar to post-apocalyptic games set in America like the *Fallout*, *Bioshock*, or *The Last of Us* franchises. KojiPro took more inspiration from the vast landscapes of Iceland than any particular place in the United States, resulting in an America that is unrecognizable (Fontaine 2019). While America remains a narrative device, the removal of any cultural signifiers turns it into a cipher from a world-building aspect, where players build and craft roads and installations that can be added and removed without thought to preexisting institutions. The America in *Death Stranding* becomes less a representation of America the place than it is of America the idea: an environment that is shaped according to the needs and desires of a constantly changing and evolving migrant (player) community.

Emergent Systems and Complex Environments

Like Kojima's graphical adventure games and titles in the MGS series, the ludic systems and environments of *Death Stranding* reinforce the themes of the game's narrative; in this case, these themes are the importance of human connection for collective survival in the face of human and natural threats. These systems are built around reliance and trust in others, courting empathy from the player toward the game's collective others via three different aspects.

The first aspect is represented through the social bonds the player makes with NPCs in *Death Stranding* and is facilitated through the game's core mechanic. Where the core mechanic of MGS's stealth gameplay was waiting, the core mechanic of *Death Stranding* is *walking*. Walking (and driving later in the game) might seem dull as a mechanic but makes sense considering it is the action that most befits the activity of a deliveryman, even if this resulted in some critics labeling *Death Stranding* a "walking simulator" (Glennon 2019). The player character Sam begins the game delivering parcels and packages to various Knot Cities across America largely on foot. What makes this challenging is that once Sam begins carrying multiple packages or walks across steep or rocky terrain, his balance will become unstable. Players must be sensitive to the haptic feedback of the PS4's DualShock controller and tilt it back and forth to steady Sam's movement. Like KojiPro's MGS games, each of the controller's buttons in *Death Stranding* is responsible for a different input that asks players to multitask; if there are too many packages for Sam to put on his back, for example, the player must continuously hold the top L and R buttons on the controller to mimic each of Sam's arms holding onto a package. If the player ignores or loses track of any of this feedback, Sam will drop his packages or, worse, tumble to the ground and throw his packages off his body, which results in the player having to again pick up each package one by one.

Players are thus given a stark choice early in the game: make multiple trips with fewer packages for an easier but more time-consuming walking experience or carry as many packages as possible while being extremely attentive to a more deliberate delivery. The latter is often the more practical choice, considering the long distances required to deliver packages as the player progresses in the game, as well as the fact that the more Sam walks, the more he wears out his boots, which then need to be replaced. But fewer trips can also result in a more stressful play experience as even the slightest lapse in concentration—amplified in areas occupied by mules or BTs—can send Sam and his packages flying and players panicking to fight off enemies while preserving the condition of the cargo. As such, while the walking mechanics of *Death Stranding* can be frustrating, they are also effective in simulating the physical exertion and concentration of the deliveryman. Kojima said he wanted "the player to become Sam, but gradually," where the player's first forays with Sam is "like a baby learning to walk" (Goldberg 2019). Upon learning how to control Sam, players can more strongly empathize and connect with this seemingly routine action that is, in reality, a balancing act requiring careful coordination.

Delivering packages is a stressful activity, but this play becomes more enjoyable as the player receives upgrades to make the walking process smoother. Appropriately, these upgrades are presented by various preppers in the game who supply tools and gadgets that enable the player character Sam to complete deliveries with greater ease. As Sam connects the Knot Cities, his journey becomes easier through the addition of powered exoskeletons, which allow the player to carry more packages with less of an effect on Sam's balance, as well as various vehicles that allow Sam to get from point A to B with less physical exertion and concentration from the player. The fact that these gadgets are supplied by the other human characters of the game upon completing missions is a simple but direct reinforcement of the game's central theme of creating strong connections. The avatars also gain something in return related to their narrative, whether that is as simple as a pizza delivery or as complex as a long-separated family member. Of course, completing missions and receiving rewards is not exclusive to *Death Stranding*, but the game's emphasis on developing strong bonds is displayed in the ways in which in-game avatars and player characters benefit one another through agreed-upon contracts or the compact between the vendor and client. As each person fulfills their end of a mutual exchange, both of their respective situations can improve.

This thematic association between cooperation and survival is reinforced through *Death Stranding*'s second connective aspect between parent and child. This bond is represented in the game through the relationship that develops between the adult Sam and the infant BB. BB is, like many video game companions, a character who assists the player character in completing missions. As the game progresses, her companion status becomes more complex as her relationship with Sam is explored through the game's narrative, mechanics, and gameplay, or what Nave Barlev has termed the "ludo-rapport model" of analyzing video game companions (Barlev 2021). This model also mirrors the visceral qualities in which BB exerts her own humanity by forcing the player to see, hear, and feel her presence or absence.

From a narrative standpoint, while BBs might look like babies, they are defined by Sam's bosses as "tools" that detect the presence of BTs in the environment. Initially, the BB that Sam equips is no different from any other in its application to complete missions, and multiple characters tell Sam not to get "too attached" to BB as her function is strictly as a piece of equipment. But as the story progresses, Sam experiences "flashbacks" of BB's past. In these cut scenes, seen from the perspective of BB, Sam watches scenes featuring BB's father, who cared for, talked with, and sang songs to her as a baby. As Sam witnesses BB's past life, he (and the player) gradually sees her as a person, eventually giving her the name "Lou" to signal his acceptance of her as a surrogate daughter.

From a mechanics standpoint, BB is also an indispensable companion that enables vision through her ludic connection to the player. Equipping BB's pod to a terrain scanner alerts players to the location of BTs through highlighting their ghostly, floating outlines. This allows players to creep past the specters (in a nod to the stealth mechanics of MGS) who would otherwise be rendered invisible. Connecting to BB means that players are able to fully see the world, as her abilities allow players to navigate landscapes that would be impossible without her. BB becomes more than a piece of equipment as players progress through the game, however, as she also responds to the actions of players with emotional outbursts that players must *hear*. Stressful encounters like wading through deep water, encountering BTs, or falling down a cliff can upset BB and make her cry uncontrollably. Players have the option of ignoring the baby's cries, but as they do not subside for an extended period, the experience is anxious and uncomfortable, like trying to continue the game during an "Alert" phase in MGS. To soothe BB immediately, players must press a button that allows the player character Sam to hold BB's pod in his arms, and gently swaying the controller side to side will eventually calm BB down (see Figure 5.5). What ties BB's emotional state even closer to the player is the fact that her wailing is heard from a more local source than the TV; continuing with Kojima's design ethos of viewing the game console as part of the experience, BB's cries emanate from the speaker on the PS4 controller. As the controller is often perched on the player's stomach or lap in a similar position to how BB is attached to Sam's abdomen, the player becomes attuned to BB in an embodied way that cannot be dismissed as easily as hearing BB cry on the screen from a distance. The player character Sam becomes

Figure 5.5 Soothing BB's painful cries requires multiple steps in *Death Stranding* (Kojima Productions 2019).

connected through their shared empathy for the emotional well-being of their bridge baby.

These mechanics help strengthen the bond between Sam and BB that is revealed through *Death Stranding*'s larger structures and gameplay. BB's cries are designed to discomfit the player but hearing them repeatedly can reduce them to background noise. Ironically, this might encourage the player to tune her out and engage in a form of virtual child abuse. To counter this negligence, Sam and BB develop a "bond level" throughout the game, where the happier and more comfortable BB is around Sam, the less stress and stamina depletion she experiences when the two are in danger. When engaging in hostile situations, Sam must be sensitive to his companion so as not to increase her stress and decrease her stamina which, once depleted, renders her incapacitated. Importantly, Kojima and his team ensured that playing without BB is highly punitive, as navigating areas with BTs becomes incredibly laborious. At one point in the game, BB is physically removed from the player character Sam, and the difficulty completing deliveries without her hammers home her practical importance but also her emotional role; traversing America alone is a lonely experience without the outlet of BB reacting to your actions.

Players thus *feel* the absence of BB and her effect on their own stress levels. The bond system results in a nurturing style of play, where players must pay attention to not only their own health and stamina but that of their infant companion. This engagement between the parental player and dependent avatar mimics what psychoanalyst Takeo Doi (1962) has called the concept of *amae*, or "to depend or presume upon another's benevolence" (1). Doi argued that *amae* is synonymous with a fundamental human desire for connection, as it "originates in the infant's natural feelings for and behavior towards its mother" through nonverbal appeals for care such as cooing, pouting, and crying (1973, 74). When BB starts to *amaeru* to Sam, players are tasked with responding to her indulgent needs. This can mean soothing her negative emotional states—exerting caution when going down hills or engaging enemies—but also bringing out more positive ones that will elicit her amusement. The environment is designed with "fun" things that will make BB giggle in delight like running full speed down a hill, touching a sign created by another player, taking a dip in a hot spring, or having Sam relieve himself with the "urination" action.[4] Later in the game, Sam can acquire items that when equipped will increase BB's bond with him, but these items and actions also simply provide the player with a basic and primal joy: the sound of an infant's laughter.

The intimate relationship that develops between Sam, BB, and the player is both an example and subversion of the father-child relationships at the heart of contemporary "dadified" games such as *The Last of Us*, *Bioshock Infinite*, and *God of War*. These games feature masculine protagonists who must protect and in turn are assisted by child avatars (Stang 2017). The child companions gradually develop strength and individuality but not at the expense of any change in player behavioral or emotional response (Murray 2019). The growth of the child avatars, moreover, is represented through their own improved proficiency at fighting and killing enemies, echoing the games' own violence-motivated narratives and gameplay. BB, on the other hand, is linked to how the player plays the game or is entirely removed from the game in certain moments. Players must adjust their behaviors accordingly to account for the presence or absence of their baby buddy.

These behaviors stand in contrast to the violent affordances of traditional masculine game heroes and instead focus on playful and nurturing affordances. Such affordances are similar to those of "care-based games," such as the digital pets known as *Tamagotchi* (Bandai 1996) popularized in the 1990s, where the "core mechanic is about taking care of or nurturing gardens or animals" (deWinter 2015, 75). But where Tamagotchi encouraged nurturing play that was primarily targeted at young girls, BB is part of a game with much darker and masculine genre elements. Like how Kojima used Solid Snake to subvert the image of the traditional action hero, Sam subverts the image of the stereotypical masculine "dad" figure that has come to characterize violent companion games. By forcing older male players to assume the matriarchal role of caretaker, Kojima "momifies" Sam, asking players to assume maternal or even nonbinary forms of gender identification.[5] *Death Stranding's* portrayal of the relationship between Sam and BB poignantly asks us who is the real hero: the intense, violent killer, or the nurturing, protective parent?

Reflexive Spaces

The player character Sam builds connections to various in-game avatars, recalling the single-player experience of most KojiPro games. But it is the third connective aspect of the game's systems that is both its most novel and, in line with previous KojiPro games, its most reflexive: a social multiplayer component, or what Kojima has labeled the game's "Social Strand System." Players have the option of playing the game on or offline, and the experience between the two is considerably different. As the game's environments become increasingly difficult to navigate, Sam must craft equipment such as ladders, ropes, and vehicles, as well as structures such as roads, bridges, and shelters through acquired materials that make travel smoother and less hazardous. On the one hand, playing offline is similar to that of most MGS titles, emphasizing the lone-wolf persona of the player character Sam who is tasked with completing missions/deliveries with only the resources gathered from the game's various NPCs. Playing online, on the other hand, connects Sam to a server of other players, and while these players can't see and interact with one another like in an MMORPG, the materials they craft are left behind and can be utilized by other players. This form of "indirect" (*kansetsuteki*) communication was Kojima's solution to the harmful consequences of constant direct communication on social media. The Social Strand System, which allows players to pick up the "strands" that other players leave behind even if they don't directly interact with them, worked like a "large time gap between two people writing and waiting for a letter from each other" (Morioka 2019). While players are not physically present in each other's game world, their presence can nonetheless be experienced in various ways that can encourage empathetic play in one another.

This style of linked play is what Ian Bogost (2004) has called "asynchronous multiplay," or multiplayer games that are played at different times. Asynchronous multiplay is distinguished by several factors, from sequential (rather than tandem) play to breaks (or "dead-time") between players, but the most important aspect that applies to *Death Stranding* is the game's "persistent state which all players affect, and which in turn affects all players" (2). Players who choose to play online will have access to materials, vehicles, and structures that continue to affect and shape the world that they share. Such asynchronous multiplay is similar to another Japanese franchise, From Software's notoriously challenging *Dark Souls* (2011) and its many sequels and spin-offs, which allows players online to access in-game hints (or tricks) from other players who have already completed specific areas of the game. This "jolly cooperation" consists of players receiving help from others in the form of "cooperative mechanics, tip sharing, and community building" (Welsh 2020). In *Death Stranding*, players can also similarly make signs that provide hints to players warning them of danger and also make jokes that subvert theatrical situations.

The use of asynchronous multiplay in *Death Stranding* is more complex, however, as it goes beyond simple commentary in the world and into actively shaping how it functions. Each player's contribution to the persistent game world is a "strand" that can then be picked up, used, iterated upon, expanded, and then left for another player to use in their journey. On a simple level, this can result in novice players accessing items or vehicles left behind by players who are far ahead in the game, helping them traverse difficult areas with greater ease. At its most sophisticated, players can pool materials and build roads, bridges, and infrastructure for the UCA much faster than they could if attempting it alone. As Kojima argues, this invisible presence of supportive others can create a powerful feeling: "You lose this feeling of solitude when you find out there's the same people all over the world" (Chen 2020). Playing online transforms the experience of *Death Stranding*, constantly reminding the player that others are assisting their journey even if they are not present. Such an idea reflects Kojima's own parasociality with TV and film characters as a latchkey kid, though here displayed in the very real actions of other players.

On an allegorical level, the Strand System can be thought of as a form of collective nation-building, but on an affective level, the Strand System transcends the idea of the nation's "imagined community" as it emphasizes in-game actions that have a direct positive effect on others. Encouraging players to build bridges is a comment on the divisiveness of building border walls and barriers, but enlisting the collective support of players to rebuild crumbling infrastructure can also be seen as a progressive argument for the validity of public works projects, where access and use of institutions becomes easier, safer, and more scenic if everyone contributes. As players get accustomed to the ability for collective action, they can also become empowered by "problem-solving in formal semantics" or their ability to directly create tangible effects in imaginary worlds (Wolf 2012, 17). Alexandre Paquet argues (2021) that *Death Stranding* has a strong potential for "thinking utopia" as "there is a direct engagement with space that bypasses the centrality of structures of power such as the nation-state" (85). As players cooperate and collaborate indirectly with one another but directly with the spaces of the game itself, the Strand System offers a unique experiment for the formation of strong collectives without intimate communities or institutional intermediaries.

There are ways for players to acknowledge the help they receive from others, however, largely in the Strand System's incorporation of and rehabilitation of social media conventions to reinforce supportive behavior. Gifting and sharing goods asynchronously is a common feature of social network and mobile games, which is often done for the purpose of building social capital (Wohn et al. 2011). Helping or sharing goods with others may not immediately translate to rewards, but it can result in increased social capital. This social capital is reflected in *Death Stranding* through giving players the ability to "like" any equipment or structure they come across in the game world (see Figure 5.6). Upon seeing structures created by others in the game, players may feel obligated to help members of

Figure 5.6 Players can contribute to building infrastructure in *Death Stranding* (Kojima Productions 2019), which then gets liked by other players for points and a general feeling of community.

their social network in turn, resulting in a "virtuous cycle where other players become more willing to help those who help them leading to the reciprocal nature of social networked gameplay" (Boudreau and Consalvo 2016, 81).

While players can give many "likes" for equipment or signposts that they find useful or witty, they cannot leave any negative feedback. Such a limitation is not surprising for Kojima, who has commented on the support he has received early in his career from enthusiastic fans but also on the harmful discourse on social media platforms today: "I go on the internet—it's all connected, and everyone is battling each other. I wish people would use the technology in a different way" (Chen 2020). It's also not surprising considering Kojima's own penchant for using social media—particularly Twitter—as a largely positive tool for expressing his own game ideas and an appreciation for the films, games, and music of other creators. The Strand System as a whole can be seen as a reflection of Kojima's social media use for progressive or at least consistently optimistic purposes. As players can give and receive multiple likes for their shared goods, they are encouraged to share and create both frequently and thoughtfully to receive reciprocal affirmation from their community. And as their creations can only be "liked" or ignored by others, the game creates a "virtuous cycle" where helpful equipment and structures encourage player empathy and appreciation. Or in Kojima's words, "You'll start thinking about others when you play and how you might be able to help them" (Powell 2019). In this way, the Strand System reinforces the bonds created in the game world by offering a positive alternative to toxicity on social media and networked video game platforms.

Aside from the Strand System, one other area of the game allows for players to indulge in Kojima's medium-reflexive spaces and sense of humor: Sam's Room, an isolated space where the player character Sam can decompress and recover his health and stamina after a long day of trekking. Sam's Room later becomes an important location where key characters deliver narrative exposition, but its role as a safe space also has the important function of ameliorating the emotional state of the player, who might tire from long, monotonous deliveries through treacherous landscapes and climates. Once Sam perches himself on his bed, players can move the camera around to elicit a reaction from Sam, who will make gestures, pose, or even spit his drink into the camera. The space is a playful area for Sam to engage with BB, poking her pod or making faces to get her to laugh. Sam's Room also has surprises for the player who continues to play the game year-round; on their birthday, for example, players will receive a special birthday cake delivered by a mysterious benefactor. While the larger blending of game spaces occurs in the game's Social Strand System, which connects players asynchronously in the evolving construction of the game world, Sam's Room also provides a respite from the continuous work of making the world a better place through a reflexive and playful dialogue with KojiPro's developers and their penchant for planting gags and "fan service" in the game world.

Conclusion

As *Death Stranding* illustrates, Kojima's progressive design has remained remarkably consistent despite the move from Konami to his own self-named studio. Kojima's teams continue to respond to new game trends and technologies, which is exemplified in this chapter's focus on portable and open world games. By de-emphasizing narrative linearity and cinematic bombast, KojiPro's portable and open world games emphasize mechanics of simulation that grant players a far greater degree of choice in how they proceed in the game world. Despite this added focus on player agency, however, these games are still built around many of the features of Kojima's earliest adventure games, from the socially relevant narratives and cinematic aesthetics to the thematic play systems and comedic reflexivity. Even the social mechanics of *Death Stranding* are heavily reinforced by and built around the game's linear narrative on rebuilding human collectives.

Fundamentally, these games also evince KojiPro's obsession with getting players to break out of their gaming environments and acknowledge the many spaces and contexts around them, redefining the limits and boundaries of video game play. This awareness extends to that of the natural world in *Boktai* and the joy of cooperative camaraderie in *Peace Walker*, to the empowerment of the individual in *The Phantom Pain* and the insistence that we continue to work together to cure toxic environments in *Death Stranding*. There is also a slight advance in the faith Kojima has placed in the hands of players. While stopping short of the total simulation of games like *Minecraft*, KojiPro relinquished a degree of control to players with the hopes that they can playfully offer solutions to problems that the developers themselves could not consider. Some players even responded by aping the ideas of *Death Stranding* to combat the global Covid pandemic; inspired by the design of BB, one parent in China ended up constructing a pod for his infant son in a case of life imitating art (Bullard 2020). Meanwhile, players, journalists, and researchers showed how even single-player video games could help to ease the isolation and depression of quarantine through enabling common points of connection with (virtual) others despite enforced social distancing (Frank 2020; Jarzyna 2020). Ultimately, these games continue Kojima's insistence that games connect players to experiences outside the game proper, encourage them to think about issues and conflicts that society actively grapples with today, and then work together to change them.

Chapter 6

KOJIPRO'S LEGACY AND FUTURE

After a career spanning over thirty years in commercial game development and with the creation of his own independent studio, Hideo Kojima is more widely celebrated as a game creator than ever before. Since leaving Konami, he was recognized with the "Industry Icon Award" at the 2016 Game Awards Show and a Lifetime Achievement Award at the 2017 Brasil Game Show. Upon the release of *Death Stranding*, Kojima was hailed as a "genius" by celebrated artists and profiled in countless articles by legacy outlets that detailed his life and work as an "auteur" (Gault 2019; Chen 2020; Okamoto 2020). But this recognition now also extends outside of the games industry: the British Academy of Film and Television Arts awarded him with a fellowship in 2020 for his "outstanding and exceptional contribution to film, games, or television," and the Agency of Culture Affairs Japan honored him in 2022 with the seventy-second Minister of Education, Culture, Sports, Science, and Technology Award for Fine Arts, only the second time a games creator has received the award. Kojima's popular impact is on display in an episode of the sci-fi anthology TV series *Black Mirror* called "Playtest." Critics and fans believed Kojima inspired the episode's Japanese game designer, Sho Saito, who creates a game that accesses the player's brain and directly targets his personal fears (Figure 6.1). These examples show how Kojima has become a name and figure that now represents and even transcends the game medium. Considering this public awareness of Kojima and his image, I would like to conclude this book with a short diversion into Kojima's genius for branding and self-promotion, elements which also appropriately inform his game design.

Kojima has in fact talked about how, when he designs a game, he considers everything from the concept and the story to the "promoting" and "supervising the merch." Part of "promoting" the game is editing of the game's promotional trailer, an aspect that he takes on himself as he considers "the trailer is part of the title" and hails directly from his interest and enthusiasm for films (Kojima 2019).

Figure 6.1 Side-by-side comparison of Hideo Kojima on the cover of PlayStation Official Magazine UK (2011) and the character of Shou Saito in *Black Mirror* (Netflix 2016).

These trailers showcase the games through a combination of gameplay and cut scenes and are often premiered at industry showcase events. Such was the case with the trailer for *MGS2*, which caused a splash at the Electronic Entertainment Expo (e3) in 2000 by showcasing game footage so detailed that some people in attendance thought they were watching prerendered cut scenes (Linneman 2017). The trailer's reception prompted Konami to produce a DVD solely of its exhibition and reception at e3, featuring the trailer itself and copious footage of Kojima presenting it to enraptured audience members. The DVD documents the social impact the trailer had at the time but also shows Konami's and Kojima's recognition that using well-edited paratexts could direct players toward features and concepts they wanted to emphasize well before the game's release.

Subsequent MGS releases saw similar promotional efforts, culminating with the promo blitz for *MGSV* that created buzz through cryptic allusions and sleights of hand. This included the creation of a fictional studio and CEO named Joakim Mogren that turned out to be a disguised Hideo Kojima himself, Joakim being an anagram of "Kojima," and Mogren containing the word "ogre," which was the original codename of *MGSV* (Mallory 2012). The creation of the fictional studio and personality, as well as the misdirection in the title for *MGSV* (originally just titled *The Phantom Pain*), was a ruse created to stir up publicity for the game, one that many fans of the series had already guessed well before the big reveal as their favorite trickster had conditioned them to find the "play" even in the trailer.

The initial promotional creativity exhibited in *MGSV* unfortunately did not continue later into the game's development, though would persist in other KojiPro forms. Kojima was apparently forbidden by Konami from doing other types of interviews or even preparing other games for development, and his subsidiary under Konami was disbanded (Hussain 2015). Following his exit from Konami in late 2015, Kojima's proclivity for publicity helped him and his team generate interest in the revival of Kojima Productions as an independent game studio, whose partnership with Sony Entertainment was announced in December of 2015 (Molina 2015). Kojima effectively harnessed the branding powers of social media while founding his new studio. He tweeted about the company securing office space and assembling staff while moving forward on their new game project. Kojima's staff produced videos for the company's YouTube channel (HideoTube) featuring Kojima and writer-editor Kenji Yano as the two talked about movies and attended game-related events. Seemingly unrelated to the making of games, these videos were an extension of various podcast and YouTube videos started by Kojima at Konami. The new videos continued with the talk show's emphasis on Kojima as a cinephile and polymathic creator and later connected to how the company promotes itself as more than just a games company. For example, one video highlighted a screening area (see Figure 6.2). The space became its own feature in the company's self-promotion, as both Kojima Productions' official account and

They have Movie Viewing events here.

Figure 6.2 Kojima Productions' website and social media continue to promote staff film viewings. Source: Kojima Productions for IGN on YouTube (2022).

Kojima's own personal account would tweet out "movie viewing days" (accompanied by popcorn) that would enrich the staff's perspectives and creativity through education in classic cinema.

When Kojima Productions finally moved into their office in 2016, Kojima, Yano, and Yoji Shinkawa gave interviews to media outlets about their new "journey." Kojima likened his studio to a "spaceship," an idea visually reflected in the fact that anyone entering the studio is first greeted by a stark white hallway with an astronaut perched in the center of the room. Kojima and the staff talked about how the open design of the facility encourages an open environment, an idea echoed in subsequent recruitment videos posted on the company's YouTube channel with current staff remarking on the fact that there are no "big walls or barriers" getting in the way of the company's "collaborative environment." The image formed of Kojima Productions from this publicity is that of a game studio interested in broader cinematically inspired experiences and dedicated to assembling like-minded creative souls who want to search out new gameplay horizons. In this subtle way, the PR for the new KojiPro recycles the early impressions Kojima had of his dev teams at Konami as eclectic renegades that don't fit neatly into other companies or industries.

This combination of promotional misdirection and claims to innovation was on display in the numerous trailers for the reconstituted Kojima Productions first game. Unlike the trailer for *MGS2*, the initial trailers for *Death Stranding* do not focus on gameplay, instead opting to introduce each of the many central characters in the game amid a backdrop of bizarre environments from shores of beached sea creatures to war-torn European cities. Premiering at high-profile industry events like e3 and the Tokyo Game Show, each of the trailers was viewed by massive throngs of attendees eagerly awaiting Kojima's latest invention. The trailer worked to build interest in the game through casting well-known celebrity actors as the characters, but the cryptic delivery of the game's genre and gameplay ensured that the media discourse around the game remained curious and full of "conspiracy theories" (Hernandez 2016). A meme from the trailer was even created from an odd sequence where the camera zooms down the protagonist's gullet, only to reveal a baby baring his butt before swiveling around to give finger guns to the camera. Kojima then appeared in interviews to talk up the game's "totally brand new genre," promising a game that players had never experienced before (Phillips 2019). The promotional campaign for *Death Stranding* was thus important in not just building interest in the game but also reassuring players that the newly independent Kojima

Productions would continue to deliver game experiences that were inscrutable and unpredictable.

Whether they succeeded in their first foray depends on the player's standpoint, as reviews for the game were among the more mixed for any Kojima-directed title. Some reviewers decried the game for its "repetitive objectives" and "glorified fetch quests" (Ogilvie 2019). Other less negative reviews said the game is "equal parts amazing and exasperating," praising its interconnected systems but criticizing a story that "doesn't fully come together in the end" (Hanson 2019). More positive reviews were glowing, with one outlet calling the PC release the game of 2020 and "one of the best games about getting from point A to point B ever made" (PC Gamer 2020). One critic familiar with Kojima's previous games and writings stated, "*Death Stranding* cites Johan Huizinga's idea that civilization is regulated by play, suggesting Sam is 'homo ludens,' the playful person" (Fukuyama 2019). Another critic acknowledged the game's flaws, while still concluding, "*Death Stranding* makes me glad that Hideo Kojima makes video games—because our hobby would be boring as hell without him" (Patterson 2019). Still, even Kojima's most strident supporters expressed disappointment with the game's flaws, particularly its lack of "serious consequences" when its systems were fully tested like in Kojima's adventure and stealth titles (Wolfe 2019).

Death Stranding is the newest game in Kojima's game oeuvre at the time of this book's publication, and so I conclude with some final thoughts about how the game strongly relates to the director's progressive game design in both its strengths and shortcomings, and the potential direction of Kojima Productions going forward. First, both fans and detractors agreed that *Death Stranding* was still a "Kojima" game, reflecting the distinctive brand that Kojima had built for himself and his games over thirty years. These Kojima-isms are frequently tied to the game's narratives—a blend of sci-fi settings, detailed world-building, and geopolitical intrigue—and aesthetics, which draw from contemporary cinema and animation techniques and representations. KojiPro's games consistently tried to advance what could be achieved in game stories and audiovisuals. Even as the games he developed got bigger, Kojima continued to maintain a tight control over this narrative and audiovisual production through writing the scripts, communicating closely with artists and voice actors, and even editing his own trailers. In some cases, this central focus on a single storyteller hampered the pacing and lucidity of games. This limitation might also be exacerbated in the current KojiPro environment, where the director doubles as the company boss.

But the fact that Kojima was able to consistently maintain this distinctive imprint on all of the games he directed is not just because of self-promotion. As documented with his earliest games for the MSX2 and PC Engine, Kojima's entry into the games industry as a planner for small teams of developers instilled in him a mindset of being aware of the many departments and processes involved in game development. Even as the budgets ballooned and the dev teams expanded, this "indie" mindset would prod him to "direct" each game he supervised and impart aspects of his humor and artistic tastes (and those of the KojiPro team) in even the most commercial of game franchises. This centrality also inherently limits the appeal of Kojima's games to a niche audience. Despite the popularity of the MGS franchise, it has a smaller social footprint and appeals to a narrower demographic than the games of Nintendo's Shigeru Miyamoto, who makes games for a broad audience from children to adults and whose most famous brands—such as *The Legend of Zelda* and *Donkey Kong*—have long been delegated to other game designers. Kojima has emphasized on many an occasion that he consciously makes games for a more limited audience, with the hopes to speak more directly and passionately to that smaller group. This explains why Kojima's fans respect and celebrate him with such intensity, cosplaying as characters from his games or camping outside of press events to catch a glimpse of him (Chan 2020). In an industry that can seem all too impersonal, Kojima injects a degree of intimacy into big-budget spectacle. This niche quality could pose a problem for KojiPro (and its agreement with Sony) going forward, as Kojima's idiosyncrasies may have trouble finding a large enough audience to justify AAA-size budgets when not attached to a recognizable franchise like MGS. However, while it might be difficult to parse the success of *Death Stranding*'s five million copies sold without knowing the game's budget (Dring 2021), these concerns might be misplaced considering a sequel to *Death Stranding* is in development, suggesting the title was far from a commercial failure.

Second, *Death Stranding* further demonstrates Kojima and KojiPro's mantra of innovating game systems. While Kojima might have entered the games industry as a wannabe film director, his early years at Konami shaped him into a game designer, with a conscious regard to how systems reinforce the themes of his increasingly complex narratives. Working on adventure games that needed the approval of his superiors and understanding of his peers made Kojima fundamentally think about how his cinematic concepts would translate to playable mechanics and navigable environments. As Kojima's team around him grew with like-minded developers, the Kojima Clan continually expanded upon and experimented with systems introduced in previous games. Each KojiPro title is rife with systems that have been tested to stand up to demanding players, creating the hands-on reputation for value-laden "service" that Kojima is known for. The masterful stealth gameplay of *MGSV* was the result of not just one game project, but a team that had grown together over decades in a single game studio with countless veteran designers and programmers able to contribute ideas and buff out problems in development. If *Death Stranding* wants in moments for this lack of refinement, it is less a mark of shame on the rookie effort of a new studio than it is a testament to the networks, technologies, and amenities afforded to commercial game development at a major game studio.

Knowing what we know about KojiPro, moreover, it also might be instructive to assess the merit of *Death Stranding* after future titles from the studio are developed. With *Snatcher* and *Policenauts*, Kojima and his team iterated with new platform technologies countless times to create the polished games they are now known for today. While elements of *Death Stranding* draw from the MGS franchise, KojiPro attempted to create multiple interconnected systems for a new type of game experience. *Death Stranding* could end up being like *Metal Gear* for the MSX2, which presaged much more sophisticated gameplay in *Metal Gear 2: Solid Snake* and *Metal Gear Solid*. Or it could be like *Peace Walker*, which allowed developers to experiment with new ideas that would be implemented in *MGSV*. Kojima has already confirmed that his studio will develop a "completely new game" for Microsoft's Xbox platform that will utilize the company's "cutting edge cloud technology," making the Social Strand System a potential dry run for much more ambitious asynchronous multiplay (McWhertor 2022). This commitment to innovation might affect the studio's ability to succeed commercially, but it has become Kojima's mantra: "For the first person, everything is hard. But I want to be the first. I want to keep being the first" (Parkin 2022).

Finally, with *Death Stranding*, we see how Kojima continues to advocate for social progress and awareness by blurring the boundaries of real and game spaces. We can see this with KojiPro's penchant for referencing real-life actors, characters, and worlds, blurring the space of the cinematic with the ludic. KojiPro's dedication to composite media design has inspired countless other titles which have emphasized complex stories and realistic character animation to create compelling game experiences. The blurring of game and other media will also continue to be a priority for the studio; KojiPro now has a Los Angeles-based division focused on film, music, and television (Makuch 2021), and its first title is a film adaptation of *Death Stranding* in collaboration with Hammerstone Studios. The director also now hosts "Hideo Kojima Presents Brain Structure," a weekly podcast where he talks about his favorite books and music, and chats with contemporary film directors. As I have argued in this book, however, a fixation on KojiPro as interactive cinema is misplaced, as Kojima and his team consistently remind players that they are not watching movies but playing games. While KojiPro's games embrace the latest computing and processing technology to recreate more "realistic" graphics or environments, they just as often undermine this realism. By redrawing the boundaries of the magic circle to interrogate players' sense of comfort, they keep players on their toes while also getting them to laugh at their own actions.

In short, Hideo Kojima's games continue to embrace alternative media forms and languages in order to push games beyond their existing conventions. For all of the proclamations about Kojima as a cinematic auteur turned game designer, this is the real legacy of Kojima and Kojima Productions' progressive game design. From urging players to stand and turn up the audio on their television sets or unplug and switch controllers to compelling them to make Codec calls that explain the history of SALT II or the feasibility of mass extinctions, this boundary-blurring results in alternative systems of play that draws players out of their comfort zones to acknowledge the world around them. And in the process, this acknowledgment, this awareness, can hopefully translate to thinking about how to advocate for broader change in society. As Snake's longtime nemesis Ocelot might say, that's pretty good.

GAMEOGRAPHY

This gameography covers every game in which Kojima is credited in its development, from his early days at Konami developing games for the PC-8801/MSX to his newest games for the Sony PlayStation 5 at Kojima Productions. I have chosen to only include games in which Kojima is credited in a creative role, or there is ample documentation of his involvement. Kojima assisted on a number of games for the MSX, but since his exact role in these games is unclear and he has not discussed his work on them in subsequent interviews, I've left them out of this gameography.

Kojima has also produced dozens of titles for Konami that have not been released outside of Japan. Though they are listed here, more detailed summaries accompany only the games which Kojima had a direct creative role (director/writer/designer) or which are influenced by his game designs. Titles are listed in English first for international releases and Japanese first for Japan-only releases.

*Penguin Adventure (**Yume Tairiku Adventure**)*	JP: 1986 EU: 1987
Platform: MSX	**Developer:** Konami
Role: Planner	

A colorful pseudo-3D platformer directed by Hiroyuki Fukui, players control Penta, a penguin tasked with bringing back the magic Golden Apple in hopes of curing the ailing Princess Penguin. Intended as a follow-up to *Antarctic Adventure*, the sequel improved on the original through the addition of RPG elements such as mini-games, upgradable equipment, and even multiple endings. Though Kojima is not listed in the game's credits, he and others have confirmed that he assisted in "planning support" soon after joining Konami. Kojima has tweeted that a number of his ideas for "boss fights and gimmicks" were used in the game.

Snatcher	JP:　　　1988/1992/1996
	US/EU:　1994
Platform: NEC PC-8801/MSX2/PC Engine/ Sega CD/Sony PlayStation/Sega Saturn	**Developer:** Konami
Role: Writer/Director	

Following the success of *Metal Gear*, Kojima asked programmers at Konami to create a simplified scripting engine to allow him a greater degree of control of directing the flow of the gameplay. The result is *Snatcher*, Kojima's (and Konami's) first graphical adventure game with a menu-based interface and one that would eventually give him the title of "director" with the port to the PC Engine. Notable for its futuristic cyberpunk world inspired by popular sci-fi films at the time, players take on the role of the detective-like Gillian Seed as he hunts down the humanoid robots known as Snatchers.

SD [Super Deformed] Snatcher	1990
Platform: MSX2	**Developer:** Konami
Role: Writer/Command Package	

A role-playing game remake of *Snatcher* that follows the original's plot in a top-down RPG setting. Kojima was not initially involved in the game's production, though his entire team was brought in to assist development in the midst of working on *Metal Gear 2: Solid Snake* as development had fallen behind schedule.

Policenauts	1994/1995/1996
Platform: NEC PC-9821/3DO/ Sony PlayStation/Sega Saturn	**Developer:** Konami
Role: Director/Writer	

The graphical adventure game follow-up to *Snatcher* with a point-and-click interface and shooting sequences. Players assume the role of Jonathan Ingram, a former astronaut thawed from twenty-five years in cryosleep, as he investigates a hidden drug- and organ-trafficking ring on the outer space colony Beyond Coast. Like *Snatcher*, the game was inspired by popular Hollywood films at the time (in this case, the buddy cop genre). *Policenauts* was ported to multiple consoles, with each port adding new features or animation.

Tokimeki Memorial Drama Series Vol. 1: Niji-iro no seishun [Rainbow-Colored Youth]	1997
Platform: Sony PlayStation/Sega Saturn	**Developer:** Konami
Role: Producer	

A graphical adventure game spin-off series of the popular dating game franchise *Tokimeki Memorial*. Kojima was only a producer for the game series, but the entire *Drama* series is heavily inspired by the design of *Policenauts*, with direction of the first two titles by KojiPro mainstay Noriaki Okamura and development mostly handled by Kojima's *Policenauts* team.

Tokimeki Memorial Drama Series Vol. 2: Irodori no love song [Love Song of Many Hues]		1998
Platform: Sony PlayStation/Sega Saturn	**Developer:** Konami	
Role: Producer		

Tokimeki Memorial Drama Series Vol. 3: Tabidachi no uta [Song for Departure]		1999
Platform: Sony PlayStation/Sega Saturn	**Developer:** Konami	
Role: Supervisor		

Beatmania		1998–2002
Platform: Sony PlayStation/Sega Saturn	**Developer:** Konami	
Role: Producer		

The "Bemani" or *Beat Mania* franchise of arcade rhythm music game series. Kojima was a producer for multiple console ports and expansions of *Beatmania*, *Beatmania IIDX*, and *Guitar Freaks*.

Zone of the Enders (Z.O.E.)		2001
Platform: Sony PlayStation 2	**Developer:** Konami	
Role: Producer/Opening Movie Creation		

An action-adventure game influenced by the style and conventions of mecha (robot) anime. Set on an outer space colony in the twenty-second century, the series deals with themes of war and exploration similar to the MGS franchise, though in service of a much more combat-oriented system as players control mechanical robots. While Kojima did not direct the game, he created a detailed backstory and world for *Z.O.E.* that formed the template for the game's structure while also providing comments and guidance throughout the game's development. For its sequel, *2nd Runner/Anubis*, Kojima's role was more at the "macro level" as he claims to have been less involved in the game's direct development. While the games derive inspiration from the MGS series in the cinematic treatment and narrative, they are more focused on combat mechanics and less emergent in their gameplay.

Zone of the Enders: 2nd Runner (Anubis: Zone of the Enders)		2003
Platform: Sony PlayStation 2	**Developer:** Konami	
Role: Producer/Planning		

Boktai: The Sun Is in Your Hand (Bokura no taiyô)	JP/NA: 2003 EU: 2004
Platform: Nintendo Game Boy Advance	**Developer:** Konami
Role: Producer/Original Concept and Design	

A departure from the big budgets of Sony PlayStation games, *Boktai* was created for portable play in mind. In a post-apocalyptic future where people have been turned into the undead, players control vampire hunter Django as he excavates crypts to exterminate powerful creatures called immortals. In a novel twist, Django's weapon is powered by actual sunlight derived from a solar sensor on the game's cartridge, forcing players to go outside during the day if they wanted to complete the game. While Kojima did not direct any of the *Boktai* games, he crafted the original concept—from the story to the idea for a solar-powered game cartridge. The game would spawn a mini-franchise with several sequels and even a comic adaptation published in Shogakukan's *Coro Coro Comic* manga magazine.

Boktai 2: Solar Boy Django (Zoku bokura no taiyô: Taiyô shônen Django)	JP/NA: 2004 EU: 2005
Platform: Nintendo Game Boy Advance	**Developer:** Konami
Role: Producer	

Shin bokura no taiyô: Gyakushû no Sabata [New Boktai: The Revenge of Sabata]	2005
Platform: Nintendo Game Boy Advance	**Developer:** Konami
Role: Producer	

Lunar Knights (Bokura no taiyô: Django & Sabata)	JP: 2006 NA/EU: 2007
Platform: Nintendo Game Boy Advance	**Developer:** Konami/Kojima Productions
Role: Producer	

Kabushiki baibai trainer kabutore! [Stock-Trading Trainer Kabutore!]	2006
Platform: Nintendo DS	**Developer:** Konami/Kojima Productions
Role: Producer	

A stock-trading simulator designed by Kojima Productions that gamifies buying and selling equities through the incorporation of adventure game elements.

Kabushiki baibai trainer kabutore! NEXT [Stock-Trading Trainer Kabutore!]	2007
Platform: Nintendo DS	**Developer:** Konami/Kojima Productions
Role: Producer	

Kabushiki baibai trainer kabutore FX [Stock-Trading Trainer Kabutore!]	2009
Platform: Nintendo DS	**Developer:** Konami/Kojima Productions
Role: Producer	

Castlevania: Lords of Shadow		2010
Platform: Sony PlayStation 3, Xbox 360, PC	**Role:** Producer/General Direction for JP Version	
Lords of Shadow was developed by the Spanish game developer MercuryStream, with Kojima Productions providing creative and localization support. Kojima also directed the port of the Japanese version of the game (including its JP trailer), overseeing the direction of the voice actors, many of whom were brought in from their work on the *MGS* series.		

P.T. [Playable Teaser]		2014
Platform: Sony PlayStation 4	**Developer:** Konami/Kojima Productions (7780s Studio)	
Role: Director/Designer		
Designed as a demo for an installment in the *Silent Hill* "survival horror" franchise, Kojima designed and directed this brilliant teaser with collaboration from director Guillermo del Toro. Set in a single dimly lit, L-shaped hallway with doors at either end, the game space is a continuous loop. Players control an unnamed protagonist (later revealed as Norman Reedus) in the first-person perspective, with "walking" and "zooming in on objects" as the only available actions. To escape the loop, players must solve cryptic puzzles through hints from the environment, with changes made to subsequent loops in the hallway each time a puzzle is solved. To increase the tension, a ghost named Lisa can appear at random times to surprise and kill the player, resetting the loop to the beginning. The teaser took social media by storm, with critics and players raving about their experience playing the game. Though intended as Kojima's contribution to the franchise, *Silent Hills* was unfortunately cancelled by Konami around the time of Kojima's departure from the company. The teaser was also removed from the PlayStation Store, further creating a mythical aura around the singular experience that could no longer be played.		

Death Stranding		2019
Platform: Sony PlayStation 4, PC	**Developer:** Kojima Productions	
Role: Director/Writer/Designer		

Kojima Productions' first effort as an independent studio was inspired by a wave of populism that swept Western countries. In a future reduced to rubble following a cataclysmic event called the *Death Stranding*, survivors of humanity hunker down in disparate underground cities to avoid toxic rainfall and floating specters. Players control Sam Porter Bridges, a deliveryman who is asked by the president of the United States to travel to each of the cities and connect them to the internet-like Chiral Network. Accompanying Sam on his journey is B.B., a "bridge baby" intubated in a tube and connected to a device which allows Sam to scan the environment for specters and other hostile beings. Play largely involves walking Sam across vast and beautiful expanses to deliver packages, stealthily creeping past specters and package thieves, and engaging in brief but kinetic combat sequences with terrorists and tar-covered monsters.

Death Stranding: Director's Cut		2021
Platform: Sony PlayStation 5, PC	**Developer:** Kojima Productions	
Role: Director/Writer/Designer		

The Metal Gear Franchise

Metal Gear		1987
Platform: MSX2	**Developer:** Konami	
Role: Designer		

Kojima's first complete game and the inaugural title of the *Metal Gear* franchise. Kojima worked with the limitations of the MSX hardware—which could only display a limited number of enemies and bullets on screen at once—to design a military combat game where the objective was to avoid combat. Players are introduced to Solid Snake, an operative of the special forces unit FOXHOUND, as he carries out a solo sneaking mission to infiltrate the mercenary nation Outer Heaven and destroy its nuke-equipped, walking bipedal tank called Metal Gear. The game introduced the franchise's trademark "stealth" gameplay of navigating the player character Snake through various environments while avoiding being spotted by or engaging in direct confrontation with patrolling enemy units.

Metal Gear 2: Solid Snake	1990
Platform: MSX2	**Developer:** Konami
Role: Designer	

The true follow-up to *Metal Gear* (with no connection to the side-scrolling *Snake's Revenge*) featured larger environments, a more ambitious plot, and greatly advanced stealth mechanics from its predecessor. Players control Snake (and a radio-based team of support) as he must infiltrate the terrorist haven Zanzibar Land in order to rescue a kidnapped bioscientist and destroy the modified Metal Gear D. *Solid Snake* featured interactive environments with responsive objects and surfaces, more varied and responsive enemy AI, and a much larger playing field spanning multiple areas and screens. To account for this expanded field, players are also given a radar grid that shows them the location of enemies so that they can plan their sneaking routes.

Metal Gear Solid	JP/NA: 1998 EU: 1999
Platform: Sony PlayStation	**Developer:** Konami
Role: Director/Writer/Producer/Original Concept and Design	

The game that put Hideo Kojima on the international map, *Metal Gear Solid* featured many gameplay concepts from *Metal Gear 2: Solid Snake* while also expanding these concepts to account for the increased processing and storage capacity of the CD-ROM-based Sony PlayStation. Renegade FOXHOUND soldiers—a dynamic group led by Solid Snake's brother Liquid Snake—have taken over Shadow Moses, a nuclear disposal compound in Alaska, and threaten to launch a nuclear attack from it on the White House with their secret weapon, Metal Gear REX. Snake is forced out of retirement to infiltrate the facility, rescue several hostages, and prevent the terrorists from carrying out a nuclear strike on the United States. This story is delivered cinematically through the incorporation of dynamic cut scenes and "Codec" radio conversations, all of which are voiced by professional voice actors. Players must also now navigate three-dimensional environments composed of polygonal graphics, though the perspective of most of these environments is often from a slanted top-down angle that cannot be changed by the player.

Metal Gear Solid: Integral	JP: 1999 NA/EU: 2000
Platform: Sony PlayStation	**Developer:** Konami
Role: Director/Writer/Producer/Original Concept and Design	

An expanded version of the original *Metal Gear Solid*, which included a "VR Disc" that consisted solely of VR training missions. This disc was released in NA and EU, respectively, as *Metal Gear Solid: VR Missions* and *Metal Gear Solid: Special Missions*.

Metal Gear: Ghost Babel	2000
Platform: Nintendo Game Boy Color	**Developer:** Konami
Role: Supervising Director/Producer	

Created through a request from Konami Europe for a Game Boy version of *Metal Gear Solid*, Kojima spearheaded *Ghost Babel* with the intention of focusing on the essence of *Metal Gear*. While not a direct remake of the PlayStation classic, it combines the overhead 2D perspective of the MSX games with new additions introduced in *Metal Gear Solid*, particularly multidirectional movement and an increased array of weapons. The game did not sell particularly well but was received very positively by critics due to its polished gameplay and sophisticated story full of conspiracy and intrigue. According to scenario writer Tomokazu Fukushima, there is as much Codec dialogue in *Ghost Babel* as there is in the CD-ROM-based *Metal Gear Solid*. While Kojima is credited as a supervising director and producer, *Ghost Babel* was directed by Shinta Nojiri, a KojiPro regular who would go on to direct several portable games in the MGS franchise.

Metal Gear Solid 2: Sons of Liberty	JP/NA: 2001 EU: 2002
Platform: Sony PlayStation 2	**Developer:** Konami
Role: Director/Writer/Producer/Original Concept and Design	

Originally titled "Metal Gear Solid III," this direct sequel to *Metal Gear Solid* finds Solid Snake infiltrating a tanker transporting a new type of Metal Gear through the Hudson River. Terrorists hijack the Metal Gear and sink the tanker with Snake on it, seemingly left for dead. Fast forward two years later and—in one of the series' most elaborate fake outs—players no longer control Solid Snake, but instead greenhorn FOXHOUND operative Raiden as he is sent into an offshore cleanup facility to neutralize a terrorist threat led by the shadowy Patriots. *Sons of Liberty* introduced a new degree of realism in its stealth action, with enemies now able to coordinate and exhibit a range of intelligent behaviors, tiered environments with multiple interactive components, and a host of abilities in the hands of player character Snake/Raiden. Despite this added control, however, *Sons of Liberty* is also a game that repeatedly removes narrative control from players by deliberately frustrating and confusing them, mirroring the game's plot that questions freedom of thought and accuracy of knowledge in a rapidly evolving information age.

The Document of Metal Gear Solid 2	2002
Platform: Sony PlayStation 2	**Developer:** Konami
Role: Director/Designer/Producer	

A wonderful making-of-disc that highlights KojiPro's desire to reveal the inner workings of *Sons of Liberty*'s development process. *Document* allows players to view/hear character models, sketches, environments, trailers, soundtracks, promo material, and scripts, with the highlight being an interactive storyboard set alongside the game's many cutscenes. A pipeline of the game's development is also featured, with statements from dozens of crew members.

Metal Gear Solid 2: Substance	JP/NA: 2002
	EU: 2003

Platform: Sony PlayStation 2/Microsoft Xbox/Microsoft Windows	**Developer:** Konami

Role: Director/Writer/Producer/Original Concept and Design

Like *Integral*, an expanded version of the original *Sons of Liberty* that features several additional cutscenes, collectible items, game modes, and an assortment of "VR missions." The NA/EU release included a skateboarding mini-game promoting Konami's upcoming *Evolution Skateboarding*, with players able to skate as Snake or Raiden.

Metal Gear Solid: The Twin Snakes	2004

Platform: Sony PlayStation 2	**Developer:** Konami

Role: Writer/Producer/Original Concept and Design

Approached by Nintendo's Shigeru Miyamoto to make a *Metal Gear Solid* for the Nintendo GameCube, Kojima obliged with *Twin Snakes*, a remake of his Sony PlayStation original codeveloped by Konami and Silicon Knights. While not directed by Kojima, it follows the original game's story and gameplay and features cut scenes helmed by action director Ryuhei Kitamura.

Metal Gear Solid 3: Snake Eater	2004

Platform: Sony PlayStation 2	**Developer:** Konami

Role: Director/Writer/Producer/Original Concept and Design

While the sequel to *Sons of Liberty*, *Snake Eater* is actually a "prequel," set in the 1960s and featuring the early exploits of Big Boss, the legendary mercenary whose genes would be used to create Solid (and Liquid) Snake. In *Snake Eater*, a young Green Beret operative codenamed Naked Snake must enter Russian territory to rescue a rocket scientist, destroy a nuclear superweapon, and assassinate a defector to the Soviet Union, the decorated soldier and his former mentor, The Boss. *Snake Eater* takes the stealth gameplay of the series to new heights, introducing a level of simulation in its environments, enemies, and player affordances not yet seen in the series. Set mostly outdoors and in the past, players have fewer gadgets and places to hide from enemies, who are equipped with a heightened degree of sensitivity, coordination, and persistence. Players must not only manage their visibility through equipping an assortment of camouflage but also must be aware of Snake's medical condition, tending to broken bones, gunshots, and even his hunger levels (the various wildlife in the jungles double as enemies to subdue and food for sustenance). The game also introduces what would become a staple in the series: the Close-Quarters-Combat (CQC) hand-to-hand combat system, allowing players more options for subduing enemies nonlethally to extract information. A masterclass in story and level design, many critics consider *Snake Eater* to be the finest overall entry in the franchise and among the very best games ever made.

Metal Gear Ac!d	JP: 2004
	NA/EU: 2005
Platform: Sony PlayStation Portable	**Developer:** Konami
Role: Executive Producer	

A grand departure from previous MGS titles, *Metal Gear Ac!d* is a turn-based strategy RPG directed by Shinta Nojiri where players use trading cards to control the character's movements and actions. Like *Ghost Babel*, while some weapons, items, and even characters including Solid Snake make appearances from other games, most of the story and cast are unconnected to the Kojima-directed MGS titles.

Metal Gear Ac!d 2	JP: 2005
	NA/EU: 2006
Platform: Sony PlayStation Portable	**Developer:** Konami
Role: Producer	

Metal Gear Solid 3: Subsistence	JP: 2005
	NA/EU: 2006
Platform: Sony PlayStation 2/Microsoft Xbox/Nintendo 3DS	**Developer:** Konami
Role: Director/Writer/Producer/Original Concept and Design	

Like *Integral* and *Substance*, an expanded version of the original *Snake Eater*, but a much bigger upgrade compared to previous expanded versions. Spread over several discs, it features not just the usual additional items and game modes but also an entirely reworked third-person camera perspective that makes the game much more navigable and less frustrating to control in its wide-open environments. The game also includes a short-lived online mode which would inspire other online efforts and a three-and-a-half-hour cut of the game's cinematics.

Metal Gear Solid: Digital Graphic Novel	2006
Platform: Sony PlayStation Portable	**Developer:** Konami
Role: Director	

An audiovisually enhanced version of the *Metal Gear Solid* comic illustrated by artist Ashley Wood. Kojima directs the music, voice acting, and additional animation, creating an extended cine-comic retelling of the original *Metal Gear Solid*. The game also includes some interaction in the form of a "scanning interface" that allows players to zoom in or out on specific images and then access more information from those images in a separate database called the "mission mode." Like most KojiPro works, the experiments with graphic artwork and interactive cutscenes introduced here would find their way into more mainline titles of the MGS franchise, particularly *Portable Ops* and *Peace Walker*.

| *Metal Gear Solid: Portable Ops* | JP/NA: 2006 |
| | EU: 2007 |

| Platform: Sony PlayStation Portable | Developer: Konami |

Role: Producer/Original Concept and Story

The fourth portable entry in the MGS franchise, *Portable Ops* returns to the more action-oriented gameplay of MGS. Unlike the *Metal Gear Ac!d* games, it also has greater continuity story-wise with the MGS series, picking up six years after *Snake Eater* and casting the player once again in the sneaking suit of Big Boss as he investigates an abandoned Soviet missile silo in Columbia. The gameplay is a mix of mechanics featured in *Snake Eater* and a novel addition called the Comrade System, which eschews the franchise's customary solo-based gameplay and instead requires players to assemble four-man cells to conduct squad-based infiltration missions. *Portable Ops* also introduced a Wi-Fi-enabled multiplayer mode that integrated with the single-player campaign in various ways. Cut scenes continue the style introduced in *Digital Graphic Novel*, with illustrations drawn by Ashley Wood.

| *Metal Gear Solid: Portable Ops Plus* | JP/NA: 2007 |
| | EU: 2008 |

| Platform: Sony PlayStation Portable | Developer: Konami |

Role: Producer/Original Concept and Story

| *Metal Gear Solid Mobile* | 2008 |

| Platform: N-Gage/Mobile Phone | Developer: Konami |

Role: Supervisor

A mobile phone MGS developed for NTT docomo's i-mode platform in Japan and Nokia's N-Gage platform outside Japan as part of Kojima Productions' 20th Anniversary Party (this was a celebration of Kojima and his team rather than the official formation of KojiPro, which was only formally created in Konami in 2005). With a story set between *Metal Gear Solid* and *Sons of Liberty* and mechanics borrowing from both *Sons of Liberty* and *Snake Eater*, *Mobile* is ambitious for the limited affordances of mobile phone tech at the time, though is unconnected to the rest of the franchise.

Metal Gear Solid 4: Guns of the Patriots		2008
Platform: Sony PlayStation 3	**Developer:** Konami	
Role: Director/Writer/Producer/Original Concept and Design		

Guns of the Patriots concludes the Solid Snake saga with a final chapter set five years after the events of *Sons of Liberty*. Though MGS veteran writer Shûyo Murata was originally in charge of the game, Kojima ended up taking the mantle once again after severe fan backlash. Set in a world ravaged by the "war economy," players once again control Snake as he sets out to assassinate Liquid Snake—whose consciousness has fused with the body of Revolver Ocelot—once and for all. One major twist is that players' beloved clone mercenary is referred to as Old Snake after suffering the effects of accelerated aging. While Snake moves better than ever due to the game's polished controls and streamlined Octocamo camouflage system, which allows him to blend smoothly into various environments, he also occasionally needs to stop to catch his breath or stretch his back if he's been running too much or crouching too long. Snake's stress level also needs to be monitored as anything from a violent encounter to a joke about his appearance can give him anxiety and lower his performance. While occasionally suffering from some of the longest cutscenes in the series, *Guns of the Patriots* wraps up the Solid Snake saga while also adroitly commenting on contemporary warfare, artificial intelligence, and the inherent repetition in video game sequels and franchises.

Metal Gear Online		2008
Platform: Sony PlayStation 3	**Developer:** Konami	
Role: Director/Writer/Producer/Original Concept and Design		

An online, multiplayer combat game developed between Kojima Productions Japan and US offices. While the game showed promise and grew a small and passionate following, it was plagued by development issues and service was terminated in 2012. The core game was reworked into an arcade version featuring head controls and stereoscopic 3D rendering called *Metal Gear Arcade* in 2010.

Metal Gear Solid Touch		2009
Platform: iOS	**Developer:** Konami	
Role: Producer/Original Concept and Story		

A third-person shooter developed for iOS based on *Guns of the Patriots* and designed by KojiPro veteran and *Boktai* director Ikuya Nakamura.

Metal Gear Solid: Peace Walker	2010
Platform: Sony PlayStation Portable	**Developer:** Konami
Role: Director/Writer/Producer/Original Concept and Design	

While Solid Snake's story was concluded with *Guns of the Patriots*, Big Boss's story was still largely untold. Set ten years after the events of *Snake Eater*, *Peace Walker* follows Big Boss to Costa Rica, where his private military company (PMC) Militaires Sans Frontiéres has been asked to save the country from soldiers armed with nuclear warheads. By far the greatest of the portable MGS games and one of the very best entries in the franchise, *Peace Walker* features a dense script written by Kojima and Murata that references Cold War politics and America's history of failed interventions in South America. It also features numerous innovative gameplay additions—co-op play, mission-based operations, collectible mini-narratives, and base-building—that would expand the direction for future MGS installments and shift Kojima's own design preferences away from linear narratives to more open-ended and customizable gameplay.

Metal Gear Rising: Revengeance	2013
Platform: Sony PlayStation 3/Microsoft Xbox 360	**Developer:** PlatinumGames
Role: Producer/Original Concept and Story	

A follow-up to *Guns of the Patriots* set four years later, players control a cybernetically enhanced Raiden as he carries out orders for a PMC. It was largely developed by PlatinumGames after KojiPro struggled with its ambitious production. While some stealth gameplay is featured, it is the most action-intensive game in the series, with some comparing its hack-and-slash combat to PlatinumGames' action franchise *Bayonetta*.

Metal Gear Solid V: Ground Zeroes	2014
Platform: Sony PlayStation 3/4	**Developer:** Konami
Role: Director/Writer/Producer/Original Concept and Design	

Set a few months after the events of *Peace Walker*, players control Big Boss as he sets out to rescue two imprisoned child soldiers held hostage in an American maximum security black site located in southern Cuba. Clearly referencing American black sites such as Guantanamo Bay, *Ground Zeroes* weaves contemporary geopolitics and the war on terror into Cold War trappings. Intended as a prologue to *The Phantom Pain*, *Ground Zeroes* is shorter than the typical MGS but features what is its single most complex environment ever created: Camp Omega, a massive and multifaceted military base with countless options for entry and infiltration. The game employs an "open world" gameplay structure where players must complete a series of objectives but in any order they so choose.

Metal Gear Solid V: The Phantom Pain		2015
Platform: Sony PlayStation 3/4	**Developer:** Konami	
Role: Director/Writer/Producer/Original Concept and Design		

Set several years after the events of *Ground Zeroes* placed Big Boss in a coma, the player now controls Venom Snake as he seeks vengeance on those who betrayed him. Taking place in the twin locales of the deserts of Afghanistan and the jungles of Zaire, *The Phantom Pain* features the most ambitious and complex stealth gameplay of the MGS series and, arguably, of any stealth game ever created. The maps are sprawling open worlds with multiple large environments scattered across both areas. More like a TV series than the continuous cinematic arc of previous games, *The Phantom Pain* allows players to select "episodes" that they can play individually and which tie into a larger overall story, but then also continue to explore different areas of the map without regard to narrative. The game also takes the base-building elements from Peace Walker and explodes them, allowing players to "fulton" weapons, vehicles, and various personnel from their locations to improve Mother Base (which can then be explored by foot). *The Phantom Pain* was a capstone to Kojima's direction of the MGS series and also his employment at Konami, as the director would leave the studio shortly after the game's release.

NOTES

Chapter 2

1   A southern-central region of Japan that includes the prefectures of Osaka, Kyoto, Hyogo, Nara, Wakayama, Mie, and Shiga.
2   Kojima was not the only one to notice the world-building in *Xevious*. The anthropologist Shinichi Nakazawa has written elegantly about the depth of the game and the enthusiasm of its players in arcades in the 1980s. See Nakazawa (2015).
3   This is a technique that Kojima has referenced in his admiration of the films of Jacques Tati, particularly *Playtime* (1967).
4   In a little-known bit of trivia, Snake is actually of English and Japanese heritage.

Chapter 3

1   Sierra would take this formula and put players into other roles and worlds inspired by Western fantasy, science fiction, and even adult-themed content, such as *Space Quest* (1986–95), *Police Quest* (1987–98), and *Leisure Suit Larry* (1987–).
2   Anastasia Salter argues Jane Jensen's horror-themed *Gabriel Knight* series contributed significantly to the adventure game genre through cinematic qualities such as full-motion video and a Hollywood voice cast (see 2018, 52–5).
3   The editors of *MSX Magazine* weren't likely lying; according to Yoshinori Sasaki, an assistant manager at Konami, "The people who played [*Snatcher*] couldn't forget it and they demanded a conversion to home systems" (EGM 1995, 176).
4   A standard compiler-compiler or parsec generator that generates code that is then executed by a parser. The parser is a subprogram that interprets player inputs and accesses a database of outcomes, such as the various descriptions and dialogues in the game.
5   The scripting language developed for *Policenauts* would even be totally implemented for the spin-off *Tokimeki Memorial Drama Series* (Konami 1997–9).
6   The back pages of certain issues of *MSX Fan*, for example, feature game screenshots of explicit female sexuality mailed in by readers. Like other boy's serial publications such as manga magazines at the time, games magazines did not just cover games, but a wide array of male-

centered coverage, from cinema to gambling to pinup models, and the consumption of sexualized women was considered just another part of "being a boy." This male-centered press and industry orientation of early video game culture is similar to that found in the United States, as documented by Carly Kocurek in her book on American arcade culture. See Kocurek 2015.

7   A great deal of commercial manga and anime in the 1980s, in fact, indulged in erotica and frank sexuality; renowned genre manga authors such as Masamune Shirow (*Ghost in the Shell*), Kouta Hirano (*Hellsing*), and Kiyohiko Azuma (*Yotsuba&!*) either got their start or continued to work in *hentai* or animated pornography. While a divide exists for media intended for children, teens, or adults, professionals may freely cross these demographic boundaries.

8   This inclusion of the staff's names also reflects their behind-the-scenes camaraderie, a product of the small team working so intensely for such a sustained period of time. The staff joked afterward that the development led to relationship issues; Yoshioka was dumped by his girlfriend, while the wife of assistant director Shinya Inoue (of Neo Kobe Pizza fame) threatened him with divorce (Konami 1992, 6–7). Some staff even faced medical ailments, and it was during this period when Kojima began to imbibe his trademark Lipovitan-D energy supplements on a regular basis.

Chapter 4

1   This divergence between narrative and play has been termed "ludonarrative dissonance" and occurs if the narratives do not align with the actions that players perform within the game world (see Hocking 2007). To take a recent example, *The Last of Us Part II* (Naughty Dog 2020) is a visually sumptuous and narratively complex game about the limits of revenge and violence that nevertheless requires players to repeatedly kill human beings in slick and grotesquely violent ways. The game does not recognize whether the player kills all enemies or none, nor does it recognize the dissonance between play that indulges in violence and a narrative that admonishes it.

2   As Kojima and his team were not typically directly involved in the English-language recording and localization process, I have left this aspect out of the book. For a look at the complex language choices involved in the localization of *MGS1*, see Blaustein (2019).

3   While this criticism of *MGS4* is not unique, it is a bit ironic in the sense that the game had the most interactive cut scenes of any in the franchise, with players able to control multiple camera angles and tap various perspectives while "watching" any of these cut scenes and lengthy dialogues.

4 Keita Moore (2017) presents a counterargument that while Snake's
   mechanics encourage the player to avoid violence and aggressive
   engagement, the narrative romanticizes not just Snake but many of the
   military enemies of the MGS franchise. In some games they are cast
   as victims, while in others their valor and sacrifice on the battlefield is
   portrayed as heroic. Moore argues this type of sympathetic portrayal has
   been used by Japanese nationalists to justify Japan's actions in the Pacific
   War. Snake reflects the series' general empathy with the perspective of the
   soldier, which would seemingly be at odds with its progressive anti-war
   sentiment. Viewed in this way, Snake occupies an ambivalent position
   with regard to the series' treatment of war.

5 The decision especially angered fans, who reacted in a way "not dissimilar
   to that of many Star Wars fans to Jar Jar Binks" (Newman 2008, 40).

6 In the Japanese version of the game, players who have save files from
   Konami titles directed or produced by Kojima such as *Policenauts* or
   Tokimeki Memorial get a special greeting from the director himself:
   "Thank you for your continued support!"

Chapter 5

1 *Metal Gear Solid 4: Guns of the Patriots* features over eight hours of cut
   scenes, with the epilogue's cinematics running at roughly seventy minutes
   total.

2 The games in the *Tokimeki Memorial Drama Series* are particularly
   noteworthy, as they use the *Policenauts* engine to greatly enhance the
   emotional storytelling and visual complexity of the *Tokimeki Memorial*
   dating sim set in a Japanese high school. The first game in the series
   replaces gun shoot-outs with soccer club penalty kicks, and the players'
   success or failure in these challenging mini-games greatly affects the
   emotional direction of the story.

3 There is unfortunately no space here to discuss this remarkable game
   and its breath-taking concept and execution in detail. See this book's
   gameography and Eisenmann (2014) for an analysis of the design of *P.T.*

4 *Death Stranding*'s array of actions for the player character Sam also
   indicate the game's propensity for simulation, allowing players to drink
   energy drinks to improve stamina but also partake in "pitstops" to relieve
   Sam after he has become too bloated. Sam's piss, however, has the added
   function of vaporizing BTs should he find himself short on ammo.

5 Viewed in this way, the game's description as a "walking simulator" also
   reflects what Dean Bowman has called the genre's ability to "domesticate"
   the masculine and military-oriented FPS through a subversion of
   "orthodox" game paradigms and a recentering on female or queer player
   identities (Bowman 2019).

WORKS CITED

Aarseth, Espen. 1997. *Cybertext: Perspectives on Ergodic Literature.* Baltimore: The John Hopkins University Press.

Aarseth, Espen. 2001. "Allegories of Space: The Question of Spatiality in Computer Games." In *Cybertext Yearbook*, edited by Markku Eskelinen and Raine Koskimaa, 152–71. University of Jyvaskyla: Research Centre for Contemporary Culture.

Anderson, Benedict. 1983. *Imagined Communities: Reflections on the Origins and Spread of Nationalism.* New York: Verso.

Anno, Hideaki. 1988–89. *Gunbuster.* Tokyo: Gainax.

Another World. 1991. Delphine Software. Video Game.

A Plague Tale: Innocence. 2019. Asobo Studio. Video Game.

Ash, James. 2015. *The Interface Envelope: Gaming, Technology, Power.* New York: Bloomsbury.

Ashcraft, Brian. 2015. "Konami's Official Word on Hideo Kojima." *Kotaku*, March 26. https://kotaku.com/konamis-official-word-on-hideo-kojima -1693789490.

Assassin's Creed. 2007. Ubisoft. Video Game.

Barlev, Nave. 2021. "Don't Leave Me Alone Here: Introducing the 'Ludo-Rapport Model for Player-Companion Interaction' in Video Games." *Transcommunication* 8.1: 1–25.

Barnett, Brian. 2020. "Geoff Keighley Talks About His Friendship With Hideo Kojima—IGN Unfiltered." *IGN*, August 27. https://www.ign.com/ articles/geoff-keighley-talks-about-his-friendship-with-hideo-kojima-ign -unfiltered.

Bateman, John A. and Karl-Heinrich Schmidt. 2012. *Multimodal Film Analysis: How Films Mean.* New York: Routledge.

Bell, Elizabeth. 2008. *Theories of Performance.* Thousand Oaks, CA: Sage Publishing.

Blaustein, Jeremy. 2019. "The Bizarre, True Story of Metal Gear Solid's English Translation." *Polygon*, July 18. https://www.polygon.com/2019/7/18 /20696081/metal-gear-solid-translation-japanese-english-jeremy-blaustein.

Bogost, Ian. 2004. "Asynchronous Multiplay: Futures for Casual Multiplayer Experience." Paper presented at *Other Players*, Copenhagen, Denmark, December 6–8. http://bogost.com/downloads/i.%20bogost%20- %20asynchronous%20multiplay.pdf.

Bogost, Ian. 2007. *Persuasive Games: The Expressive Power of Videogames.* Cambridge, MA: MIT Press.

Boktai: The Sun is in Your Hand. 2003. Konami. Video Game.

Bolter, Jay David and Richard Grusin. 1999. *Remediation: Understanding New Media.* Cambridge, MA: MIT Press.

Boluk, Stephanie and Patrick LeMieux. 2017. *Metagaming: Playing, Competing, Spectating, Cheating, Trading, Making, and Breaking Videogames.* Minneapolis: University of Minnesota Press.

Boudreau, Kelly and Mia Consalvo. 2016. "The Sociality of Asynchronous Gameplay: Social Network Games, Dead-Time, and Family Bonding." In *Social, Casual, and Mobile Games: The Changing Gaming Landscape*, edited by Michele Willson and Tama Leaver, 77–88. New York: Bloomsbury.

Bowman, Dean. 2019. "Domesticating the First-Person Shooter: The Emergent Challenge of *Gone Home's* Homely Chronotope." *Press Start* 5.2: 150–75.

Bramwell, Tom. 2004. "Hideo Kojima Discusses the Development of Metal Gear Solid 3." *Eurogamer*, April 14. https://www.eurogamer.net/articles/news140404mgs3.

Brooker, Peter. 1994. "Key Words in Bertolt Brecht's Theory and Practice of Theatre." In *The Cambridge Companion to Bretcht*, edited by Peter Thomson and Glendyr Sacks, 185–200. Cambridge: Cambridge University Press.

Brooker, Will. 2009. "Camera-Eye, CG-Eye: Videogames and the 'Cinematic.'" *Cinema Journal* 48, Spring: 122–8.

Brusseaux, Denis, Nicolas Courcier, and Mehdi El Kanafi. 2018. *Metal Gear Solid: Hideo Kojima's Magnum Opus.* Toulouse: Third Editions.

Bullard, Benjamin. 2020. "This Awesome Dad Made A Real-Life Death Stranding 'Baby Jar' Pod And Suit For Quarantine Life." *SyFyWire*, March 27. https://www.syfy.com/syfywire/death-stranding-inspired-baby-jar-pod.

Burch, Ashly and Anthony Burch. 2015. *Metal Gear Solid.* Los Angeles: Boss Fight Books.

Cameron, James. 1984. *The Terminator.* Los Angeles, CA: Orion Pictures.

Campbell, Colin. 2006. "Japan Votes on All Time Top 100." *Next Generation*, March 3. Accessed via *Internet Archive.* https://web.archive.org/web/20120223200621/http://www.edge-online.com/features/japan-votes-all-time-top-100.

Carpenter, John. 1981. *Escape from New York.* Film. Los Angeles, CA: Avco Embassy Pictures.

Carter, Marcus, Martin Gibbs, and Mitchell Harrop. 2012. "Metagames, Paragames and Orthogames: A New Vocabulary." In *FDG'12: Proceedings of the International Conference on the Foundations of Digital Games*, edited by Magy Seif El-Nasr, Mia Consalvo, Steven Feiner. Raleigh, NC, May.

Chami, Tarak. 2016. *A Hideo Kojima Book: From Mother Base with Love.* Self-published.

Chan, Khee Hoon. 2020. "The Cult of Hideo Kojima." *Eurogamer*, February 26. https://www.eurogamer.net/articles/2019-12-09-hideo-kojima-on-tour.

Chaplin, Charlie. 1936. *Modern Times.* Los Angeles, CA: United Artists.

Chen, Adrian. 2020. "Hideo Kojima's Strange, Unforgettable Worlds." *The New York Times*, March 3. https://www.nytimes.com/2020/03/03/magazine/hideo-kojima-death-stranding-video-game.html.

Clements, Jonathan. 2013. *Anime: A History.* London: BFI Press.

Cohen, David. 2008. *Screenplays.* New York: HarperCollins.

Comolli, Jean-Louis and Jean Narboni. 1990. "Cinema/Ideology/Criticism (October 1969)." In *Cahiers du Cinema, 1969–1972: The Politics of Representation*, edited by Nick Browne, 58–67. London: Routledge.

Condry, Ian. 2009. "Anime Creativity: Characters and Premises in the Quest for Cool Japan." *Theory Culture Society* 26: 139–63.

Consalvo, Mia. 2009. "There is No Magic Circle." *Games and Culture* 4.4: 408–17.

Conway, Steven. 2010. "A Circular Wall? Reformulating the Fourth Wall for Videogames." *Journal of Gaming and Virtual Worlds* 2.2: 145–55.

Csikszentmihalyi, Mihaly. 1990. *Flow: The Psychology of Optimal Experience*. New York: HarperCollins.

Daliot-Bul, Michal. 2014. *License to Play: The Ludic in Japanese Culture*. Honolulu, HI: University of Hawaii Press.

Dark Souls. 2011. From Software. Video Game.

Death Stranding. 2019. Kojima Productions. Video Game.

deWinter, Jennifer. 2015. *Shigeru Miyamoto*. New York: Bloomsbury.

deWinter, Jennifer. 2019. "Authorship." In *How to Play Video Games*, edited by Matthew Thomas Payne and Nina B. Huntemann, 177–84. New York: NYU Press.

Domsch, Sebastian. 2013. *Storyplaying: Agency and Narrative in Video Games*. Berlin: de Gruyter.

Doi, Takeo. 1962. "*Amae*: A Key Concept for Understanding Japanese Personality Structure." *Psychologia* 5: 1–7.

Doi, Takeo. 1973. *The Anatomy of Dependence*. New York: Kodansha International.

Donkey Kong. 1981. Nintendo. Video Game.

Donner, Richard. *Lethal Weapon*, Film. 1987. Burbank, CA: Warner Bros. Pictures.

Dorimaga. 2003. "Hiroi Oji x Kojima Hideo: Totteoki no Hatsutaidan" [Hiroi Oji x Kojima Hideo: The first meeting you have been waiting for]. *Dorimaga* 12, June 27: 33–8.

Dring, Christopher. 2021. "Death Stranding has Sold 5 Million Copies on PS4 and PC." *gamesindustry.biz*, July 26. https://www.gamesindustry.biz/articles/2021-07-23-death-stranding-has-sold-five-million-copies-on-ps4-and-pc.

Dulin, Ron. 1995. "Sega CD: Snatcher." *VideoGames*, January: 69.

Duncan, Margaret. 1988. "Play Discourse and the Rhetorical Turn: A Semiological Analysis of *Homo Ludens*." *Play and Culture* 1: 28–42.

Dyer-Witheford, Nick and Greig de Peuter. 2009. *Games of Empire: Global Capitalism and Video Games*. Minneapolis: University of Minnesota Press.

Edge. 2004. "Kojima Versus the Big Robots." *EDGE Magazine* 136, April: 68–74.

Edge Staff. 2015. "The Codec is Metal Gear Solid's Most Important Item." *Games Radar*, July 27. Accessed August 23, 2020. https://www.gamesradar.com/codec-metal-gear-solids-most-important-item/.

EGM Staff. 1995. "Special Feature: Snatcher." *Electronic Gaming Monthly*, January: 174–6.

EGM Staff. 2003. "Electronic Gaming Monthly's 100 Best Games of All Time." *Electronic Gaming Monthly*, June 11. Accessed via *Internet Archive*. https://web.archive.org/web/20030611191341/http://gamers.com/feature/egmtop100/index.jsp.

Eisenmann, Viktor. 2014. "P.T. (Silent Hills Teaser) Game Analysis." *Game Developer*, September 18. https://www.gamedeveloper.com/design/p-t-silent-hills-teaser-game-analysis.

Fagerholt, Erik and Magnus Lorentzon. 2009. "Beyond the HUD User Interfaces for Increased Player Immersion in FPS Games." MA Thesis. Goteborg, Sweden: Chalmers University of Technology. https://publications.lib.chalmers.se/records/fulltext/111921.pdf.

Famitsu Staff. 1999. "Metal Gear: Ghost Babel." *Weekly Famitsu Magazine* 572, December: 226–9.

Famitsu Staff. 2014. "PS4 Creator Interview: 'Gêmu no mirai wa tanoshii' to kanjite hoshii! Metal Gear Solid V: Ground Zeroes/Phantom Pain (KONAMI) Kojima Hideo intaabyû" [PS4 Creator Interview: I want people to feel: "The Future of Games is Fun!" *Metal Gear Solid V: Ground Zeroes/Phantom Pain* (KONAMI) Kojima Hideo Interview], February 13. https://www.famitsu.com/news/201402/13047011.html.

Fernández-Vara, Clara. 2008. "Shaping Player Experience in Adventure Games: History of the Adventure Game Interface." In *Extending Experience: Structure, Analysis, and Design of Computer Game Experience*, edited by Olli Leino, Hanna Wirman, and Amyris Fernandez, 210–27. Rovaniemi, Finland: Lapland University Press.

Finney, Jack. 1955. *The Body Snatchers*. New York: Dell Books.

Flanagan, Mary. 2009. *Critical Play: Radical Game Design*. Cambridge, MA: MIT Press.

Fontaine, Andie Sophia. 2019. "Hideo Kojima's Death Stranding Is Totally Set In Iceland." *The Reykjavik Grapevine*, November 19. https://grapevine.is/news/2019/11/19/hideo-kojimas-death-stranding-is-totally-set-in-iceland/.

Frank, Adam. 2020. "Playing 'Death Stranding,' Even in Isolation, You're Not Alone." *NPR*, May 14. https://www.npr.org/2020/05/14/855475333/playing-death-stranding-even-in-isolation-youre-not-alone.

Frasca, Gonzalo. 2003. "Simulation Versus Narrative: Introduction to Ludology." In *The Video Game Theory Reader*, edited by Mark J. P. Wolf and Bernard Perron, 221–37. London: Routledge.

Freybe, Konstantin, Florian Ramisch, and Tracy Hoffman. 2019. "With Small Steps to the Big Picture: A Method and Tool Negotiation Workflow." *4th Digital Humanities in the Nordic Countries Conference*. University of Copenhagen, March.

Fukasaku, Kinji. 1973. *Jingi Naki Tatakai* [Battles Without Honor or Humanity]. Tokyo: Toei Studios.

Fukuyama, Koji. 2019. "Death Stranding Review." *IGN*, November 1. https://jp.ign.com/death-stranding/39469/review/death-stranding.

Fuqua, Antoine. 1998. *The Replacement Killers*, Film. Culver City, CA: Sony Pictures.

Galloway, Alexander. 2004. "Social Realism in Gaming." *Game Studies* 4.1. http://www.gamestudies.org/0401/galloway/.

Galloway, Alexander. 2006. *Gaming: Essays on Algorithmic Culture*. Minneapolis: University of Minnesota Press.

GameFan. 1996. "Viewpoint." *GameFan*, April: 12–13.

Gamefest. 2012. "A Conversation with Video Game Designer Hideo Kojima." *Smithsonian American Art Museum*, March 17. Accessed February 12, 2019. https://americanart.si.edu/videos/gamefest-conversation-video-game -designer-hideo-kojima-154170.

Game Hihyô. 1996. "Dezain suru gêmu tachi" [The Games that Design]. *Game Hihyô* [Game Criticism], October: 54–84.

GameSpy. 2003. "25 Most Overrated Games of All Time." *GameSpy*, September 3. Accessed via Internet Archive. https://web.archive.org/ web/20040818131303/http://archive.gamespy.com/articles/september03 /25overrated/index25.shtml.

Garfield, Richard. 2000. "Metagames." *Gamasutra*, May 11. Accessed via Internet Archive. https://web.archive.org/web/20080227154137/https:// www.gamasutra.com/features/gdcarchive/2000/garfield.doc.

Garratt, Patrick. 2007. "MGS4 is for the Fans, Says Kojima." *VG247*, June 4. https://www.vg247.com/mgs4-is-for-the-fans-says-kojima.

Gates, James. 2018. "An Introduction to Hideo Kojima." *Culture Trip*, June 30. https://theculturetrip.com/asia/japan/articles/an-introduction-to-hideo -kojima/.

Gault, Matthew. 2019. "'We're Not Thinking About Others.' What Hideo Kojima Wants You to Learn From *Death Stranding*." *Time*, November 8. https://time.com/5722226/hideo-kojima-death-stranding/.

Gee, James Paul. 2009. "Playing Metal Gear Solid 4 Well: Being a Good Snake." In *Well Played 1.0: Video Games, Value, and Meaning*, edited by Drew Davidson, 117–23. Pittsburgh, PA: ETC Press.

Gekkan PC Engine. 1993. "K-Kiss Returns: 3rd Stage." *Gekkan PC Engine*, May: 124–5.

Genette, Gerard. 1997. *Paratexts: Thresholds of Interpretation*, trans. Jane E. Lewin. Cambridge: Cambridge University Press.

Gerow, Aaron. 2007. *Kitano Takeshi*. London: British Film Institute.

Giaponne, Krista Bonello Rutter. 2015. "Self-Reflexivity and Humor in Adventure Games." *Game Studies* 15.1. http://gamestudies.org/1501/articles/bonello_k.

Gifford, Kevin. 2009. "Kojima Reflects on Snatcher, Adventure Games." *1up .com*, November 4. Accessed via Internet Archive. https://web.archive.org/ web/20121022181649/http://www.1up.com/news/kojima-reflects-snatcher -adventure-games.

Glennon, Jen. 2019. "'Death Stranding' is the Anti-Uncharted, for Better or Worse." *Inverse*, November 9. https://www.inverse.com/article/60782-death -stranding-review-uncharted-walking-simulator.

Glennon, Jen. 2020. "'Death Stranding' is the Anti-Uncharted, for Better and Worse." *Inverse*, November 9. https://www.inverse.com/article/60782-death-stranding-review-uncharted-walking-simulator.

Goldberg, Harold. 2019. "A Video Game Auteur's Quest for Connection." *Vulture*, November 27. https://www.vulture.com/2019/11/hideo-kojima-death-stranding.html.

Golden Joystick. 2015. *A Hideo Kojima Book: The Ultimate Guide to Metal Gear Solid*. Bath: Future Publishing Ltd.

Gray, Jonathan. 2010. *Show Sold Separately: Promos, Spoilers, and Other Media Paratexts*. Cambridge, MA: MIT Press.

Greely, Henry. 1993. *The Code of Codes: Scientific and Social Issues in the Human Genome Project*. Cambridge, MA: Harvard University Press.

Green, Amy. 2017. *Posttraumatic Stress Disorder, Trauma, and History in Metal Gear Solid V*. New York: Palgrave Macmillan.

Greenbaum, Aaron. 2021. "Why The Breakup Between Konami and Kojima Was Worse Than You Thought." *Looper*, January 28. https://www.looper.com/322205/why-the-breakup-between-konami-and-kojima-was-worse-than-you-thought/.

Hades. 2020. Supergiant Games. Video Game.

Hanson, Kyle. 2019. "Death Stranding Review." *Attack of the Fanboy*, November 1. https://attackofthefanboy.com/reviews/death-stranding-review/.

Harris, John. 2007. "Game Design Essentials: 20 Open World Games." *Gamasutra*, September 26. https://www.gamasutra.com/view/feature/1902/game_design_essentials_20_open_.php.

Hartzheim, Bryan Hikari. 2016. "The Auteur Theory." *The Routledge Encyclopedia of Modernism*, September 6. https://www.rem.routledge.com/articles/auteur-theory-the.

Hartzheim, Bryan Hikari. 2017. "Solid Snake." In *100 Greatest Video Game Characters*, edited by Jaime Banks, Robert Mejia, and Aubrie Adams. New York: Rowman and Littlefield, 180–2.

Hawkins, Matthew. 2011. "Kojima Loves to Joke Around, but Deadly Serious about Disdain for NES *Metal Gear*." *GameSetWatch*, June 13. http://www.gamesetwatch.com/2011/06/kojima_loves_to_joke_around_but_deadly_serious_about_disdain_for_nes_metal_gear.php#more.

Hernandez, Patricia. 2016. "Kojima's New Game, *Death Stranding*, Already Has Conspiracy Theories." *Kotaku*, June 14. https://kotaku.com/people-are-trying-to-decipher-the-trailer-for-hideo-koj-1781954066.

Higgin, Tanner. 2010. "'Turn the Game Console off Right Now!': War, Subjectivity, and Control in *Metal Gear Solid 2*." In *Joystick Soldiers: The Politics of Play in Military Video Games*, edited by Nina B. Huntemann and Matt Thomas Payne, 252–71. New York: Routledge.

Hitman. 2000. IO Interactive. Video Game.

Hocking, Clint. 2007. "Ludonarrative Dissonance in Bioshock: The Problem of What the Game is About." *Click Nothing*, October 7. https://clicknothing.typepad.com/click_nothing/2007/10/ludonarrative-d.html.

Hodgson, David S. J. 1998. *Metal Gear Solid: Official Mission Handbook*. Tampa, FL: Millennium Publications.

Huizinga, Johan. 1949. *Homo Ludens: A Study of the Play Element in Culture*. London: Routledge.

Hussain, Tamoor. 2015. "Kojima Productions Has Disbanded, Says Metal Gear Solid Voice Actor." *Gamespot*, July 12. https://www.gamespot.com /articles/kojima-productions-has-disbanded-says-metal-gear-s/1100 -6428811/.

Hutchinson, Rachael. 2019. *Japanese Culture Through Videogames*. London: Routledge.

Hutchinson, Rachael. 2019. "Fukasaku Kinji and Kojima Hideo Replay Hiroshima: Atomic Imagery and Cross-Media Memory." *Japanese Studies* 39.2: 169–89.

IGN Staff. 2022. "The Top 100 Games of All Time." *IGN*, January 1. https:// www.ign.com/articles/the-best-100-video-games-of-all-time.

Isbister, Karen. 2017. *How Games Move Us: Emotion by Design*. Cambridge, MA: MIT Press.

Ishimaru, Keiji and Keita Nekoyanagi. 2004. "The Picture of Hideo Kojima." In *Metal Gear Solid Naked*, edited by Hideo Kojima, 56–69. Tokyo: Kadokawa Shoten.

Itoi, Kay. 2001. "Hideo Kojima." *Newsweek*, December 30. https://www .newsweek.com/hideo-kojima-148239.

Itoh, Project. 2008. "MGS shiriizu he to uketsugareru Policenauts" [*Policenauts*, the Bridge to the *MGS* Series]. *Policenauts* PSOne Books Re-Release Official Website. Accessed March 23, 2019. https://www.konami .com/mg/archive/other/psonebooks/policenauts/column01.html.

Iwamoto, Yoshiyuki. 2006. *Japan on the Upswing: Why the Bubble Burst and Japan's Economic Renewal*. New York: Algora.

Jarzyna, Carol Laurent. 2020. "Parasocial Interaction, the COVID-19 Quarantine, and Digital Age Media." *Human Arenas* 4. https://doi.org/10 .1007/s42087-020-00156-0.

Jenkins, Henry. 2007. "Transmedia Storytelling 101." *Aca-Fan*, March 21. http://henryjenkins.org/blog/2007/03/transmedia_storytelling_101.html.

Johnson, Kenneth. 1976. *The Bionic Woman*, Television show. Universal City, CA: MCA TV.

Juul, Jesper. 2002. "The Open and the Closed: Games of Emergence and Games of Progression." In *Computer Games and Digital Cultures Conference Proceedings*, edited by Frans Mäyrä, 323–9. Tampere: Tampere University Press.

Juul, Jesper. 2011. "The Whereabouts of Play, or How the Magic Circle Helps Create Social Identities in Virtual Worlds." In *Online Gaming in Contexts: The Social and Cultural Significance of Online Games*, edited by Garry Crawford, Victoria Gosling, and Ben Light, 130–40. London: Routledge.

Kalata, Kurt. 2011. "Snatcher." *Hardcore Gaming*, May 8. http://www .hardcoregaming101.net/snatcher/.

Kato, Aniki. 2014a. "'Imasugu, MSX no dengen wo kire!' Konami no MSX gêmu densetsu 4" ["Turn Off Your MSX Now!" The Legend of Konami's MSX Games 4]. March 13. https://weekly.ascii.jp/elem/000/000/206/206388/.

Kato, Aniki. 2014b. "'Snatcher no teki wa Metal Gear?!' Konami no MSX gêmu densetsu 5" ["Snatcher's Enemy is Metal Gear?!" The Legend of Konami's MSX Games 5). April 17. https://weekly.ascii.jp/elem/000/000/214/214490/.

Katsumata, Tomoharu. 1972. *Mazinger Z*, Television show. Nerima: Toei Animation.

Kent, Steven. 2005. "Hideo Kojima: Game Guru, Movie Maniac." Originally published by Gamespy, November 3. Archived by Metal Gear Solid.net. Accessed December 12, 2018. http://www.metalgearsolid.net/features/hideo-kojima-game-guru-movie-maniac.

Kikuchi, Nepone. 2016. "How Should we Interpret the Story of MGSV? The Expert Speaks! (Yano Kenji Interview English Version)." *Famitsu*, February 26. https://www.famitsu.com/news/201602/26099526.html.

Kikuchi, Nepone and Katsuhiko Hayashi. 2019. "Long-Distance Empathy: An Interview with Hideo Kojima About Death Stranding." *Famitsu*, November 2. https://www.famitsu.com/news/201911/02185866.html.

King, Geoff and Tanya Krzywinska. 2006. *Tomb Raiders and Space Invaders: Videogame Forms and Contexts*. London: I.B. Tauris.

King's Quest. 1984. Sierra. Video Game.

Klinger, Barbara. 2003. "'Cinema/Ideology/Criticism' Revisited: The Progressive Genre." In *Film Genre Reader III*, edited by Barry Keith Grant, 75–91. Austin: University of Texas Press.

Kocurek, Carly. 2015. *Coin-Operated Americans: Rebooting Boyhood at the Video Game Arcade*. Minneapolis: University of Minnesota Press.

Kohler, Chris. 2005. *Power-Up: How Japanese Video Games Gave the World an Extra Life*. New York: Brady Games.

Kohler, Chris. 2008. "Metal Gear Solid 4: The Spoiler-Free Review." *Wired*, July 7. https://www.wired.com/2008/07/mgs4-review/.

Kohler, Chris. 2016. "The Legendary Creator of *Metal Gear Solid* on His Weird New Game." *Wired*, June 22. https://www.wired.com/2016/06/hideo-kojima-death-stranding-interview/.

Kojima, Hideo. 1987. *Metal Gear Design Doc*. Unpublished. Archived by Metal Gear MSX. Accessed January 22, 2019, via. http://www.ne.jp/asahi/hzk/kommander/mg1arc.html.

Kojima, Hideo. 1990. *Metal Gear 2: Solid Snake Design Doc*. Unpublished. Archived by Metal Gear MSX. Accessed January 25, 2019. http://www.ne.jp/asahi/hzk/kommander/mg2arc.html.

Kojima, Hideo. 1993a. "Ima akasareru MSX hiwa 2: Waga seishun no MSX [MSX saigo no kishu]" [Inside Stories of the MSX Now Revealed 2: The MSX of My Youth (The Last Machine, MSX)]. *Beep! Mega Drive*, April: 69.

Kojima, Hideo. 1993b. "Ima akasareru MSX hiwa 3: Waga seishun no MSX [MSX saigo no kishu]" [Inside Stories of the MSX Now Revealed 3: The MSX of My Youth (The Last Machine, MSX]). *Beep! Mega Drive*, May: 81.

Kojima, Hideo. 1998a. *World of the Metal Gear Solid*. Tokyo: Konami Corporation/Sony Magazines Deluxe.

Kojima, Hideo. 1998b. *Metal Gear Solid 2 Grand Game Plan Translation*. Junker HQ. Accessed August 28, 2020. http://junkerhq.net/MGS2gameplan.pdf.

Kojima, Hideo. 2002. *Metal Gear Solid 2 Sons of Liberty: THE MAKING*. Tokyo: Konami Corporation/Sony Magazines Inc.

Kojima, Hideo. 2004. "Study of Video Game Modern Sciences at the Turn of the Century, Development Department 2 (from a 1989 Internal Memo 'Konami Paradigm')." In *Metal Gear Solid Naked*, edited by Hideo Kojima, 64. Tokyo: Kadokawa Shoten.

Kojima, Hideo. 2008. *My Body is Composed of 70% Movies: The Films that Created Kojima Hideo*. Tokyo: Sony Magazines.

Kojima, Hideo. 2009. "Solid Game Design: Making the Impossible Possible." Keynote at Game Developers Conference (GDC) 2009 presented at San Francisco, CA, March.

Kojima, Hideo. 2017. "Hideo Kojima on War, Video Games and 'Death Stranding.'" *Glixel*, August 23. http://www.rollingstone.com/glixel/features/kojima-death-stranding-aims-to-be-a-new-sort-of-game-of-war-w499148.

Kojima, Hideo. 2019. "What I'm Editing now is the Launch Trailer. It'll be the Last One Until the Release. Normally Such Launch Trailer is Handled by Outsourcing CGI Studio Using the Movie Director to Make it Gorgeous with Full CGI or Live Action. I do by Myself as the Trailer is a Part of the Title." *Twitter*, October 3. https://twitter.com/HIDEO_KOJIMA_EN/status/1179415576743161859.

Kojima, Hideo. 2020. "'Bokura no taiyo.' Keitai gêmuki desae okunai de asobu jidai. Touji wa sumaho mo GPS mo nakatta. Gêmu wa subete puroguramu no ryousan copii nanode, yûzâ wa onaji naiyou wo asobu. Soko ni yûz tokuyu no youso wo iretakatta. Sumukuni, chiiki, kisetsu, asobubasho, jikantai, shisetsu. Sore ni yotte, nichijou seikatsu ni micchaku shita asobi ga umareru" ["Boktai." An era where cell phone games are played indoors. At the time, there were no smartphones or GPS devices. Games were all mass-produced copies, so all players played the same content. It was here that I wanted to insert components unique to the player. Where they lived, their regions, seasons, play spaces, time zones, facilities. Based on this, a play would emerge that adheres to their daily lives]. *Twitter*, July 17. https://twitter.com/Kojima_Hideo/status/1283903424661053440.

"Kojima Hideo." 2000. In *Game Maestro Vol. 2: Producers/Directors*, edited by Shida Hidekuni, 56–79. Tokyo: Mainichi Communications.

Kolata, Gina. 2013. "Human Genome, Then and Now." *The New York Times*, April 15. https://www.nytimes.com/2013/04/16/science/the-human-genome-project-then-and-now.html.

Kollar, Phil. 2010. "Metal Gear Solid: Peace Walker Inspired by Pokémon, SimCity." *GameInformer*, June 3. https://www.gameinformer.com/b/news/archive/2010/06/03/metal-gear-solid-peace-walker-inspired-by-pokemon-simcity.aspx.

Konami. 1989. Liner Notes for *Snatcher (Radio Play)*, by Konami KuKeiHa Club. King Records 276A-7713. Archived at *Junker HQ*. Accessed March 22, 2019. http://junkerhq.net/Snatcher/SRP/linernotes.html.

Konami. 1991. Liner Notes for *Metal Gear 2: Solid Snake Original Soundtrack*, by Konami KuKeiHa Club. King Records KICA-7501.

Konami. 1992. Liner Notes for *The Syber Punk Adventure Snatcher: Zoom Tracks*, by Konami KuKeiHa Club. King Records KICA-7610. Archived at *Junker HQ*. Accessed March 22, 2019. http://junkerhq.net/Snatcher/SZT/linernotes.html.

Konami. 1998. *Metal Gear Solid CLASSIFIED*. Tokyo: Konami Media Entertainment.

Konami. 2000. *Metal Gear: Ghost Babel Konami Perfect Guide*. Tokyo: Konami Media Entertainment.

Konami. 2005a. *Metal Gear Solid 3 Snake Eater: SHEDDING*. Tokyo: Konami Media Entertainment.

Konami. 2005b. *Metal Gear Solid 3 L*. Tokyo: Konami Media Entertainment.

Konami. 2008. "Policenauts, the Place Where Many Staff Met." *Policenauts* PSOne Books Re-Release Official Website. Accessed March 28, 2019. https://www.konami.com/mg/archive/other/psonebooks/policenauts/interview01.html.

Konami CP Department, ed. 1996a. *Policenauts Sega Saturn Konami Official Guide*. Tokyo: NTT Publishing.

Konami CP Department, ed. 1996b. *Policenauts Sega Saturn Konami Official Perfect Guide*. Tokyo: NTT Publishing.

Konami Europe. 2003. *The Making of Metal Gear Solid 2: Sons of Liberty*. France: Fun TV.

Konami Look. 2000. *Autumn*. Tokyo: Konami Media Entertainment.

Kondo, Naoji. 2001. *Hikikomori kêsu no kazoku enjo* [Family support for hikikomori]. Tokyo: Kongou Shuppan.

Kress, Gunther. 2010. *Multimodality: A Social Semiotic Approach to Contemporary Communication*. Abingdon: Routledge.

Krichane, Selim. 2020. "Hideo Kojima as 'Author' in the West: Towards a Historical and Discursive Analysis of Video Game Authorship." *Replaying Japan 2020 Conference*, August 11.

Lebling, P. David, Marc S. Blank, and Timothy A. Anderson. 1979. "Zork: A Computerized Fantasy Simulation Game." *Computer* 12.4: 51–9.

Liebe, Michael. 2008. "There is No Magic Circle. On the Difference Between Computer Games and Traditional Games." In *Conference Proceedings of the Philosophy of Computer Games 2008*, edited by Stephan Gunzel, Michael Liebe, and Dieter Mersch, 56–67. University of Potsdam, May.

Linneman, John. 2017. "Metal Gear Solid 2 was the Game That Changed Everything for PS2." *Eurogamer*, April 23. https://www.eurogamer.net/articles/digitalfoundry-2017-metal-gear-solid-2-df-retro.

Lynch, David. 1984. *Dune*, Film. Universal City, CA: Universal Pictures.

Makuch, Eddie. 2021. "Kojima Productions Opens a Film and TV Business." *Gamespot*, November 22. https://www.gamespot.com/articles/kojima-productions-opens-a-film-and-tv-business/1100-6498243/.

Mallory, Jordan. 2012. "The Phantom Pain Speculation Round-Up: Metal Gear?!" *Engadget*, December 9. https://www.engadget.com/2012-12-08-the-phantom-pain-speculation-round-up-metal-gear.html.

Maniac Mansion. 1987. LucasFilm Games. Video Game.

Martin, Craig. 2014. "Reinterpreting Article Nine Endangers Japan's Rule of Law." *Japan Times*, June 27. https://www.japantimes.co.jp/opinion/2014/06/27/commentary/japan-commentary/reinterpreting-article-9-endangers-japans-rule-of-law/.

Mashita, Akira. 1992. "Inside *Snatcher*." In *Snatcher Official Guidebook (Gekkan PC Engine Special Edition)*, 100–11. Tokyo: Shogakukan.

McCarthy, Dave. 2008. "Metal Gear Solid 4: Guns of the Patriots UK Review." *IGN*, May 30. https://www.ign.com/articles/2008/05/30/metal-gear-solid-4-guns-of-the-patriots-uk-review.

McTiernan, John. 1988. *Die Hard*. Film. Century City, CA: 20th Century Fox.

McWhertor, Michael. 2022. "Hideo Kojima is Working on a New Xbox Game." *Polygon*, June 12. https://www.polygon.com/23164776/hideo-kojima-productions-xbox-game.

Mendoza, Kelly. 2009. "Surveying Parental Mediation: Connections, Challenges, and Questions for Media Literacy." *Journal of Media Literacy Education* 1: 28–41.

Metal Gear. 1987. Konami. Video Game.

Metal Gear 2: Solid Snake. 1990. Konami. Video Game.

Metal Gear: Ghost Babel. 2000. Konami. Video Game.

Metal Gear Solid. 1998. Konami. Video Game.

Metal Gear Solid 2: Sons of Liberty. 2001. Konami. Video Game.

Metal Gear Solid 3: Snake Eater. 2004. Konami. Video Game.

Metal Gear Solid: Portable Ops. 2006. Konami. Video Game.

Metal Gear Solid 4: Guns of the Patriots. 2008. Konami. Video Game.

Metal Gear Solid: Peace Walker. 2010. Konami. Video Game.

Metal Gear Solid V: Ground Zeroes. 2014. Konami. Video Game.

Metal Gear Solid V: The Phantom Pain. 2015. Konami. Video Game.

Military Wiki. 2014. "Close Quarters Combat." *Wiki Article*, November. Accessed December 5, 2020. https://military.wikia.org/wiki/Close_quarters_combat.

Molina, Brett. 2015. "Ex-Konami Designer Kojima Signs with Sony." *USA Today*, December 16. https://www.usatoday.com/story/tech/gaming/2015/12/16/ex-konami-designer-kojima-signs-deal-sony/77422464/.

Monster Hunter. 2004. Capcom. Video Game.

Montfort, Nick and Ian Bogost. 2009. *Racing the Beam: The Atari Video Computer System*. Cambridge, MA: MIT Press.

Moore, Keita. 2017. "The Game's the Thing: A Cultural Studies Approach to War Memory, Gender, and Politics in Japanese Videogames." University of Hawaii, Manoa, MA thesis.

Morioka, Daichi. 2019. "Kojima Hideo-shi ga idomu shingata gêmu 'Death Stranding' no shousan" [The chance of success for Hideo Kojima's new game challenge, "Death Stranding"]. *Nikkei XTrend*, October 17. https://xtrend.nikkei.com/atcl/contents/18/00205/00004/?P=2.

Morton, Drew. 2016. *Panel to the Screen: Style, American Film, and Comic Books During the Blockbuster Era*. Jackson: University Press of Mississippi.

Ms. Pac-Man. 1981. Nintendo. Video Game.

MSX Fan. 1990. "Fan Attack: Solid Snake." *MSX Fan*, September: 10–19.

MSX Fan. 1995. "The Messages of Farewell: Bokutachi no MSX" (Our MSX). *MSX Fan*, August: 4–9.

MSX Magazine. 1987. "MSX Soft Top 20." *MSX Magazine*, October: 83.

MSX Magazine. 1989. "Snatcher: Cybâpankku no sekai nano desu" (Snatcher: It's a Cyberpunk World). *MSX Magazine*, March: 26–7.

MSX Magazine. 1990. "Interview: Konami's Development Division." *MSX Magazine*, August: 44–7.

MSX Magazine. 2003. "Kojima Hideo Interview." In *MSX Magazine Eikyûhozonban 3* [MSX Magazine Permanent Preservation Edition 3], 152–5. Tokyo: ASCII.

Muraoka, Hideki. 1998. *Gekkan Famitsu Bros. October 1998: Metal Gear Solid*. Tokyo: ASCII.

Murray, Soraya. 2018. "Landscapes of Empire in *Metal Gear Solid V: The Phantom Pain*." *Critical Inquiry* 45.1: 168–98.

Murray, Soraya. 2019. "The Last of Us: Masculinity." In *How to Play Video Games*, edited by Matthew Thomas Payne and Nina Huntemann, 101–9. New York: NYU Press.

Nakamura, Takumi. 2020. "'Death Stranding' wa shingata koronaka no sekai wo yogen shiteita? Ima koso 'Desusuto' wo purei subeki riyû [Did "Death Stranding" predict the world under coronavirus? The reason why you should play "DS" now]. *Real Sound*, April 18. https://realsound.jp/tech/2020/04/post-540637.html.

Nakazawa, Shinichi. 2015. "The Game Freaks Who Play with Bugs—In Praise of the Game *Xevious*." Translated by Jérémie Pelletier-Gagnon and Tsugumi Okabe. *Kinephanos* 5.1: 175–201.

Newman, James. 2004. *Videogames*. London: Routledge.

Newman, James. 2008. *Playing with Videogames*. London: Routledge.

Niizumi, Henry. 2009. "Kojima Talks Peace Walker." *Gamespot*, September 25. http://tgs.gamespot.com/story/6230488/kojima-talks-peace-walker.

Nikkan SPA! 2013. "'Metal Gear' no AI wa Geinin wo mezashiteiru (Gêmu kurieitâ Korekado Yuji)" ["Metal Gear" AI is aiming for comedy (Game

creator Yuji Korekado)]. *Nikkan SPA!*, May 19. https://nikkan-spa.jp
/412710.

Noon, Derek and Nick Dyer-Witheford. 2010. "Sneaking Mission: Late
Imperial America and Metal Gear Solid." In *Utopic Dreams and Apocalyptic
Fantasies: Critical Approaches to Researching Video Game Play*, edited by J.
Talmadge Wright, David G. Embrick, and András Lukács, 73–95. Lanham,
MD and Plymouth: Lexington Books.

O'Donnell, Casey. 2014. *Developer's Dilemma: The Secret World of Video Game
Creators*. Cambridge, MA: MIT Press.

Ogilvie, Tristan. 2019. "Death Stranding Review." *IGN*, November 1. https://
www.ign.com/articles/2019/11/01/death-stranding-review.

Okamoto, Daisuke. 2020. "Nihon ni honmono no kurieitâ wa irunoka?
Kojima Hideo kantoku ga 'sakkasei' ni kodawaru riyû" [Is there a true
creator in Japan? The reason why director Kojima Hideo is insistent over
"authorship"]. *Livedoor*, May 29. https://news.livedoor.com/article/detail
/18332936/.

Onoue, Koji. 2016. "Kojima Hideo to sanman-ji taidan: Ima dakara
kataritsukusu, boku to hon" [A 3000-word Talk with Kojima Hideo: Books
and Me, What I Can Talk About Now]. *Shimirubon*, November 30. https://
shimirubon.jp/columns/1675611.

Otsuka, Eiji. 2010. "World and Variation: The Reproduction and Consumption
of Narrative." Translated by Marc Steinberg. *Mechademia Fanthropologies*
5: 99–116.

Paquet, Alexandre. 2021. "Delivering Packages in Apocalyptic Times: Utopia
and Collectives in *Death Stranding*." *Replaying Japan* 3: 77–86.

Parish, Jeremy. 2013. "Making Bad Hardware Design Fun: Remembering
Boktai." *USGamer*, August 15. https://www.usgamer.net/articles/making
-bad-hardware-design-fun-remembering-boktai.

Parkin, Simon. 2012. "Hideo Kojima: Video Game Drop-Out Interview." *The
Guardian*, May 23. https://www.theguardian.com/technology/gamesblog
/2012/may/23/hideo-kojima-interview-part-1.

Parkin, Simon. 2015. "Hideo Kojima's Mission Unlocked." *The New Yorker*,
December 17. https://www.newyorker.com/tech/annals-of-technology/
hideo-kojimas-mission-unlocked.

Parkin, Simon. 2022. "'I Want to Keep Being the First': Hideo Kojima on
Seven Years as an Independent Game Developer." *The Guardian*, October
26. https://www.theguardian.com/games/2022/oct/26/i-want-to-keep
-being-the-first-hideo-kojima-on-seven-years-as-an-independent-game
-developer.

Patterson, Mollie L. 2019. "Death Stranding Review." *EGM*, November 1.
https://egmnow.com/death-stranding-review/.

PCGamer Staff. 2020. "Game of the Year 2020: Death Stranding." *PCGamer*,
December 31. https://www.pcgamer.com/game-of-the-year-2020-death
-stranding/.

Penguin Adventure. 1986. Konami. Video game.

Phelps, Andrew. 2020. "Gaming Fosters Social Connection at a Time of Physical Distance." *The Conversation*, April 14. https://theconversation.com/gaming-fosters-social-connection-at-a-time-of-physical-distance-135809.

Phillips, Tom. 2019. "Kojima Mulls Death Stranding Genre, Says it's Something 'Totally Brand New.'" *Eurogamer*, June 5. https://www.eurogamer.net/articles/2019-06-05-kojima-mulls-death-stranding-genre-says-its-something-totally-new.

Phoenix Wright: Ace Attorney. 2001. Capcom. Video Game.

Policenauts. 1994. Konami. Video game.

Portopia Renzoku Satsujin Jiken [The Portopia Serial Murder Case]. 1983. Enix/Chunsoft. Video Game.

Powell, Steffan. 2019. "Death Stranding: Hideo Kojima Explains his New Game." *BBC*, November 4. https://www.bbc.com/news/newsbeat-50172917.

Professor Layton and the Curious Village. 2007. Level-5. Video Game.

Rasmussen, Eric E. 2014. "Proactive vs. Reactive Media Mediation: Effects of Mediation's Timing on Children's Reactions to Popular Cartoon Violence." *Human Communication Research* 40: 396–413.

Roberts, David. 2016. "Quiet Embodies Metal Gear's Complex Relationship with Women." *Gamesradar*, October 12. https://www.gamesradar.com/quiet-embodies-metal-gears-complex-relationship-women/.

Roth, Martin. 2017. *Thought-Provoking Play: Political Philosophies in Science Fictional Videogame Spaces from Japan*. Pittsburgh, PA: ETC Press.

Rouse, Richard. 2005. *Game Design: Theory and Practice*, 2nd edn. Plano, TX: Wordware.

Rox, Nick. 1994. "Snatcher: Review." *GameFan*, December: 46–7.

Ruh, Brian. 2013. *Stray Dog of Anime: The Films of Mamoru Oshii*. New York: Palgrave Macmillan.

Saito, Mutsushi, ed. 1996. *Policenauts Official Visual Data Book*. Tokyo: Tokyo: Kodansha.

Sakurai, Masahiro. 2004. "Metal Gear as a Game." In *Metal Gear Solid Naked*, edited by Hideo Kojima, 106–9. Tokyo: Kadokawa Shoten.

Salen, Katie and Eric Zimmerman. 2003. *Rules of Play: Game Design Fundamentals*. Cambridge, MA: MIT Press.

Salter, Anastasia. 2014. *What is Your Quest? From Adventure Games to Interactive Novels*. Iowa City: University of Iowa Press.

Salter, Anastasia. 2018. *Jane Jensen*. New York: Bloomsbury.

Scharre, Paul. 2023. *Four Battlegrounds: Power in the Age of Artificial Intelligence*. New York: W. W. Norton & Co.

Schiesel, Seth. 2008. "Making a Game That Acts Like a Film." *New York Times*, July 5. https://www.nytimes.com/2008/07/05/arts/05meta.html.

Schnabel, Keith. 2020. "Every Way Death Stranding Predicted The Future, Explained." *Screenrant*, November 10. https://screenrant.com/death-stranding-pandemic-future-predictions-2020-virus-kojima/.

Schreier, Jason. 2015. "Metal Gear Solid V: The Phantom Pain: The Kotaku Review." *Kotaku*, September 4. https://kotaku.com/metal-gear-solid-v-the -phantom-pain-the-kotaku-review-1728728287.

Scott, Ridley. 1982. *Blade Runner*, Film. Burbank, CA: Warner Bros. Pictures.

Screenrobot. 2019. "Hideo Kojima—Video Gaming's First Auteur." *Screenrobot*, July 9. https://screenrobot.com/hideo-kojima-video-gamings -first-auteur/.

SD Snatcher. 1990. Konami. Video Game.

Sega Saturn Magazine. 1996. "The Saturn Version Became the Cutest After All." *Sega Saturn Magazine*, September: 200–1.

Semenenko, Aleksei. 2004. "Quentin Tarantino's Milk Shake: On the Problem of Intertext and Genre." In *Intertextuality and Intersemiosis*, edited by Marina Grishakova, Markku Lehtimäki, 134–50. Tartu: Tartu University Press.

Sheridan, Connor. 2020. "Metal Gear Solid 5 Players on PS3 Finally Disarm All Their Nukes and Kojima Seems Pleased." *Gamesradar*, July 29. https:// www.gamesradar.com/metal-gear-solid-5-players-on-ps3-finally-disarm -all-their-nukes-and-kojima-seems-pleased/.

Shmuplations. "Ace Attorney: Justice For All—2002 Developer Interview." [from the GSLA]. http://shmuplations.com/justiceforall/.

Shmuplations. "Boktai—2003 Developer Interview" [originally featured in the April 2003 issue of *Nintendo Dream*]. *Shmuplations*. https://shmuplations .com/boktai/.

Shmuplations. "Zone of Enders: The 2nd Runner—2003 Developer Interview" [from the *Visual Works of Anubis*]. *Shmuplations*. http://shmuplations.com /zoneofenders/.

Sim City. 1989. Maxis. Video Game.

Simmons, Rachel. 2016. "How Social Media is a Toxic Mirror." *Time*, August 19. https://time.com/4459153/social-media-body-image/.

Snake's Revenge. 1990. Konami. Video Game.

Snatcher. 1988. Konami. Video Game.

Snyder, Daniel. 2012. "How Hideo Kojima Became a Legendary Video Game Designer." *The Atlantic*, March 21. https://www.theatlantic.com/ entertainment/archive/2012/03/how-hideo-kojima-became-a-legendary -video-game-designer/254831/.

Stamenkovic, Dusan, Milan Jasevic, and Janina Wildfeuer. 2017. "The Persuasive Aims of Metal Gear Solid: A Discourse Theoretical Approach to the Study of Argumentation in Video Games." *Discourse, Context, and Media* 15: 11–23.

Stang, Sarah. 2017. "Big Daddies and Broken Men: Father-Daughter Relationships in Video Games." *Loading . . . The Journal of the Canadian Game Studies Association* 10.16: 162–74.

Stanton, Rich. 2015a. "Metal Gear Solid: The First Modern Video Game." *Eurogamer*, August 12. https://www.eurogamer.net/articles/2015-08-12 -metal-gear-solid-the-first-modern-video-game.

Stanton, Rich. 2015b. "Metal Gear Solid 3: From Russia with Love." *Eurogamer*, August 30. https://www.eurogamer.net/articles/2015-08-30-metal-gear -solid-3-from-russia-with-love.

Stanton, Rich. 2015c. "Metal Gear Solid 4: Rinse, Repeat, Resolve?" *Eurogamer*, November 15. https://www.eurogamer.net/articles/2015-11-15 -metal-gear-solid-4-rinse-repeat-resolve.

Stanton, Rich. 2015d. "Metal Gear Solid V—How Kojima Productions is Blowing Apart the Open-World Video Game." *The Guardian*, June 11. https://www.theguardian.com/technology/2015/jun/11/metal-gear-solid-v -phantom-pain-kojima-preview.

Steinberg, Marc. 2015. "8-Bit Manga: Kadokawa's Madara, or, The Gameic Media Mix." *Kinephanos* 5.1: 40–52.

Stemmler, Claudius. 2019. "'A Hideo Kojima Game': A Brief Overview of Stylistic Traits." *In Media Res*, August 5. http://mediacommons.org/imr/ content/hideo-kojima-game-brief-overview-stylistic-traits;

Sturges, John. 1963. *The Great Escape*, Film. Beverley Hills, CA: United Artists.

Suellentrop, Chris. 2010. "Bioshock 2: The Rare Video-Game Sequel that Builds on the Original (And Not Just by Adding Better Guns)." *Slate*, February 23. https://slate.com/technology/2010/02/bioshock-2-the-rare -video-game-sequel-that-builds-on-the-original-and-not-just-by-adding -better-guns.html.

Super Mario Bros. 1985. Nintendo. Video Game.

Svelch, Jaroslav. 2018. *Gaming the Iron Curtain: How Teenagers and Amateurs in Communist Czechoslovakia Claimed the Medium of Computer Games.* Cambridge, MA: MIT Press.

Taitai. 2013. "Ishii Jiro and Other Successful Creators Talk About Adventure Games." *4Gamer.net*, November 9. https://www.4gamer.net/games/074/ G007427/20131108107/.

Taiyoung, Ryu. 2012. "Kojima, Hideo (1963–)." In *Encyclopedia of Video Games: The Culture, Technology, and Art of Gaming*, edited by Mark J. P. Wolf, 348–50. Santa Barbara, CA: Greenwood.

Takahashi, Dean. 2015. "How Pokémon Go Will Benefit from Niantic's Lessons from Ingress on Location-Based Game Design." *GamesBeat*, December 16. https://venturebeat.com/2015/12/16/how-niantic-will-marry -animated-characters-with-mobile-location-data-in-pokemon-go/.

Takei, Yohei. 2008. "All About Hideo Kojima: Director of the Hit Software *Metal Gear Solid.*" *Yomiuri Shimbun*, June 11: 8.

Tamagotchi. 1996. Bandai. Video Game.

Tamburro, Paul. 2016. "Let's Talk About THAT Quiet Scene in Metal Gear Solid." *Crave*, July 27. http://www.craveonline.com/culture/900837-lets-talk -quiet-scene-metal-gear-solid-v.

Tati, Jacques. 1967. *Playtime*, Film. Paris: Specta Films.

Thearkhound. 2019. "Famitsu #403: Hideo Kojima Interview (Metal Gear Solid)." *The Ark Hound*, December 13. https://thearkhound.tumblr.com/ post/189640385948/the-following-is-translation-of-an-interview-with.

The Games Machine. 1987. "Metal Gear." *The Games Machine*, December/ January 1987–88: 61.

The Last of Us. 2013. Naughty Dog. Video Game.

The Last of Us Part II. 2020. Naughty Dog. Video Game.

The PlayStation. 1996. "Notes of Policenauts: Kojima Hideo Policenauts wo kataru" (Notes of Policenauts: Hideo Kojima talks about Policenauts). *The PlayStation* 21, February 9: 152–5.

Therrien, Carl. 2019. *The Media Snatcher: PC/CORE/TURBO/GRAPHX/16/C DROM2/SUPER/DUO/ARCADE/RX.* Cambridge, MA: MIT Press.

Thompson, J. Lee. 1961. *The Guns of Navarone*, Film. Culver City, CA: Columbia Pictures.

Thorsten, Marie. 2012. *Superhuman Japan: Knowledge, Nation, and Culture in US-Japan Relations*. London: Routledge.

Tieryas, Peter. 2017. "*Snatcher* is Cyberpunk Noir at its Best." *Kotaku*, June 16. http://kotaku.com/snatcher-is-cyberpunk-noir-at-its-best-1795989020.

Tokimeki Memorial. 1994. Konami. Video Game.

Tom Clancy's Splinter Cell. 2002. Ubisoft. Video Game.

Tomino, Yoshiyuki. 1979. *Mobile Suit Gundam*, Television show. Tokyo: Sunrise.

Totilo, Stephen. 2009. "Hideo Kojima Talks *Metal Gear Solid: Peace Walker* And How You Can Help Him." *Kotaku*, September 25. https://kotaku.com/hideo-kojima-talks-metal-gear-solid-peace-walker-and-h-5367724.

Tschang, F. Ted, ed. 2007. "Balancing the Tensions Between Rationalization and Creativity in the Video Games Industry." *Organization Science* 18.6: 989–1005.

Vo, Alex. 2019. "Death Stranding Director Hideo Kojima's Five Favorite Films." *Rotten Tomatoes*, December 20. https://editorial.rottentomatoes.com/article/death-stranding-director-hideo-kojimas-five-favorite-films.

Wardrip-Fruin, Noah. 2020. *How Pac-Man Eats*. Cambridge, MA: MIT Press.

Watts, Jonathan. 2002. "Public Health Experts Concerned about 'Hikikomori.'" *Lancet* 359.9312: 1131.

Weise, Matthew. 2009. "The Rules of Horror: Procedural Adaptation in *Clock Tower, Resident Evil*, and *Dead Rising*." In *Horror Video Games. Essays on the Fusion of Fear and Play*, edited by Bernard Perron, 238–66. Jefferson, NC: McFarland.

Welsh, Ori. 2008. "Metal Gear Solid 4: Guns of the Patriots Review." *Eurogamer*, May 30. https://www.eurogamer.net/articles/metal-gear-solid-4-guns-of-the-patriots-review.

Welsh, Timothy. 2020. "(Re)Mastering Dark Souls." *Game Studies* 20.4. http://gamestudies.org/2004/articles/welsh.

Westbrook, Logan. 2011. "Hideo Kojima Cleans Out Closet, Finds *Metal Gear* Treasures." *The Escapist*, January 21. http://www.escapistmagazine.com/news/view/107149-Hideo-Kojima-Cleans-Out-Closet-Finds-Metal-Gear-Treasures#&gid=gallery_99&pid=7.

Willett, John. 1964. *Brecht on Theatre: The Development of an Aesthetic.* London: Methuen.

Wilson, Greg. 2006. "Off With Their HUDs!: Rethinking the Heads-Up Display in Console Game Design." *Gamasutra*, February 6. https://www.gamasutra.com/view/feature/130948/off_with_their_huds_rethinking_.php.

Wilson, Jeffrey. 2012. "The 10 Most Influential Video Games of All Time: 7. Metal Gear Solid." *PC Magazine*, April 11. Accessed via *Internet Archive.* https://web.archive.org/web/20120411203024/http://www.pcmag.com/slideshow_viewer/0%2C3253%2Cl%3D251652%26a%3D251651%26po%3D4%2C00.asp?p=n.

Wohn, Donghee Yvette, Cliff Lampe, Rick Wash, Nicole Ellison, and Jessica Vitak. 2011. "The 'S' in Social Network Games: Initiating, Maintaining, and Enhancing Relationships." In *System Sciences (HICSS), 2011 44th Hawaii International Conference on*, 1–10, IEEE.

Wolf, Mark J. P. 2012. *Building Imaginary Worlds: The Theory and History of Subcreation.* New York: Routledge.

Wolfe, Terry. 2018. *The Kojima Code: 1987–2003.* Victoria, CA: Tellwell.

Wolfe, Terry. 2019. "Going Astray in Death Stranding." *Mr. Wolfe's Meta Gear*, December 3. https://metagearsolid.org/2019/12/going-astray-in-death-stranding/#more-7185.

Xevious. 1982. Namco. Video Game.

Yamashita, Akira. 1988. *Micon BASIC Magazine Super Soft Magazine Deluxe Vol. 10: Challenge! A.V.G & R.P.G.* Tokyo: ASCII.

Yamashita, Akira. 1994. "Policenauts." *Micon BASIC Magazine*, August: 160–2.

Yarwood, Jack. 2021. "Creating the Iconic Soundtrack for *Metal Gear Solid 2: Sons of Liberty*." *Game Developer*, September 21. https://www.gamedeveloper.com/audio/creating-the-iconic-soundtrack-for-metal-gear-solid-2-sons-of-liberty.

Yokoi, Gumpei and Take Makino. 1997. *Yokoi Gumpei Game-kan.* Tokyo: ASCII.

INDEX

Note: Page numbers followed by "n" refer to notes.